# The Collapse of Fortress Bush

Alasdair Roberts

# The Collapse of Fortress Bush

*The Crisis of Authority in American Government*

**New York University Press** • *New York and London*

NEW YORK UNIVERSITY PRESS
New York and London
www.nyupress.org

Library of Congress Cataloging-in-Publication Data
Roberts, Alasdair (Alasdair Scott)
The collapse of fortress Bush : the crisis of authority in American
government / Alasdair Roberts.
p.   cm.
Includes bibliographical references and index.
ISBN-13: 978-0-8147-7606-3 (cloth : alk. paper)
ISBN-10: 0-8147-7606-X (cloth : alk. paper)
1. United States—Politics and government—2001– 2. United States—
Foreign relations—2001– 3. Bush, George W. (George Walker), 1946–
4. Bush, George W. (George Walker), 1946– —Friends and associates.
5. Authority. 6. Executive power—United States. 7. Political leadership—
United States. 8. September 11 Terrorist Attacks, 2001. 9. War on
Terrorism, 2001– 10. United States—Social conditions—1980–   I. Title.
E902.R625  2008
973.93—dc22          2007034068

New York University Press books are printed on acid-free paper,
and their binding materials are chosen for strength and durability.

Manufactured in the United States of America
10 9 8 7 6 5 4 3 2 1

In framing a government which is to be administered by men over men, the great difficulty lies in this: You must first enable the government to control the governed; and in the next place oblige it to control itself.

—James Madison, *The Federalist No. 51*

# Contents

# Preface

The aim of this book is to ask why the U.S. government reacted to the 9/11 crisis and its aftermath as it did. This is obviously an important question—for Americans who want assurance that the nation will be defended against future attacks, for allied countries that share similar risks, which may be aggravated or diminished by U.S. policy, and for many other countries, and foreign citizens, who are affected directly by the exercise of American power.

Within the United States there is a widely held understanding about the proper answer to this question. It includes claims about what happened and why. The conventional view says that the 9/11 attacks led to radical changes in government policy in many areas. One of the objectives of the administration, largely achieved, was said to be an unprecedented and dangerous concentration of executive authority. These radical changes were said to have come about because key personalities—President George W. Bush, Vice President Richard Cheney, Defense Secretary Donald Rumsfeld, Attorney General John Ashcroft, and a coterie of advisers—had sharply defined views about the need for change and were adroit at exploiting the opportunity created by the 9/11 attacks.

It is easy to see why this interpretation of what happened after 9/11 gained popularity. As a rule, stories about radical disruptions of the status quo are more newsworthy than stories of incremental change, and stories about the clash of personalities are more easily conveyed than stories about weaknesses in institutions or systems of government. We like tales about struggles between heroes and villains in which the stakes are very large.[1] Furthermore, this particular story, which can be framed as one about popular resistance against an overreaching executive, plays on a rhetorical tradition that is deeply rooted in American history and culture.

For critics of the Bush administration, this conventional narrative about the 9/11 crisis and its aftermath is both alarming and reassuring. It is alarming because it suggests that well-established norms about the aims and techniques of government policy have been over-thrown. But it is also reassuring because it offers the possibility of re-versal. If the fault lies in the predispositions of key players, then the objective is to change the roster of players—not necessarily an easy project, but still one that might be executed within a few election cy-cles. Not coincidentally, the conventional narrative is also an efficient means of mobilizing potential allies in that political struggle.

The purpose of this book is to argue that the conventional under-standing of what happened after 9/11 is misguided in two ways. First, I intend to challenge the proposition that "everything was different" after the attacks. I will mark the continuities and discontinuities in federal policy and argue that in many ways the intriguing point is how policy *did not* shift radically. I will also argue that a proper expla-nation for the trend in government policy after 9/11 requires an un-derstanding of the limits on executive action that arise from the design of governmental institutions, political culture, and the pressures of a market economy. At the turn of the millennium, the United States was a highly advanced liberal state that also maintained a highly advanced defense establishment. In both respects it was unique among devel-oped nations. The 9/11 attacks revealed how this sort of state operates in a moment of crisis.

The policies of the Bush administration have enraged many peo-ple in the United States and abroad, and this anger has sometimes col-ored readers' response to this text. One complaint is that the effect of this work is to justify or excuse the policies of the Bush administra-tion. I am thought to have done this by telling a story in which cir-cumstances are shown to encourage certain kinds of behavior and dis-courage others. President Bush, in this view, could be regarded as a product of his environment—an agent following a script determined by external factors, with diminished culpability for his actions. There is a small grain of truth in this complaint. Context—institutional, po-litical, cultural, and economic—determines the costs and benefits of alternative courses of action. I argue that context has changed over time, also changing the calculus of executive decision making. Certain kinds of executive action have become relatively more difficult, and others relatively easier.

This hardly means that the policy responses that we observed over the past five years were defensible or inevitable. Saying that choices are made within a context is not the same as denying the possibility of choice. Great leaders use their authority to challenge constraints and encourage citizens to reconsider the usual way of doing business. President Bush invoked this conception of leadership when he said that "a time of war is a time of sacrifice." But President Bush did not take this idea seriously and did not challenge the American public to take it seriously either.

There is another way of making this point that is perhaps more agreeable to critics of the Bush administration. The U.S. system of government, in its current configuration, has virtues, but it is also prone to certain kinds of failure, such as unduly militaristic responses to crises or poorly planned and coordinated responses. Skilled leaders understand the tendencies of the system and accommodate its frailties. Unskilled leaders do not, and as a result they make mistakes, often with terrible consequences. But the *kinds* of mistakes that unskilled leaders are likely to make are broadly determined by institutional, cultural, and economic considerations.

In short, my argument may help to explain President Bush's behavior, but it does not excuse it. Nonetheless, the argument does suggest that prescriptions for reform that dwell principally on the need to replace old leaders with new ones are likely to be inadequate. In a state distinguished by the two characteristics of *entrenched liberalism* and *neomilitarism*—terms that I will define in the first chapter—there are persistent biases toward noxious and dangerous policies. The constraints imposed by such a system of governance must be recognized and dealt with.

The final draft of this book was prepared in June 2007 and accommodates developments until that date.

# 1

# A Crisis of Authority

For the first time since the resignation of Richard M. Nixon more than thirty years ago, Americans have had reason to doubt the future of democracy and the rule of law in our own country.

—Joe Conason, *It Can Happen Here*, 2007[1]

EACH OF US remembers when the 9/11 crisis began: on the crisp autumn morning in 2001 when two airliners were hijacked and smashed into the twin towers of New York's World Trade Center, causing mass death and panic in the world's financial hub. A third airliner crashed into the Pentagon, the headquarters of the most powerful military force on earth. A fourth airliner, aimed at the White House or Congress, fell instead in a field in western Pennsylvania. This was our first digital-age security crisis: a terrible trauma, apprehended instantly and universally. It was a *security* crisis because it raised a series of questions that related directly to the protection of the U.S. homeland. Were more attacks on the way? Could the nation deter future assaults? If not, were we prepared to respond to the aftermath?

Americans looked to their national government for answers to these questions. This was evident in opinion polls, which showed a remarkable turnabout in the public's usual perceptions about their federal government. Two weeks after the 9/11 attacks, President George W. Bush received the highest approval rating ever recorded in the seventy-year history of the Gallup poll. According to a *Washington Post* survey completed in October 2001, 64 percent of Americans professed to trust "government in Washington to do what is right"—a level not seen in comparable surveys since the mid-1960s.[2] It seemed that the terrorist threat had impelled Americans to reconsider their distaste for central government.[3]

This effect did not last long. At some point in the five years that followed, the 9/11 crisis ceased to be a security crisis. It became some-

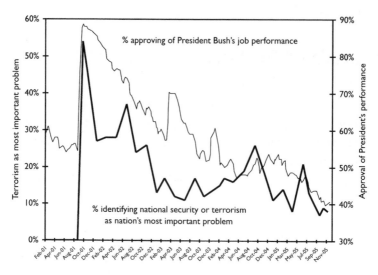

FIG. 1.1. Concern about terrorism and support for the president. (Gallup poll)

thing uglier: a crisis of authority. The public's preoccupation with terror attacks dissipated. By fall 2005, Americans regarded rising gas prices as a more serious social problem. On the fourth anniversary of the 9/11 attacks, concern about terrorism did not spike, as it had in preceding years.[4] The public's faith in the president, and in the federal government more generally, waned. Public discourse, at home and overseas, was seized instead with fears about the concentration and abuse of power within the executive branch of the U.S. government.

Abroad, sympathy for victims of the 9/11 attacks was displaced by anger at the willingness of the United States to wield its diplomatic and military might with scant regard for its traditional allies or international law. The United States had ceased to be a superpower, as it had been for the preceding fifty years; it was now an *hyperpuissance,* or hyperpower, according to a French foreign minister,[5] or—if one preferred Germanic etymology—the Überpower.[6] It had become, for some, the world's leading rogue state,[7] a rampaging elephant,[8] a nation that had declared a war on law,[9] a selfish and dangerous giant,[10] an unchallengeable behemoth,[11] a colossus with attention-deficit disorder,[12] and a simple-minded goliath.[13]

The point was not simply that the United States was the predominant global power. The complaint was also, and perhaps principally, that there appeared to be no discipline on the exercise of that power. The nation had slipped the restraints imposed by the political and military realities of the Cold War. There was growing agreement, as Francis Fukuyama observed, that "the irresponsible exercise of American power is one of the chief problems in contemporary politics."[14]

Comparable anxieties were aired at home, where the Bush administration was alleged to have launched a "rolling coup" against the U.S. Constitution.[15] "The biggest story of the Bush presidency," said Dan Froomkin of the *Washington Post,* is its "dramatic expansion of executive power."[16] The distinguished historian Arthur Schlesinger Jr. lamented the resurgence of an "imperial" presidency.[17] The bipartisan Constitution Project warned against the growth of "permanent and unchecked presidential power."[18] The president had run amok,[19] said others, executing policies that infringed radically on civil liberties,[20] and put the United States on the path to autocracy,[21] dictatorship,[22] totalitarianism,[23] and the Big Brother state.[24] The Bush administration was said to have browbeat Congress and the courts—and also the federal bureaucracy, until it was populated by "robotrons [who] just do what they're told."[25]

The president and his allies, said Princeton University professor Paul Krugman, were "engaged in an authoritarian project, an effort to remove all the checks and balances that have heretofore constrained the executive branch [and] create a political environment in which nobody dares to criticize the administration or reveal inconvenient facts about its actions."[26] As the fifth anniversary of the attacks neared, the editors of the *New York Times* affirmed that we had crossed from one sort of crisis to another:

> It is only now, nearly five years after September 11, that the full picture of the Bush administration's response to the terror attacks is becoming clear. Much of it, we can see now, had far less to do with fighting Osama bin Laden than with expanding presidential power. Over and over again, the same pattern emerges: *Given a choice between following the rules or carving out some unprecedented executive power, the White House always shrugged off the legal constraints.*[27]

The Bush administration, through its rhetoric and conduct, encouraged these complaints. The president and vice president believed that three decades of legislative reforms had badly weakened the executive branch, and they often said so. They wanted to restore "a strong, robust executive authority" and exert American influence more forcefully overseas.[28] The administration often imagined the American presidency as Gulliver, the giant restrained by the threads of a thousand Lilliputians. Its advisers articulated constitutional doctrines that justified a broader view of presidential power.[29] And in the four years that followed 9/11, the Bush presidency pursued policies that tested some of the limits to its authority.

Nevertheless, a broad-brushed complaint of authoritarianism does not fit the facts. In the five years that followed 9/11, the Bush administration also treated the American electorate gingerly, avoiding significant disruptions to daily life or overt infringements of citizens' rights and delivering a series of popular tax cuts. It operated one of the smallest nondefense bureaucracies in modern U.S. history.[30] It handled the business sector just as delicately, refusing to impose mandates that might disturb the rhythms of a market economy. The administration was attentive to the prerogatives of state governments, even on subjects that touched directly on homeland security.

"We've been very active and very aggressive defending the nation and using the tools at our disposal," Vice President Cheney told reporters in 2005.[31] As a general proposition this was manifestly untrue. There were many instances when the critical feature of administration policy was, in fact, the *refusal* to act aggressively and use the tools at its disposal. The Bush administration also encountered practical and political limits to its authority. Congress, although often deferential, could still be roused to take action against executive-branch initiatives. It undertook inquiries when the administration did not want them, insisted on reorganizations that the administration said were unnecessary, and modified or prohibited programs that the administration claimed were essential to national security.

There were other constraints. At critical moments, civil servants and political advisers did not act like robotrons. Instead, they spoke out against rash policies. Attempts to reorganize and coordinate within the federal bureaucracy were stymied by familiar problems of bureaucratic rivalry. The administration was embarrassed repeatedly by disclosures about covert operations and infighting over policy. Hurricane Katrina revealed the continued inability of federal agencies to collaborate with one another, as well as with their state and local counterparts. Still more evidence of the limits on executive power followed. The Supreme Court compelled the administration to reverse its policies on the treatment of suspected terrorists captured during the War on Terrorism. On the fifth anniversary of 9/11, allied forces were mired in Iraq and Afghanistan. Rash talk about the Axis of Evil had been replaced with diplomatic initiatives to curb nuclear proliferation in Iran and North Korea.

Important constraints on the exercise of authority—institutional, political, cultural, and economic—continued to operate in the five years that followed the 9/11 attacks. Furthermore, there is a pattern to these constraints. In 2001, the United States was a highly advanced liberal state, which happened also to be a military superpower. In its internal design, the U.S. system of government reflects a profound ambivalence about the exercise of executive power, even in a moment of emergency. Complaints about the rise of authoritarianism reflected this ambivalence. Indeed, these complaints can be better understood as symptoms of this underlying ambivalence about executive power, rather than as unalloyed statements of fact.

The critical question after 9/11 was how the American polity would manage this ambivalence in a moment of crisis. The answer is troubling. The American system of government, in the form in which it existed in the early years of the new millennium, found it extraordinarily difficult to pursue domestic measures essential to homeland security, and it was easily distracted by military actions that had the effect of exacerbating security threats.

## Entrenched Liberalism

The American state is designed on classical liberal principles.[32] Its aim is to thwart the concentration of governmental power and maximize individual freedom. As we all know, the writers of the Constitution pursued this goal by splitting public authority among three branches of government (executive, legislative, and judicial) and three levels of government (federal, state, and local).[33] The nation is constructed as a compound republic, as James Madison said: power has been divided so that no part of government can dominate another.[34] (The political scientist Walter Dean Burnham later said that the Constitution was designed to "defeat any attempt to generate domestic sovereignty.")[35]

Not only is authority fragmented *within* government; governmental authority as a whole is checked in two ways: by the constitutional entrenchment of basic rights for citizens and the refusal to give government an extensive role in the management of the economy.

The degree to which the United States is distinguished by these initial constitutional choices could easily be underestimated at the start of the twenty-first century. After the Cold War it became commonplace to emphasize the extent to which systems of government were converging around the world. In many countries, state planning collapsed and gave way to market reforms, and new constitutions were adopted that promised protection for the fundamental rights of citizens. The twentieth century, Francis Fukuyama has argued, ended with the "unabashed victory of economic and political liberalism."[36]

Still, the United States remains a special case, even among established liberal democracies. It is, as Irving Kristol has said, "the capitalist nation par excellence."[37] The United States maintains one of the smallest public sectors in the developed world, with roughly one-third of gross domestic product (GDP) committed to government spending. (In Europe, the proportion is usually closer to half of GDP.) Moreover, the United States regulates its economy more lightly than do most other countries in the Organization for Economic Cooperation and Development (OECD).

The United States is usually grouped with other developed English-speaking nations—such as the United Kingdom and Australia— that share a market orientation.[38] A strong commitment to the market society, many Europeans say, is the hallmark of the Anglo-Saxon approach to governance.[39] However, the United States is an unusual case even among the Anglo-Saxon countries because of constitutional features that contribute to the fragmentation of power. Other English-speaking nations are parliamentary democracies, in which there is no formal constitutional separation between the executive and legislative branches. In parliamentary systems, the executive has more sway over legislators, and over the bureaucracy as well. Several other English-speaking countries are also unitary rather than federal states. Only Canada has an enumeration of rights within its constitution, as the United States does, but Canada's charter of fundamental rights is newer by almost two centuries.[40]

Figure 1.2 provides a sense of the unusual place of the United States among the world's advanced democracies. The United States

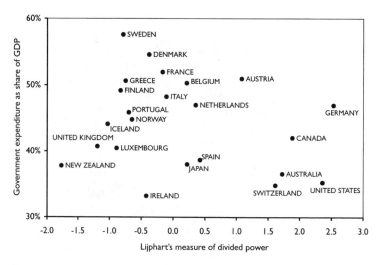

Fig. 1.2. American exceptionalism.

relies more heavily on the market to produce goods and services, a fact that is roughly captured by government expenditure as a share of GDP. Its constitution is also designed to fragment authority more extensively, a reality captured by the measure of divided power developed by Professor Arend Lijphart.[41]

The antistatist ethos of the United States is reflected in its culture as well as its institutions.[42] In cross-national surveys, Americans claim to be more strongly committed to the principle of self-reliance, and more skeptical of collective action, than almost all other nationalities.[43] Samuel Huntington suggests that the element of American political culture that most clearly distinguishes the nation from the European democracies is its "antipower ethic." "Opposition to power, and suspicion of government as the most dangerous embodiment of power," says Huntington, "are the central themes of American political thought."[44]

Throughout American history, the president has been the lightning rod for anxieties about the concentration of political power. A nation born in revolt against a monarch has re-created that struggle ever since, with successive presidents taking the place of George III. In this sense, complaints against President Bush's authoritarian impulses were not new: rather, they gained power by redeploying habits of argument already familiar to the majority of Americans. There were

THE HANDS OF DICTATORSHIP!

FIG. 1.3. The *Los Angeles Times* criticizes President Franklin Roosevelt, February 1937.

intriguing parallels, for example, between liberal attacks on President Bush and conservative attacks on President Franklin Roosevelt six decades earlier. Roosevelt, like Bush, wrestled with a national crisis in his first term but was widely condemned in his second term for kingly and dictatorial ambitions (figs. 1.3 and 1.4).[45]

The structure of American government is not static. However, the evolution of the U.S. system of governance has, in many respects, had the effect of entrenching the distinctive qualities of the initial design. (Political scientists will recognize this as an argument about *path dependence.* Initial choices about institutional arrangements are more deeply entrenched over time and increasingly difficult to reverse.)[46] For example, we remain attached to the idea that U.S. citizens have basic, inalienable rights, but the content of basic rights has broadened, constitutional and legislative safeguards for those rights have improved, and the community of advocacy groups that monitors the violation of rights has expanded. Popular consciousness of rights has increased as well.

The same process of reinforcement over time has operated elsewhere. The three branches of government have larger staffs, longer histories, and more-sophisticated internal structures, and all these considerations complicate efforts to change the behavior of each branch and its relationship to the others. The same can be said of agencies within the executive branch. State and local governments have also grown in size, sophistication, and confidence. The market economy (and the lobby that represents corporate interests) has gained in breadth, complexity, and wealth. The mechanisms that generate and replicate popular culture—including old themes such as the antipower ethic—are more efficient than ever before. This may be one reason why distrust of major institutions (a symptom of the antipower ethic) is more intense today than it was four decades ago.

The current condition of U.S. government is not only the result of gradual entrenchment over time. The architecture of government also changed in important ways as a result of the political and economic crises that confronted the United States during the late 1960s and 1970s. Anger over the abuse of power by the Nixon administration led

FIG. 1.4. Cartoonist George Danby criticizes President George W. Bush in the *Bangor Daily News,* June 2006.

TABLE 1.1
Post-Nixon Checks on the Executive

| | | |
|---|---|---|
| Federal Advisory Committee Act | 1972 | Regulates operation of advisory committees, including open meeting requirement |
| Congressional Budget and Impoundment Control Act | 1974 | Establishes Congressional Budget Office; limits the president's right to block the use of appropriated funds |
| Freedom of Information Act | 1974* | Establishes right to government documents |
| Privacy Act | 1974 | Establishes rules on handling of personal information and a right to obtain one's own personal information |
| Government in the Sunshine Act | 1976 | Requires that meetings of government boards and committees be open to the public |
| Civil Service Reform Act | 1978 | Provides protection to employees who make disclosures of information regarding official misconduct |
| Ethics in Government Act | 1978 | Creates financial-disclosure rules for senior officials and restrictions on postemployment lobbying |
| Foreign Intelligence Surveillance Act | 1978 | Regulates electronic surveillance by federal agencies in the context of foreign intelligence gathering |
| Inspector General Act | 1978 | Created independent audit and investigative offices in major federal departments and agencies |
| Presidential Records Act | 1978 | Affirms public ownership of presidential records, provides right of access to documents |
| General Accounting Office Act | 1980 | Expands investigatory powers of the Comptroller General |

* FOIA was adopted in 1966 but was significantly strengthened after Nixon's resignation.

to the adoption of a battery of laws that regulate the executive branch, or created new counterweights to executive power (table 1.1).[47] In later years, presidents attempted to weaken these controls, but they were not always successful and in notable cases the post-Nixon constraints were strengthened rather than weakened. In many cases the passage of a law fostered a new constituency of friendly legislators, nongovernment organizations, academics, and journalists, who resisted attacks on these new controls. The ideas embedded in these statutes—such as the principle of transparency in government operations, the government employee's right to "blow the whistle" on misconduct, the principle that official positions should not be abused for personal gain, and the idea of efficiency in administration—are now more deeply embedded in public consciousness, even if they are not always honored in practice. Indeed, our heightened awareness of these principles may make us more conscious of abuses than before.

Equally critical is the post-Nixon shift in attitudes about governmental management of the economy.[48] President Nixon was a Republican, but his ideas about the federal government's role in management of the economy are anathema to postmillennial Republicans. Nixon was a pragmatist, prepared to intervene forcefully in the market if there were political advantages in doing so. ("I am a Keynesian," Nixon famously said in January 1971.)[49] When the inflation rate began to rise in the late 1960s and early 1970s, Nixon responded by imposing the nation's first peacetime controls on wages and prices, temporarily in 1971 and again in 1973, after the Arab oil embargo. Nixon also imposed a 10 percent surcharge on imported goods in 1971 to protect the value of the U.S. dollar. Federal regulation also grew substantially during the Nixon years. Two federal agencies that are now the object of Republican enmity—the Occupational Safety and Health Administration (OSHA) and the Environmental Protection Agency (EPA)—were among the children of the Nixon era, both established in 1970. Nixon's chief economic adviser later said that the Nixon administration imposed "more new regulation . . . than any other presidency since the New Deal."[50]

The failure of attempts to revive the U.S. economy in the 1970s eventually led to a shift in assumptions about the relationship between government and the market. The economy was in a deep crisis, Ronald Reagan said in his first inaugural address, that would not be resolved until the integrity of the market system was restored. ("Government is not the solution to our problem," Reagan said. "Government *is* the problem. . . . It is my intention to curb the size and influence of the Federal establishment.")[51] This deep commitment to market principles, and skepticism about the efficacy of government intervention, eventually became known as neoliberalism.[52] It included a commitment to tax reduction, discipline in fiscal and monetary policy, a retreat from "command-and-control" regulation with an emphasis on less-intrusive tactics to achieve federal priorities, and active promotion of expanded global trade.[53] By the 1990s, even Democrats had adapted to the neoliberal agenda. It had become the dominant public philosophy.[54]

## Neomilitarism

This picture of the predicament of the United States—as a determinedly liberal state, constantly negotiating the boundaries of governmental authority and deeply ambivalent about executive power—is familiar but in important respects very misleading. The U.S. federal government is also distinctive among the central governments of other developed countries because of the dominance of its defense establishment.

The overwhelming military capacity of the United States is generally understood: the country is estimated to account for two-fifths of the planet's total military expenditure.[55] It is said by some European critics to suffer from a complex that they call *gigantisme militaire*, a pathological preoccupation with the accumulation of military might in excess of actual need.[56] This is not a completely accurate diagnosis. After all, the United States is a wealthy country, which accounts for one-fifth of world income. Even if it acquired military capacity in strict proportion with its income, it would still be the dominant world power. In fact, an important feature of U.S. defense policy is the extent to which it has learned how to project force without imposing substantially on the national economy. U.S. defense expenditures accounted for 4 percent of GDP in 2006. The country's last major rival, the Soviet Union, committed almost one-fifth of GDP to national defense in the waning years of the Cold War.[57]

Nonetheless, the defense establishment dominates the U.S. federal bureaucracy. In 2005, roughly two-thirds of the federal government's operating budget was dedicated to national defense.[58] At least half the federal workforce—including 1.4 million uniformed military personnel and 900,000 civilians—are engaged in defense-related work. Two-thirds of the federal government's contractor workforce, perhaps another three or four million employees, also work in the defense sector.[59]

The dominance of the defense establishment is uncommon in two respects. First, it is unusual in U.S. history. Although the United States built up substantial military forces at several points in its early history —during the Civil War and the First World War, for example—these forces were quickly dispersed after relatively short conflicts. When Franklin Roosevelt was inaugurated as president in 1933, the non-defense component of the federal government, although small, still dwarfed the defense sector. Circumstances were wholly reversed after the Second World War. The United States built up massive military capabilities during the war and began to demobilize afterward, but it quickly reversed course after the advent of the Cold War in 1947–48. For the last half century, the defense bureaucracy has outmatched the nondefense bureaucracy by a ratio of at least two to one.

The dominance of the defense establishment within the architecture of central government also distinguishes the United States from other developed nations. The prime minister of the United Kingdom, for example, oversees a very different bureaucratic landscape. The British defense establishment accounts for little more than one-tenth of the UK central government's expenditure and employment.[60] Of course, there are good reasons for this. The British Empire has dissipated, and central government in the United Kingdom has taken on welfare-state functions that are dealt with by state governments or the private sector in the United States. There was a time when the British prime minister shared the predicament of a contemporary U.S. president. In terms of the tilt of administrative capabilities—measured by the allocation of workers and spending on operations—the U.S. federal government today is comparable to the UK government of the eighteenth and early nineteenth centuries, as the empire approached its zenith.[61]

In many respects, the defense and nondefense components of U.S. government are organized on distinct principles. Whereas the nondefense sector is highly federalized, and thus dependent on the cooperation of state and local governments, the defense sector is highly centralized.[62] Legislators and courts are also more likely to defer to the leadership of the executive when national-security considerations are invoked. Added to these attributes is another critical element: legitimacy. Although Americans are generally distrustful of governmental institutions, the military is a conspicuous exception. In 2001, roughly two-thirds of Americans said that they trusted their military quite a lot or a great deal.[63] Americans place greater confidence in the military than do citizens of most European countries.[64]

The structure of the defense establishment changed in two fundamental ways in the last quarter of the twentieth century. The military adopted new technologies that dramatically increased the potency of American forces, reduced manpower requirements, and lowered the human cost of warfare (that is, in U.S. fatalities and casualties). The U.S. military also abandoned the draft, thereby binding itself to the use of only persuasion, rather than coercion, to acquire the soldiers needed to fight America's wars.

As we shall see, this shift was justified on classical liberal principles, by the same individuals who advocated the program of neoliberal economic reforms pursued after 1980. In succeeding years, the U.S. government spent billions of dollars on recruitment advertising that promoted the virtues of military service. As the military's call on U.S. national resources declined—and as it actively promoted military service—its reputation rebounded.

Every nation that seeks to maintain a powerful military force wrestles with the question of how to extract the human and material resources needed to sustain that force. Autocratic regimes, indifferent to liberties and exercising broad control over the economy, obviously have an easier time in extracting resources. The task is more challenging in a state that is democratic, strongly committed to personal liberties, and hostile to "big government." The crisis that confronted the U.S. military in the early 1970s arose largely because its commitments—broad, expensive, and labor-intensive engagements overseas—lacked public support and could not be sustained. In the quarter century that followed, the U.S. military devised a new *modus operandi* calculated to assure long-term public support. Technological change, a retreat from conscription, and the development of more-sophisticated forms of advertising and recruitment were key components of this strategy, which I call *neomilitarism*.[65] This novel strategy provided U.S. forces with enhanced legitimacy and also greater autonomy. *Military* engagements overseas no longer implied equally extensive *societal* engagement in such conflicts.

The features of the postmillennial defense establishment skew the way in which federal policymakers respond to major public problems. Policymakers, understandably, want to respond to problems quickly and firmly. In the abstract there are many different ways in which any particular problem might be solved.[66] But as a practical matter, the range of feasible responses is limited by existing administrative capabilities: that is, what government already has the capacity to do well.[67] Broadly speaking, the advantages of the defense establishment—its power, autonomy, and legitimacy—create strong incentives to *militarize* policy problems by construing them as issues that require a military response.[68]

The tendency toward militarization of policy problems has been evident for years. For example, the U.S. military has been pushed into the "traditionally nonmilitary areas" of disaster response and humanitarian relief.[69] The defense establishment has assumed diplomatic functions that can no longer be borne by a State Department hobbled by budget reductions.[70] It has been enlisted in the federal government's campaign to curb the drug trade (which was declared a threat to national security) and also in the effort to control the flow of illegal immigration across the U.S.-Mexico border. Under the Clinton administration, it began to expand its responsibilities in domestic counterterrorism as well. In 2000 the Clinton administration even attempted to militarize the sphere of public health, declaring the AIDS epidemic to be a national-security threat.

The military has also been used more extensively for conventional military operations. In the post-Vietnam era, leaders of the defense establishment tried to articulate rules of engagement (such as the Weinberger doctrine and, later, the Powell doctrine) that would restrain the use of the nation's armed forces. However, a critical restraint on the use of force had been the fear of reprisal by the Soviet Union; with its collapse, the Weinberger and Powell doctrines gave way as well. American troops were deployed to Somalia in 1992 and Haiti in 1994, and attacks were made against Afghanistan and Sudan in 1998. Throughout the 1990s the United States engaged in the Balkans, sending forces to Bosnia in 1995 and Kosovo in 1998. And U.S. military engagement with Iraq, another former client of the Soviet Union, escalated throughout the 1990s.

## A Test of Governance

The September 11 attacks were often compared to December 7, 1941, the last day on which a major attack was made on U.S. territory, at Pearl Harbor. The comparison is flawed in several respects. One is the speed with which news reached most Americans. Pearl Harbor was attacked at a time when news still traveled slowly throughout the country. Driving across the United States after Pearl Harbor, journalist Alister Cooke found "a lot of people sitting in their homes not 'stunned' as the newspapers have it but fuzzily wondering where Pearl Harbor was."[71]

The advent of the digital age gave the September 11 attacks a different character. The nation's horror was immediate and unmediated. In a 2006 survey, 95 percent of Americans said that they could remember exactly where they were at the moment of the attacks five years earlier.[72] "Unlike any news I can remember, news of September 11 was almost exactly simultaneous with the events themselves," recalls novelist Jonathan Raban.

> Somehow, in the eighteen minutes since the first strike on the north tower, everybody knew, and everybody was watching CNN. . . . If you happened to live in Seattle, or Portland, or San Francisco, you were not excluded. . . . September 11 was unique in this: other shocking and violent events in the American past were relatively specialized and local—the assassinations of presidents, the destruction of a naval fleet, the mass murder of children at a school, the fiery annihilation of an eccentric cult, the blowing-up of a federal building. Except when they occurred in your neighborhood or line of work, they were about other people. September 11 was different.[73]

In fact, September 11 was one of a series of events—from the 2000 elections to Hurricane Katrina—that received saturated media coverage during the Bush years. Even after discounting for these extraordinary events, *average* cable-news viewership during the first five years of the Bush administration was almost double what it had been in the last three years of the Clinton administration (fig. 1.5).

This rapid diffusion of information and images put intense pressure on the federal government to show that it was responding vigorously to the attacks. In a way, the assaults on New York and Washington were a horrific trigger for a natural experiment in governance. How would an advanced liberal state, with an extraordinary military capacity, react to this attack on its homeland? The case was arguably different from the attack on Pearl Harbor, and not just because news had traveled so much more swiftly. So much had changed in fifty years, including the institutional safeguards for individual rights, the

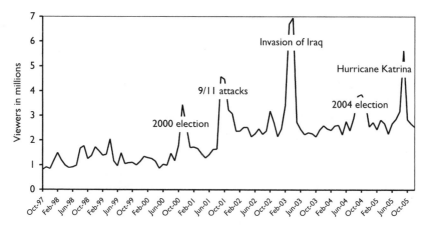

FIG. 1.5. Media saturation in the new millennium. Total primetime viewership for the major cable news networks, by month. (Nielsen Media Research)

prevailing attitude about state interference in the economy, and the nation's standing military capacity. Once shaken, how would the federal government respond?

One view, encouraged by the administration, was that September 11 triggered radical changes in U.S. government policy. The attacks "changed everything," said the White House press secretary.[74] "The way I think of it," Vice President Dick Cheney said in October 2001, "It's a new normalcy."[75] September 11, said National Security Advisor Condoleezza Rice, "forever changed the lives of every American."[76] "History starts today," Deputy Secretary of State Richard Armitage told a Pakistani official after the attacks.[77]

The proposition that "everything was different" after 9/11 entered into common parlance. Even the administration's critics seemed to concede that the 9/11 attacks led to "radical turns in foreign and domestic policy."[78] Advocates for civil liberties agreed with Cheney that the country had entered a "new normal," although they dissented sharply on the wisdom of "dramatic changes" wrought since 9/11.[79] Proponents of limited government bemoaned homeland-security measures that they said constituted the largest expansion of federal responsibilities in a half century.[80] Critics of Bush's foreign policy damned it as "radically disruptive of world order."[81] The conventional wisdom said that the Bush administration had successfully exploited the "window of opportunity" created by the attacks to adopt policies that substantially expanded presidential authority in domestic and foreign affairs.[82]

This conventional wisdom, however, was badly misguided. Everything did not change after 9/11: the considerations that shaped government policy before the attacks were not so easily overcome. The administration did not seize *every* opportunity to stretch its powers, as its critics later suggested. It acted boldly where it was easiest to do this and where bold action was more likely to be broadly supported. It retreated when confronted with stiff resistance from influential constituencies. It acted overtly when it believed that constraints on its actions were ambiguous or malleable and covertly when constraints were more fixed.

*Civil liberties.* This was clearly the case with regard to the Bush administration's treatment of civil liberties after 9/11. It was commonplace for critics to compare the 9/11 crisis to earlier security crises that were accompanied by serious intrusions on civil liberties of U.S. citizens. However, the analogy was misleading. The 9/11 crisis was notable for the extent to which it did *not* repeat many earlier excesses— such as treason and sedition trials, denaturalization proceedings, internments, blacklists, and programs to disrupt domestic protest movements.

None of this is meant to suggest that there were not serious threats to civil liberties after 9/11. But the differences from earlier crises are more interesting than the similarities. An elaborate combination of laws and policies, buttressed by a sophisticated coalition of advocacy groups, largely prevented a repeat of earlier excesses, which typically involved overt infringements of long-recognized rights, such as the right to free speech or the right to be protected against arbitrary imprisonment. In *this* crisis, the most serious challenge to citizens' liberties was posed by difficult-to-detect infringements of privacy rights, made possible by dramatic innovations in information and communications technology. The imperiled right—privacy—was one whose constitutional status was not settled until the latter part of the twentieth century. Moreover, these were often *covert* programs—partly because the administration understood that public disclosure would trigger fierce protests.

For noncitizens, by contrast, the 9/11 crisis resulted in substantial intrusions on long-established rights, such as indefinite detention, abduction, and abuse. In fact, we could reasonably make a comparison between the *alien's* experience of the 9/11 crisis and the *citizen's* experience of earlier security crises. This was a second sense in which the 9/11 crisis was distinctive: harms were displaced more fully onto foreigners. The Bush administration vigorously and openly asserted its prerogatives over the handling of aliens. The differentiation of citizens and aliens was carefully calculated and again provided a backhanded testament to domestic constraints on presidential action. Aliens could be treated more roughly than citizens because their legal status was ambiguous, and their significance in domestic politics was marginal.

*Homeland security.* After the debacle of Hurricane Katrina, Americans did not doubt that bureaucratic changes intended to improve domestic security and preparedness have been distinguished by torpidity rather than radicalism. The Department of Homeland Security (DHS), formally established in January 2003, seemed even three years later to remain a legal fiction: a loose composite of agencies fraught with disputes over resources and authority, even though all were under the nominal command of the president. An effort to reorganize the seventeen agencies within the federal intelligence community encountered similar difficulties. Attempts to mesh the work of federal, state, and local agencies were complicated by sharp disputes about the proper role of the federal government. These problems were not new, and they were not simply the result of bad judgment by poorly qualified appointees. Rather, they were the most recent illustrations of the chronic difficulty in coordinating action within disparate federal, state, and local bureaucracies.

The task of improving the performance of homeland-security bureaucracy was also aggravated by budget shortfalls. This was the product of two important constraints on presidential action: the reluctance of the American public to pay for big government and the administration's reluctance to undermine consumer confidence during an economic downturn. Americans paid substantially less for government services in 2006 than they did in 2001, and many agencies responsible for protecting the nation against domestic crises found their mission compromised as a result.

*Managing the market economy.* An expanding market economy also complicated federal action. Many of the most attractive targets for terrorist attack—airlines, chemical plants, natural-gas terminals, nuclear plants, transmission lines, computer systems—are privately owned. So are transportation systems that could serve as conduits for the conveyance of terrorists and weapons across U.S. borders. Although the federal government could have demanded that vulnerable industries adopt safety measures, it wielded its powers cautiously throughout the 9/11 crisis. This was the result of political and practical considerations. Industry lobbies campaigned against costly security measures, while federal policymakers worried about disrupting economic growth and wrestled with the question of how best to secure the substructure of an advanced market system. Not surprisingly, that substructure continued to grow in size and complexity during the crisis, continuing its sprawl across national borders and creating even more vulnerabilities.

*Foreign affairs.* It was in the field of foreign policy that presidential authority seemed to be exercised most vigorously after the 9/11 attacks. In October 2001, American military forces invaded Afghanistan, overthrowing its Taliban government but failing in their effort to capture Osama bin Laden and al Qaeda forces based in eastern Afghanistan. Eighteen months later, the United States launched Operation Iraqi Freedom, toppling the government of Saddam Hussein. The expansion of military activity was accompanied by the articulation of a new policy on the use of American military forces. The "radical new doctrine" announced by the White House in September 2002 promised that the United States would act preemptively against nations or groups that threatened national security.[83] The administration explicitly enumerated the "rogue states" that were the object of its attention. The Axis of Evil, as President Bush called it, initially included Iraq, North Korea, and Iran.[84]

The president's Manichean language, coupled with the promise of preemptive military action, alarmed many observers. Once again, however, it is possible to be misled by overheated rhetoric, this time uttered by the Bush administration. The practice of preemptive intervention is not new to U.S. foreign policy. What may have been new was the willingness to acknowledge the principle explicitly—to do overtly what had previously been done covertly.

Furthermore, the application of the principle was bounded even after 9/11. The United States had been preparing for conflict in Iraq for the preceding decade, and American public opinion was well primed to support the use of force. Also, operations in Iraq and Afghanistan did not put substantial stress on American society, by historical standards. At their post-9/11 peaks, key indicators of strain—

military spending as a percentage of GDP, the number of active-duty personnel, the annual number of military deaths—were lower than averages during the preceding half century. Outside Afghanistan and Iraq, American foreign policy continued on conventional lines, despite the articulation of new doctrine. The threat of nuclear proliferation in Iran and North Korea produced diplomacy, not military intervention.

Although the post-9/11 interventions did not constitute a radical shift in U.S. policy, it is still accurate to say that the problem of responding to the terror threat was quickly militarized after the 2001 attacks. There were alternative ways of framing the challenge—for example, as one that required sophisticated police and intelligence work and criminal prosecution. Instead, the 9/11 attacks triggered a Global War on Terrorism. "We're fighting the enemy abroad," said the Bush White House, "so that we don't have to fight them here."[85]

Bush's assertion was characterized by critics as escapism—a wrongheaded perception that the terror threat could be dealt with by "overseas efforts to topple rogue states."[86] But for a president whose authority in domestic policy was fiercely contested, militarization offered two substantial advantages. The first was the capacity to act decisively. The second was legitimacy. President Bush attempted to clothe himself in the garb of the military with the hope of drawing on the esteem with which it was regarded. Bush did this figuratively— and also literally, when in May 2003 he landed on the deck of the USS *Abraham Lincoln* in an S-3B Viking aircraft, outfitted in a navy flight suit. This was taken as hubris, arrogance, and cowboy swagger.[87] But it is more accurately regarded as a sign of weakness. The heads of other developed democracies do not feel the need to meet the media in military garb. This was evidence of the president's inability to command authority on his own account.

Even in its overseas engagements, however, the Bush administration was undone by bureaucratic constraints and its own inability to wield command competently. Planning processes were undermined by interdepartmental rivalries and the administration's own distrust of the career bureaucracy. The executive branch did not have the administrative capabilities that were necessary to achieve the president's goals, and the White House did not have the capacity to anticipate or fix that deficiency. As evidence of policy failures mounted, the Bush administration's vaunted discipline gave way to widely publicized recriminations among key advisers. Fortress Bush, as it was called, proved to be a mirage.[88] The White House could not exercise authority properly even in the domain where its prerogatives were well-established.

## Crisis and Consequences

This problem of consolidating and exercising authority was central to the 9/11 crisis. For federal policymakers the challenge was to marshal and wield authority within a system that is designed to thwart that project. For the public, the challenge was to work out its own ambivalence about governmental power. On one hand, the public wants to be protected; on the other hand, it does not like big government, and it does not trust government to use its discretion properly. As the crisis matured, this ambivalence was addressed more explicitly—partly because the perceived danger had receded and partly because the public became better informed about the way in which the Bush administration had responded to the challenge of marshaling authority and about the consequences of its policies. The 9/11 crisis became a full-blown crisis of authority.

This crisis turned on the claim that the president had exploited the 9/11 attacks as an opportunity to accumulate and abuse power. This claim was not modulated: there were no caveats about the kind of power that the president had seized or about his success or failure in accumulating authority in different spheres. Either the Bush administration was engaged in a full-fledged authoritarian project, or it was not. It was building an imperial presidency, marked by a dangerous concentration of power over foreign and domestic affairs, or not.

This way of viewing the Bush administration—as disciplined, calculating, and powerful—had the virtue of rhetorical efficiency, because it invoked old and familiar fears about overreaching chief executives. But it also had the defect of being substantially mistaken. A more accurate view would recognize that the president is faced with critical constraints as well as powerful capabilities. The restrictions are those that typify entrenched liberalism. Some arise from the evolution of institutions intended to diffuse political power and protect citizens' rights. Other constraints arise because of the commitment to a neoliberal economic policy and the growth of a complex, globalized market economy. The capabilities are those made available by a sophisticated defense establishment, itself reinvented in the post-Vietnam years and no longer checked by any rival superpower.

The United States has become a peculiar system of governance: in one sense, deliberately crippled, to protect political and economic freedoms; in another, overmuscled, as a result of a prolonged contest between superpowers. After 9/11, the United States chose to "take the fight to the enemy" because it had the capacity to do so—and also because it would have been politically or constitutionally impracticable to take equally bold action at home. Thus, overseas criticism of U.S. policy that concentrated on its undisciplined power missed a critical point: U.S. policy is driven by a kind of weakness, as well as strength. Moreover, this combination of debility and power encouraged behavior that actually undermined the long-term interests of the United States. Key elements of the nation's post-9/11 policy—war in Iraq, indefinite detention of aliens, prisoner abuse, extraordinary renditions—encouraged Islamic radicalism and aggravated threats to U.S. security.

At home, meanwhile, the federal government missed opportunities to safeguard against future attacks. It did not resolve the long-run fiscal tensions that compromise the effort to secure the U.S. homeland. It failed—even after five years—to establish clear policies on the difficult questions that arose after 9/11, such as the proper boundaries of surveillance, the propriety of preventive detention, or the interrogation and trial of suspected terrorists. The tactics that the Bush administration used to short-circuit domestic resistance after 9/11—such as the reliance on covert policies or the overstretching of old and ill-suited laws—had the effect of corroding trust in central government and undermining the possibility of negotiating clear rules on these questions. The constraints and incentives that shaped the response to 9/11—and that could be expected to shape the response to future attacks—remained substantially unchanged.

# 2

# Citizens and Aliens

If you're a citizen, you get the Cadillac system of justice. If you're a foreigner or a green-card holder, you get the beat-up Chevy version.
—Professor Neal Katyal on the Military Commissions Act of 2006[1]

IN SOME RESPECTS, the 9/11 crisis seemed very familiar to Americans. It was the sixth security crisis to grip the nation in a century. The first was triggered by the entry of the United States into the First World War in 1917; this was followed by the Great Red Scare of 1919–1921, a panic caused by the Bolshevik revolution and labor unrest following the war. The Second World War and the Red Scare that followed in 1947–1954 constituted the third and fourth crises. The fifth was the "law and order" crisis of the late 1960s and early 1970s, a decade that witnessed a string of political assassinations, devastating urban riots, mass protests, and a surge in violent crime and domestic terrorism.[2]

During each of these crises, the U.S. government took actions that seriously restricted the rights and freedoms of U.S. citizens. Foreigners living in the United States or abroad often had their rights compromised as well; but the important point is that they did not bear this burden alone. Citizens suffered with them. Well before the 9/11 attacks it was a commonplace of American political discourse that security crises compelled American citizens to accept serious tradeoffs between collective safety and individual liberty.

Many Americans perceived the 9/11 crisis in just this way, as a reprise of these earlier struggles between security and citizens' rights. The federal government's response to the 9/11 attacks, the historian Alan Brinkley said, was "a familiar story."[3] Legal scholar Geoffrey Stone saw "disturbing—and all-too-familiar—patterns in some of our government's reactions,"[4] while the journalist Haynes Johnson emphasized "parallels between the past and present."[5] History was repeating itself, said the *Sacramento Bee*.[6] The steps taken after 9/11 were "chillingly familiar," said the *San Francisco Chronicle*.[7] The *Seattle Times* felt a sense of *déjà vu*.[8] "We have been here before," said *The Progressive*.[9]

A natural consequence of this emphasis on historical parallels was a tendency to describe the effect of federal policies in stark terms: as a "war on our rights" or a "war on our freedoms."[10] "Our civil liberties and our freedoms," the producer of a prize-winning documentary film said in 2004, "have been trampled upon by our government since 9/11."[11] After 9/11, said a prominent civil libertarian, the nation fell into "the greatest civil liberties crisis since the Palmer Raids and other World War I–era abuses."[12] Like the generations who had lived through earlier crises, Americans were thought to be paying a heavy price because of the preoccupation with collective security.

The analogy to earlier crises was easy but misleading. The basic rights of citizens that were usually weakened during earlier crises were not assaulted in the same way after 9/11. This was a testament to the strength of the legal and political checks on executive power built up over the preceding century, largely in response to governmental excesses during those earlier crises. After 9/11, the most substantial threat to citizens' rights arose from governmental surveillance, profiling, and data-mining programs—programs that exploited recent innovations in communications and information technology and that threatened a recently affirmed entitlement, the right to privacy. For citizens, the critical question after 9/11 was how to balance the right to privacy with the country's security interests, given new technological capabilities. This was a distinctively postmillennial predicament.

The depressing reality is that the nation proved incapable of establishing policies to resolve this predicament that met the twin tests of transparency and legitimacy. The Bush administration was rightly condemned for undertaking programs covertly, rather than seeking congressional sanction for its policies. On the other hand, the administration also confronted a public (and a civil-liberties community) that was deeply hostile to potential intrusions on privacy rights and that routinely exaggerated the threats posed by federal initiatives. The question is not simply whether the Bush administrative *should* have attempted to seek endorsement of its policies; the answer to this question is clearly in the affirmative. The question that is less easily resolved is whether the Bush administration *could* have obtained agreement on surveillance, profiling, and data-mining policies in an environment typified by such sensitivity about the violation of civil liberties.

The post-9/11 rights crisis was also distinguished from earlier crises in another way: by the disproportionate harm borne by foreigners. While citizens worried about high-tech intrusions on privacy rights, aliens dealt with more elemental problems—such as deportation, abduction and indefinite detention, abuse and torture. Citizens once suffered from some of these threats in moments of crisis, but they are now protected by a robust civil-liberties regime. Aliens, by contrast, are not. The Bush administration exploited this reality, asserting authority most boldly where it judged that the legal and political impediments to the expansion of its power were weakest. Here, again, the conventional rhetoric failed us. The "war on *our* liberties" paled in comparison to the brutal assault on the human rights of aliens.

## False Analogies

The exercise of judging whether this crisis was more or less severe than earlier crises in terms of the infringement of citizens' rights may seem, at first, distasteful and unnecessary. A violation of fundamental rights is an absolute wrong; one can reasonably argue that it is immaterial whether there have been worse abuses in the past. A government policy does not become less noxious simply because earlier governments behaved even more egregiously.

This is undoubtedly correct. At the same time, however, it is legitimate to take an overall view and ask whether a political system tends, in moments of stress, to generate policy outcomes just as it did in earlier crises. To do this we must aggregate and weigh abuses. If we conclude that abuses in one period were more severe or frequent than in a later period, we do not deny the significance of each of the abuses in that later period. We are merely glad that they were not worse. The task of aggregating and weighing abuses is, in any case, often undertaken. Any editorialist or civil libertarian who asserted after 9/11 that history was repeating itself was making just that calculation. And so it is reasonable to ask whether their comparison of past and current abuses was justified.

In fact, the equation of the recent crisis and the previous crises was not defensible. In important respects we underestimated the extent to which legal and societal changes protected us from the raw abuses that typified earlier crises. The post-9/11 debate on civil liberties was, in some aspects, a simulacrum of earlier debates—similar in form and intensity but unequal in substance.

This was true, for example, with regard to the debate over free speech after 9/11. The crisis meant "hard times for the First Amendment," just as in earlier years, said civil-rights lawyer Floyd Abrams.[13] Advocates of free expression noted the pressures put on journalists or other citizens who criticized the president or rationalized the actions of the hijackers in the weeks following the attacks. As late as 2003, the country-music group the Dixie Chicks was boycotted after lead singer Natalie Maines criticized President Bush during a London concert, an incident that seemed to show that "dissent was not allowed" after 9/11.[14] Filmmaker Michael Moore reported that Hollywood executives had been warned not to "expect any more invitations to the White House" if they funded his film *Fahrenheit 9/11*.[15]

The Bush administration seemed to encourage this campaign against dissent. Shortly after 9/11, White House spokesman Ari Fleischer, responding to comments made by comedian Bill Maher, warned that "Americans . . . need to watch what they say, [and] watch what they do," a caution that was widely taken as a "chilling" attack on free speech and a "thuggish" attempt at censorship.[16] Soon after, Attorney General John Ashcroft warned that critics who "scare peace-loving people with phantoms of lost liberty" were giving aid to terrorists.[17] Ashcroft, Professor David Cole later said, "treated dissent and criticism as if it was treason."[18]

We can agree that Fleischer and Ashcroft should not have said what they did. At the same time, however, we must remember precisely what it means to consider dissent as treason. During the First World War, for example, the United States truly did regard dissent in this way. In 1918, Eugene V. Debs was arrested after a fiery speech that defended socialists already detained for protesting the draft. Debs, a native of Terre Haute, was a four-time presidential candidate who in 1912 polled more votes in several states than incumbent president Taft. He was sent to Atlanta Federal Penitentiary for a ten-year sentence.[19]

FIG. 2.1. Eugene V. Debs in Atlanta Federal Penitentiary, April 1921. (Reproduced with permission of the Indiana State University Library)

Hundreds of other citizens were also convicted for sedition during the First World War. Bill Haywood, a native of Salt Lake City, was convicted with other radical unionists and sent to the Leavenworth Penitentiary. The son of a chief justice of the New Hampshire Supreme Court was convicted for mailing a chain letter defending German war policy; a Vermont clergyman was sentenced to fifteen years' imprisonment for arguing that Christians should not fight; a Californian filmmaker received a ten-year sentence for a movie that depicted British atrocities during the Revolutionary War.[20] The federal government also acquired the power to revoke the citizenship of naturalized Americans who made disloyal statements. A German American living in New Jersey was stripped of citizenship acquired thirty years earlier and deported after refusing to contribute to a Red Cross war drive. Such cases, Attorney General Thomas Gregory reported with satisfaction, "had a marked effect on naturalized citizens of disloyal tendency throughout the country."[21]

During the nation's first Red Scare, dissent was again treated as if it were treason. Justice Department raids resulted in the arrest of more than four thousand suspected radicals. Over one thousand citizens caught in the raids were prosecuted under the growing number of state-sedition and criminal-syndicalism laws.[22] Some, but hardly all, were diehard radicals. In California, Mrs. Anita Whitney—"a graduate of Wellesley, social worker, suffragist, and Socialist"—was sent to San Quentin Prison.[23] There were other penalties for free speech. Victor Berger, a colleague of Debs, was barred from his seat in Congress after the 1918 election and again after the ensuing special election in 1919.[24] The New York State legislature also barred five properly elected Socialists.[25]

The pattern was repeated during the Second World War and second Red Scare. The Smith Act of 1940 included an antisedition clause that allowed imprisonment of citizens who advocated overthrow of the U.S. government. These antisedition provisions were deployed in two major prosecutions during the war: against American Trotskyites who advocated strike action during wartime and later against Americans alleged to sympathize with Nazi Germany.

During the early years of the Cold War, loyalty tests denied work to citizens who voiced progressive opinions or joined one of eighty organizations identified as subversive by the attorney general.[26] State and city governments as well as private employers adopted their own loyalty programs, even though few of their functions affected national security. It was later estimated that almost fourteen million American workers became subject to loyalty tests.[27] The Smith Act was also revived as a tool for crushing dissent; the federal government successfully prosecuted the leadership of the Communist Party of the USA for advocating the overthrow of the government.

In earlier crises, dissent truly was treated as treason; during the 9/11 crisis, by contrast, it was not.[28] The public reaction to Ari Fleischer's warning that Americans should "watch what they say" was so quick and sharp that he recanted two days later.[29] The response to Ashcroft's chastisement of civil libertarians who "scare peace-loving people with phantoms of lost liberty" was equally strong. (The editors of the *Maine Campus*, a university newspaper, felt free to retort, "The only reason why we lost liberty, you jackass, is because you took it away from us!")[30] It is true that social and economic pressures were placed on individuals who articulated unpopular views; this is certainly troubling, but it is not the same as governmental suppression of dissent. Moreover, social and economic pressures sometimes had limited effect.[31] Bill Maher's contract with ABC Television was not renewed in 2002, but Maher soon won an award for championing free speech and a new show on HBO Television. The Dixie Chicks flouted their boycott by appearing naked on the cover of *Entertainment Weekly* (fig. 2.2). And Moore's indictment of Bush's policies became a box-office "juggernaut," according to the trade journal *Variety.*[32]

Of course, there is an obvious reason why infringements on speech rights were less serious after 9/11 than during earlier crises: American society had learned from its mistakes and built stronger bulwarks against governmental abuses. When Eugene Debs was arrested in 1919, guarantees for freedom of expression were relatively weak: the Supreme Court actually upheld Debs's conviction in a terse decision. Throughout the 1920s, the Court consistently affirmed the constitutionality of state-sedition and criminal-syndicalist statutes.[33] Nonetheless there was evidence of a slow shift in judicial temperament. A series of dissenting opinions, including a powerful statement by Justice Louis Brandeis in the 1927 case *Whitney v. United States,* laid the foundation for more-liberal decisions by the Court in the future. During the Second World War, the Court blocked attempts to deport Americans suspected of Nazi or Communist sympathies, insisting that naturalized citizens could not be penalized for "sinister-sounding views which native born citizens utter with impunity."[34] By the end of the 1950s—and not without serious missteps along the way—the Court had been transformed into a vigorous proponent of free speech, overturning sedition laws, loyalty tests, penalties for refusal to collaborate in legislative Red hunts, and travel bans on Americans suspected of Communist ties.[35]

A similar adjustment of law and public attitudes occurred on another critical issue: preventive detention of citizens who are perceived to pose security threats. One of the most grievous civil-liberties abuses

FIG. 2.2. The Dixie Chicks on the cover of *Entertainment Weekly*, May 2, 2003.

of the twentieth century related to the detention of American citizens who were believed to pose such a threat. Shortly after the country's entry into the Second World War, the U.S. military removed 112,000 Japanese Americans from Pacific Coast states. Detainees were compelled to sell most of their assets, often at great loss, and transferred under armed guard to internment camps in the U.S. interior, where they were held under harsh conditions:

> Most [camps] were set up on remote, arid lands where the climate was blisteringly hot in summer and frigid in winter and where dust storms were common. . . . Comfort and privacy were all but

impossible to secure in the uninsulated, barren and hastily constructed barracks into which the families were crowded. The camps were surrounded by barbed wire and armed guards, and in some cases guards shot "escaping" internees and beat "troublemakers."[36]

Over seventy thousand of these detainees were U.S.-born citizens. (Most of the others were immigrants who had been barred by law from acquiring citizenship, even though they had lived in the United States for decades.) In contemporary terms, this wartime policy was equivalent to the removal of the whole population of Jersey City, New Jersey, or St. Petersburg, Florida.

During the war, the Supreme Court twice upheld the constitutionality of the federal decision to intern Japanese Americans.[37] Nonetheless, the country slowly recoiled from wartime excesses. Although Congress affirmed the president's authority to detain suspected security risks only a few years later—in the Emergency Detention Act of 1950[38]—this power was more carefully circumscribed: there had to be reasonable grounds for holding a detainee and a right of appeal against the government's decision. The Emergency Detention Act was eventually repealed in 1971. Chief Justice Earl Warren, who as the wartime governor of California had supported the internments, said in 1974 that he "deeply regretted" his wartime actions.[39] President Gerald Ford took the symbolic step of revoking Roosevelt's internment order in 1976, and Congress provided restitution to surviving detainees in 1988.[40]

After 9/11, the U.S. military sought to detain two U.S. citizens indefinitely: Yaser Esam Hamdi and José Padilla.[41] Some saw "painfully obvious" similarities to the internment of Japanese Americans, but the differences in circumstances were substantial.[42] The fact that all the post-9/11 citizen-detainees could be named easily (as the Japanese American detainees could not) was one of these important contrasts. Another was the judicial response. In June 2004, the Supreme Court ruled that the government had failed to respect "the privilege that is American citizenship" when it denied Hamdi the opportunity to challenge his detention before an independent tribunal.[43] The Court signaled that it was ready to reach a similar conclusion in Padilla's case as well.[44] The government responded by negotiating an agreement with Hamdi in which he renounced his citizenship and was deported to Saudi Arabia. Padilla was transferred to civilian custody and charged with conspiracy to kidnap and murder. The government's treatment of Hamdi and Padilla was not defensible; however, it was not proportionate to the harms done to U.S. citizens in the past or to noncitizen detainees after 9/11.

Indeed, one of the distinctive features of the 9/11 crisis was the complete absence of serious discussion among policymakers about legislation that would allow the short-term detention of citizens or aliens suspected of plotting terrorist acts.[45] The British government, by contrast, did introduce such controls, in its Prevention of Terrorism Act of 2005.[46] Although U.S. academics made proposals for similar legislation, these were criticized, accurately, for a "distinct air of unreality" in the American context.[47] This is not to say that the U.S. government did not actually pursue a policy of preventive detention after 9/11; it did, largely by stretching powers already given to federal agencies under immigration law. But the burden of this policy fell mainly on aliens, not citizens.[48]

## Shredding the Constitution

The constitutional and legislative checks against violation of civil liberties were stronger in 2001 than during any previous security crisis. Defending these safeguards is a civil-liberties lobby that is more extensive and vigorous than ever before. At the center of this network is the American Civil Liberties Union (ACLU), a nongovernmental organization that was established in reaction to governmental excesses during the First World War and the first Red Scare.[49] In the modern era, the ACLU has become bolder about resisting the expansion of governmental authority in moments of crisis. During the Second World War, for example, the ACLU largely supported the Roosevelt administration's policies. The ACLU's leadership affirmed the constitutionality of the internment of Japanese Americans and refused to intervene in wartime sedition cases. The organization's membership and income largely stagnated during the war.[50]

By 2001, the ACLU was accustomed to taking a much harder stance against federal intrusions on civil liberties. It also received broader public support in a moment of crisis. The ACLU's membership surged to a record high in the year after the 9/11 attacks.[51] Contributions to its national and state charitable foundations jumped by

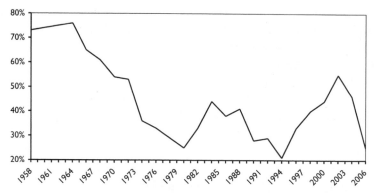

FIG. 2.3. Slumping trust: percentage of survey respondents who trust the federal government to do what is right "just about always" or "most of the time." (American National Election Studies, University of Michigan)

over 50 percent between 2000 and 2005.[52] The ACLU was also allied with many newer groups, such as the Electronic Frontier Foundation, "a high-tech ACLU" founded in 1990, and its offshoot, the Center for Democracy and Technology, which dogged the administration on profiling and surveillance programs.[53]

The influence of this civil-liberties community is amplified because of a broader shift in American political culture: the marked decline in the public deference to federal authority. Suspicion of government is, of course, one of the core elements of American political culture, as noted in chapter 1. Nevertheless, there is evidence that distrust has intensified since the Second World War. In the 1950s and early 1960s, surveys found that roughly two-thirds of adult Americans trusted the federal government to do what is right all or most of the time. The following decade was marked by a phase shift in public attitudes. In surveys taken since 1974, little more than one-third of adult Americans express the same level of trust. Periods of strong economic growth and crises such as 9/11 cause transient spikes in professed trust, but the overall downward shift appears durable.[54]

There is no simple explanation for this downward shift.[55] In the short run, attitudes about government are clearly affected by Americans' judgments about the performance of their political leaders and the state of the economy. The longer-run fall in trust is more difficult to explain. It may be a side effect of rising economic uncertainty, itself a consequence of economic liberalization, or perhaps also the consequence of the public's gradual disengagement from civic and political affairs. Distrust might also grow as a consequence of the exploitation of antigovernmental sentiments by political candidates or because the engines of popular culture—television, movies, the Internet—are now more efficient in amplifying the antistatist strains that have always been present in American life.

Whatever the cause, more-intense distrust means that the American public is primed to respond to alarms about imminent threats to their liberties. This was evident in 1995, when the Clinton administration—acting in response to the bombing of the Murrah Federal Building in Oklahoma City—proposed antiterrorism legislation that contained provisions similar to those later included in the Patriot Act. Civil libertarians condemned the Clinton proposals as one of the "worst assaults on civil liberties in decades."[56] Conservative groups including the National Rifle Association also attacked the bill. So, too, did editorialists: the *Houston Chronicle*, for example, criticized the legislation as a "frightening" and "grievous" assault on civil liberties.[57] Such complaints resonated with the general public. Surveys conducted during the debate over the proposed legislation showed that 55 percent of Americans believed that the federal government was *already* violating their constitutional rights, and 70 percent expected that the federal government would violate their rights in the future.[58] It took Congress over a year to approve the legislation—but not before it had, in the view of FBI director Louis J. Freeh, "stripped the bill of just about every meaningful provision."[59]

Popular suspicion of federal authority remained robust on the eve of the 9/11 attacks, and even afterward. A 2000 NPR/Kaiser Foundation poll found that nearly half of Americans saw the federal government as a threat to their rights and freedoms.[60] In May 2001, a Gallup poll estimated that 52 percent of adult Americans believed their federal government to be "so large and powerful that it poses an *immediate* threat to the rights and freedoms of ordinary citizens."[61] In the aftermath of the 9/11 attacks, 40 percent of Americans still felt that the federal government had "too much power," according to a Gallup poll, and a comparable proportion continued to believe that the federal government poses an immediate threat to their rights and freedoms.[62] A 2005 Yankelovich poll found that 38 percent of Americans "worried a lot" that the United States would violate their rights in the pursuit of national security.[63]

In such an unreceptive climate, a federal policymaker convinced of the need for strengthened law-enforcement powers might easily be lured to the conclusion that any transient opportunity to push through reforms ought to be exploited to the fullest. This, of course, is precisely what the federal Justice Department did in the shadow of 9/11. Attorney General John Ashcroft later said that the Justice Department prepared a "full blown legislative proposal" within four days of the 9/11 attacks. It was able to assemble the bill so quickly because much of its content had been drafted five years earlier.[64] Within three weeks the department had sent the three-hundred-page bill to Congress; within another three weeks the bill, known as the Patriot Act, was signed into law.[65] Nonetheless, the Patriot Act, like the 1995 legislation, was the subject of fierce attacks. Senator Patrick Leahy warned that Congress was "bending or even shredding" constitutional rights, and the American Library Association cautioned that the law posed a "present danger" to constitutional rights.[66] Other civil libertarians protested during Congress's review of the law that it posed "an unprecedented invasion of privacy."[67] Hundreds of local councils passed resolutions protesting the federal government's assault on constitutional rights.[68]

For many people, the Patriot Act raised the specter of the law-and-order crisis of the late 1960s and early 1970s, during which the Johnson and Nixon administrations dramatically expanded federal programs to monitor and undermine domestic protest movements.[69] The FBI's COINTELPRO program, first established to monitor the Communist Party of the USA, was redirected to "expose, disrupt, misdirect, discredit, or otherwise neutralize" the civil-rights and antiwar movements.[70] The Central Intelligence Agency established its own programs to monitor domestic antiwar campaigns, amassing dossiers on thousands of Americans engaged in lawful protest. Activists were also targeted by a covert CIA mail-opening program, and the National Security Agency established its own surveillance project, MINARET, to monitor overseas phone calls made by citizens engaged in the antiwar movement. The U.S. Army established a domestic surveillance program as well, encompassing "virtually every group engaged in dissent in the United States," sometimes including covert observation

FIG. 2.4. Poster opposing the Patriot Act distributed
by the American Civil Liberties Union, depicting an
FBI agent as a half-human, half-robot Redcoat.

and infiltration. It was later estimated that one hundred thousand
Americans became subjects of Army surveillance.[71]

Media and congressional investigations throughout the 1970s
revealed the breadth of these efforts and provoked broad public
outrage.[72] Surveillance programs were terminated and new controls
adopted to prevent their recurrence.[73] In 1976, President Gerald Ford
issued an order limiting the ability of the CIA, the National Security
Agency (NSA), and military intelligence to engage in surveillance of

U.S. citizens.[74] In the same year, Attorney General Edward Levi issued guidelines limiting the FBI's power to monitor or investigate protest groups without strong evidence of criminal conduct. (The guidelines were weakened under the Reagan administration, to require only a "reasonable indication" of criminal activity; they were also modified by the Bush administration in 2002.)[75] In 1978, Congress adopted the Foreign Intelligence Surveillance Act, which imposed limits on the federal power to engage in surveillance or conduct searches for evidence in cases involving national security.[76]

The expansion of federal surveillance during the law-and-order crisis marked an important shift in government policy. Increasingly unable to rely on traditional and overt methods of maintaining order (such as imprisonment for sedition, blacklisting, denaturalization, or travel bans), the federal government relied on methods that were less easily detected. It was able to do this because there were few checks against the expansion of these alternative methods. Such activities had not yet been problematized—that is, defined as a sphere of activity that raised profound questions about the boundaries of governmental action—and legal constraints were relatively weak. This ceased to be true after the law-and-order crisis. The abuses of that era heightened public awareness of the dangers of surveillance and produced a new web of normative and legal restrictions on federal intelligence and law-enforcement agencies.

These restrictions were tested in later years, and they were tested again after 9/11. But a distinction must be drawn between *challenges* to these restrictions and the wholesale *overthrow* of such restrictions. The claim that the Patriot Act marked an "unprecedented" invasion of privacy implied that mechanisms for constraining federal power had been completely overthrown—and that we had returned to an era marked by massive and indiscriminate surveillance, infiltration of protest groups, and harassment of political opponents. This was hyperbole. To state the point again, this is not a defense of changes contained within the law; it is only to put the matter in proportion. The Patriot Act raised important questions that were given short shrift during its rushed passage through Congress. Nonetheless, the Patriot Act only modified, and did not abandon, the policies constructed to protect civil liberties following the law-and-order crisis. Indeed, as time passed, critics eventually conceded that some changes contained within the bill were unobjectionable, consisting of updates to legislation to accommodate technological changes such as the advent of cell phones and electronic mail.

By 2005, debate centered primarily on two provisions of the Patriot Act. One was section 215, which allows the FBI to ask the Foreign Intelligence Surveillance Court for an order to obtain documents relating to counterterrorism investigations without meeting the usual standard of showing probable cause that a crime has been committed. At the time, Senator Russell Feingold worried that section 215 would allow the FBI to "go on a fishing expedition and collect information on virtually anyone."[77] Librarian associations made section 215 the centerpiece of their campaign against the Patriot Act, arguing that the government would be able to "sweep up vast amounts of information about people who are not suspected of a crime."[78] "A lot of this reminds me of the Red Scare of the 1950s," said a library administrator in the University of California system.[79]

The librarians' campaign, which played on the collision between the dark specter of government surveillance and the evident wholesomeness of the public library, proved highly effective. By 2005, section 215 was known as the "library provision," even though it actually encompassed documents held by any business or nonprofit organization. Senator Bernard Sanders of Vermont introduced a Freedom to Read Protection Act to restore "the right to read without government surveillance," which gained broad public support.[80] "When the government has secret, unlimited access to anything you read, any website you surf at the library," wrote columnist Ellen Goodman, "it creates the sense that we are all being watched."[81] Civil libertarians were ready to seize on any evidence that seemed to show abuses of this new power. Federal agents were lambasted for interviewing a student at the University of Massachusetts who had borrowed Mao Tse-Tung's *Little Red Book* for a history seminar. "Think of the chilling effect on free speech," wrote Senator Edward Kennedy, "when a government agent shows up at your home after you request a book from the library."[82]

In fact, the student had fabricated the story.[83] Indeed, section 215 did not give the government "unlimited access to anything you read," as the law itself made clear. The FBI's internal procedures created additional checks. Internal documents released in 2005 suggest that FBI agents were frustrated by the reluctance of the bureau's Office of Intelligence Policy and Review to approve applications to the Foreign

Intelligence Surveillance Court for the use of section 215.[84] (A study later found that it took roughly nine months to obtain approval of an application in 2003–2004.)[85] The Justice Department reported that it used section 215 only thirty-five times in the Patriot Act's first three years. It was never used against a public library.[86]

Section 215 may have been used infrequently because federal investigators found it more convenient to rely on section 505 of the Patriot Act, which expanded the FBI's ability to use another investigative tool, the National Security Letter, to collect business records that are judged to be relevant to terrorism investigations.[87] These letters could be issued by FBI field supervisors without court review, and organizations were banned from disclosing the fact that they had received such letters. It was reported in 2005 that the FBI was issuing thirty thousand letters for its terrorism investigations a year—an unprecedented intrusion, the *Washington Post* said, "into the lives of ordinary Americans."[88]

The report turned out to be an overstatement. An audit later found that the FBI issued roughly half this number of National Security Letters—that is, fifteen thousand a year—between 2003 and 2005.[89] Because several letters could be issued in a single investigation, the number of individuals who were the object of FBI scrutiny was likely much smaller, and perhaps half of these were actually non-U.S. persons.[90] It proved difficult to amass evidence of concrete harm to citizens that could be traced to the use of letters.[91] By 2005, the courts had also stepped in to constrain the use of National Security Letters. Two federal courts ruled that the expanded authority given to the FBI under the Patriot Act violated the constitutional guarantees against unreasonable search and seizure and that the ban on discussing letters violated guarantees on freedom of expression.[92]

Congressional enthusiasm for stiffer investigative powers was never wholehearted and waned quickly. Conservatives in the House of Representatives insisted that a sunset provision be added to the Patriot Act, causing it to lapse in four years unless Congress voted for its renewal.[93] When news leaked in 2003 that the Justice Department was drafting a follow-on to the Patriot Act, dubbed the Domestic Security Enhancement Act, the fierce public reaction quickly led the Bush administration to disavow the bill.[94] Congress failed to renew the Patriot Act within the initial time limit of December 2005 because of bipartisan concern about abuses by intelligence and law-enforcement agencies.

The renewed Patriot Act adopted in March 2006 tightened controls on the use of section 215 orders and National Security Letters. Internal approval processes were made more onerous, gag rules were modified to assure the right to consult with lawyers, and procedures for appealing against orders and letters were added. Congress also required an independent audit on whether these powers had been abused and created another five-year sunset limit for section 215.[95] (The audit found significant weaknesses in internal safeguards for the use of National Security Letters but also concluded that "in most cases the FBI was seeking to obtain information that it could have obtained properly if it had followed applicable statutes, guidelines and internal policies.")[96] Later in 2006, the ACLU abandoned its court challenge to section 215, taking credit for "improvements [that] succeeded in stemming the damage" from the original draft of the law.[97]

## A Postmillennial Rights Crisis

The debate over the Patriot Act, although marred by hyperbole, nonetheless flagged a central civil-liberties concern for citizens throughout the 9/11 crisis: the threat to privacy. It does nothing to diminish the significance of this issue to point out that it is a distinctly modern concern, for two reasons.

The first reason is the relative youth of the threatened entitlement. A conception of personal privacy has long been held to be implicit in the Constitution's Bill of Rights, most notably in the Fourth Amendment's guarantee against unreasonable search and seizure. But legal and popular understandings of the right to privacy became considerably more robust in the 1960s and 1970s. For more than a century there was held to be no constitutional bar to the warrantless interception of telegraph and telephone communications in the United States, as long as the property of a citizen was not physically entered.[98] In the 1960s, the Supreme Court became uneasy about the failure of constitutional law to keep pace with "fantastic advances in the field of electronic communication," and in 1967 it reversed its earlier decisions, ruling for the first time that wiretapping without a warrant was unconstitutional even if the property of the person being monitored was not entered.[99] Comprehensive restrictions on wiretapping and electronic surveillance were adopted by Congress in 1968. The Court's contemporaneous decision in *Griswold v. Connecticut*, although it dealt with birth control rather than surveillance, also reinforced the public's appreciation of privacy as a "fundamental personal right" guaranteed by the Constitution.[100] By the mid-1980s, over three-quarters of Americans believed that the Constitution guaranteed a right to privacy.[101]

The second reason is the newness of the technologies that aggravate the threat to privacy.[102] The technological revolution of the late twentieth century has dramatically increased the capacity to collect, distribute, and analyze vast amounts of personal information. It is the private sector, rather than government, that has been more aggressive in exploiting the potential of these new technologies; economic liberalization has sharpened the incentives for businesses to collect details about the behavior of current and prospective customers. American businesses also have more freedom to amass personal information than their foreign counterparts do, because the United States has no general privacy-protection law for the private sector, unlike other advanced market democracies.[103] (The 1974 Privacy Act only regulates the federal government itself.) Once data has been collected in the private sector, however, it is a tempting target for government agencies, who may try to acquire large amounts of digitized personal information from businesses or contract with the private sector to sift and analyze data on the government's behalf. For example, rules governing National Security Letters are important not simply because these letters appear to be used more frequently but also because a single letter might encompass a large stockpile of digitized personal information.

There are, of course, privacy threats that arise within the public sector alone. New technologies have made it vastly easier to share intelligence among national, state, and local agencies and to covertly monitor electronic communications. (Although it should also be noted that the technological revolution has also vastly increased the *volume* of private communications that might be monitored. For example, international telephone traffic tripled between 1994 and 2003, and domestic mobile-phone usage quadrupled in the same period. Worldwide email messaging is estimated to have increased sixfold in just three years, from 1999 to 2003.)[104] Government agencies are also tempted to deploy data-mining technologies to sift their own stockpiles of digitized personal information.

Congress, far from deferring to executive-branch initiatives, has often intervened to check initiatives that it thought would intrude on privacy rights. An early illustration was its reaction to Operation TIPS, a hotline for private-sector workers such as letter carriers or truckers to report suspicious activity, launched by the Justice Department shortly after the 9/11 attacks. Broadly condemned as a "snooping regime that Joseph Stalin would have appreciated," the program was prohibited by Congress in November 2002.[105]

A similar fate befell Total Information Awareness (TIA), an experimental system proposed by the Defense Advanced Research Projects Agency that would test the feasibility of analyzing massive databases of personal information to detect patterns of suspicious behavior.[106] Like TIPS, TIA was a clumsily executed initiative that quickly attracted public scorn. Congress imposed a ban on much of the TIA program in September 2003.[107] When it was revealed in early 2006 that the Department of Homeland Security was quietly developing a new program, ADVISE, that appeared to resemble TIA, Congress reacted quickly, directing the Government Accountability Office and the department's inspector general to investigate the potential privacy impacts.[108] Yet another ill-named venture, the Multistate Anti-Terrorism Information Exchange (MATRIX), combined commercial and government databases of personal information for use by law-enforcement agencies. Federal funding for the state-run program was terminated in 2005 because of complaints about violation of privacy rights.[109]

Attempts to improve screening of airline passengers also raised privacy concerns. As the protocol of the Transportation Security Administration (TSA) for checking passengers became more demanding, complaints mounted. For years, the federal government avoided passenger pat-downs, often used in other countries, which it predicted would collide with "cultural differences" in the United States.[110] When the frequency of pat-downs was increased in 2004 following suicide bombings on Russian aircraft, the ACLU warned that the pat-downs might constitute a form of sexual harassment.[111] Acting on a complaint from Representative Ed Markey, who called the pat-downs humiliating and discriminatory, the inspector general for the Department of Homeland Security launched an inquiry. A year later the inspector general concluded that there was nothing wrong with TSA procedures.[112] TSA also experimented with body-scanning technologies that might eliminate the need for pat-downs, but civil libertarians urged Congress to prohibit the routine use of such technologies.[113]

The distinctive culture of the United States was also cited as a reason for doubting the practicability of passenger-screening methods developed by the Israeli airline El Al, which involve close observation of the behavior of passengers and their reaction to questioning by security personnel.[114] When the TSA announced in 2006 that it was experimenting with a diluted version of El Al's techniques, civil libertarians raised the fear of racial profiling.[115] The technique, said the ACLU, contains "a number of highly subjective elements left to the discretion of the individual officer."[116] The *Detroit Free Press* protested that the TSA's efforts were "rife for abuse."[117]

The federal government's attempt to use profiling systems to concentrate attention on high-risk passengers also stumbled badly because of the inability to accommodate complaints about administrative errors and privacy violations. Before 9/11, the federal government had a rudimentary system for identifying passengers who might be security risks.[118] This system expanded in a haphazard way after 9/11, and many Americans who were subjected to delays or questioning because they had names similar to those on the list reacted angrily to the imposition. In widely publicized litigation, the ACLU charged that federal screening procedures violated the constitutional rights of innocent citizens. In a decision that received much less media attention, a federal court ruled that the ACLU had failed to demonstrate that enough harm had been done to sustain a constitutional challenge.[119]

However, a policy can be badly flawed without raising constitutional difficulties, and there were clearly serious defects in procedures for identifying suspicious passengers and for aiding travelers who were targeted in error.[120] The TSA attempted to develop a new screening system, CAPPS II, but was criticized for failing to meet privacy concerns and for secretly arranging for acquisition of personal data from the airline industry to test the system.[121] In 2003, Congress prohibited the testing or deployment of CAPPS II until privacy issues were properly addressed. The next year, the Bush administration abandoned CAPPS II, proposing a more modest alternative, Secure Flight. ("They're trying to do something that won't cause the public to shoot them," a government official explained.)[122] Nonetheless, privacy concerns persisted.[123] In early 2006 the administration delayed the launch of Secure Flight, acknowledging that the program remained a "source of frustration" for legislators and privacy advocates.[124] In 2007 the administration still faced a legislative ban on deployment of a new passenger-screening technology.[125]

Meanwhile, the Department of Homeland Security found itself embroiled in yet another controversy, over the expansion of its Automated Targeting System (ATS). Initially used by customs officials to screen incoming cargo, the ATS was expanded to perform "risk assessments" of millions of travelers crossing U.S. borders, including airline passengers. Privacy advocates complained that the department had carefully avoided public statements about the program in an effort to squelch debate about privacy intrusions.[126] The ATS, critics said, would assign "secret terrorist ratings" to U.S. citizens and circumvent congressional restrictions on the deployment of Secure Flight.[127] DHS officials angrily rebuffed the complaints, dismissing ATS's critics as "paranoids."[128]

The remarkable fact is that the federal government had failed, even five years after the 9/11 attacks, to deploy a passenger-screening system that met the twin tests of effectiveness and public acceptability. This was not the hallmark of a political system characterized by strong executive authority and congressional passivity. Indeed, a bipartisan collection of legislators, backed by privacy and civil-liberties groups, were reliable and influential critics of programs that appeared to threaten the privacy of U.S. citizens.

This is not to say that the large issues about the balance between privacy and security were satisfactorily resolved. On the contrary, recurrent controversies over the right to privacy provided mounting evidence of the need to develop better law on the use of powerful new technologies.[129] Over five years, the country largely failed to address this question. Instead, a less healthy syndrome appeared to be at work —a cycle in which disclosures about poorly designed federal initiatives fueled superheated rhetoric and rough congressional interventions, which in turn encouraged federal officials to develop new programs secretively, thus laying the groundwork for the next turn of revelation, scandal, and congressional intervention.

## Big Brother

This dynamic appeared to be at work in December 2005, when the *New York Times* revealed that the National Security Agency, acting on a presidential directive issued shortly after 9/11, had launched a surveillance program to uncover foreign terrorist networks that had penetrated the United States.[130] Without obtaining the warrants usually required for electronic monitoring of conversations within the United States by the 1978 Foreign Intelligence Surveillance Act, the NSA had tapped email traffic and phone calls sent from, or received by, suspects in other countries. President Bush, balking at the media's description of the NSA's activity as a domestic spying exercise, called it the Terrorist Surveillance Program, or TSP.[131] The administration alleged that major changes in communications technology made strict compliance with the 1978 law impractical.[132] Nevertheless, there was strong evidence that the Bush administration had violated the law by establishing the TSP and failing to notify congressional leaders about it.[133]

The reaction was intense but familiar, reprising well-established rhetoric about untrammeled executive power. The *Times* itself called the TSP one of the most graphic examples of wartime abuses of liberties in all of American history and "a giant step toward totalitarianism."[134] Senator Edward Kennedy said the NSA had behaved like "Big Brother run amok."[135] The TSP, said another critic, showed that "the capacity is there to make tyranny total in America."[136] Former vice president Al Gore condemned a "massive spying program" aimed at "huge numbers of American citizens," equal to the federal government's abuses during the law-and-order crisis.[137] Former senator Gary Hart, who investigated those abuses during the 1970s, drew the same comparison. The TSP was further evidence, said Hart, that the "first victim of American war is the liberty of Americans"—a remarkable statement about a conflict that had already caused at least thirty thousand military and civilian deaths.[138]

Such language had an effect on public opinion. Surveys taken in early 2006 suggested that well over 40 percent of adult Americans—that is to say, roughly ninety million people—believed that the federal government might be wiretapping their telephone conversations.[139] In fact, the *Times*'s report said only that the calls and messages of "hundreds, perhaps thousands" of U.S. residents had been briefly monitored over the preceding three years.[140] The overwhelming majority of calls and messages proved to be false leads; fewer than ten U.S. residents a year aroused enough suspicion to warrant closer scrutiny.[141]

It was also clear from news reports that the institutional and legal legacy of the law-and-order crisis had prevented the administration from "running amok." The NSA itself resisted attempts by the White

House to include purely domestic communications because of its concern about legal constraints on its activity.[142] In 2004 the program was briefly suspended and audited in response to concerns expressed by the Foreign Intelligence Surveillance Court and the Department of Justice.[143] By 2005 the program was subject to oversight by the NSA's general counsel and inspector general as well as the Justice Department.[144] The post-Nixon regime, embedded in institutional arrangements and the bureaucratic ethos, had resisted the Bush administration's assault on it. This does not mean that the program was lawful or that the internal checks were adequate. However, it does suggest that a strict equation to the nadir of the law-and-order crisis was misguided.

The NSA program was also distinguished by its nonintrusive character. The Bush administration's intention had been that Americans should never know of the program's existence. This is one respect in which the TSP was not typical of a Big Brother state, in which the authorities intend that you should be *constantly aware* of pervasive surveillance.[145] Indeed, the inevitable court challenge over the constitutionality of the TSP was complicated by the task of demonstrating that the plaintiffs—lawyers, scholars, and journalists working with foreigners who might be targeted for surveillance—were actually harmed by the TSP. The plaintiffs argued that the injury occurred when communications with clients and sources were disrupted after December 2005 disclosure, because of their "well-founded belief that their communications are being intercepted."[146] Curiously, however, it was the leak, and not the program, that was the *immediate* cause of this injury. The plaintiffs' "well-founded belief" would never have arisen if the program continued to operate, as the administration intended, in total secrecy.

Of course, the fact that harm was not immediately tangible in this case does not mean that the harm was nonexistent or that the TSP was not problematic. There is, however, a critical distinction between the threat posed by the TSP and the threats that typified earlier security crises. The citizen-victims of earlier crises—Americans convicted of sedition, stripped of citizenship and deported, blacklisted, denied the right to travel, or harassed by federal authorities—were immediately and acutely aware that their rights had been infringed. Even during the law-and-order crisis, intelligence gleaned from surveillance triggered more-tangible harms, such as harassment of civil-rights leaders, disruption of protest movements, and attacks on political opponents.[147] That these more tangible consequences did not appear to be re-created after 9/11 was, again, a consequence of the lingering effect of post-Nixon limitations. For the maintenance of collective security, the federal government was inventing devices whose operation and consequences could not be observed.

The administration eventually attempted to justify the secrecy surrounding the TSP by an appeal to national security. The president himself condemned the leak of the program's existence as a "shameful act [that] is helping the enemy."[148] "The *New York Times* has tipped off al Qaeda," complained *Commentary* magazine, "that we have been listening to every one of its communications that we have been able to locate."[149] But it seems doubtful that al Qaeda, or any other Islamist terrorist group, was surprised by disclosure of the TSP. Four years earlier, the Justice Department itself published an al Qaeda training manual that had been seized by British police in 2000. The manual warned al Qaeda's recruits about the need for tight security when making telephone calls because of "significant technological advances" in government monitoring.[150]

Attorney General Alberto Gonzales advanced another, and equally plausible, explanation for the secrecy that cloaked the program. Gonzales told journalists that the administration had been advised by legislators that congressional approval "was not something we could likely get, certainly without jeopardizing the existence of the program, and therefore, killing the program. And so a decision was made . . . that we should continue moving forward" without approval.[151] "There was a conscious choice," another official told the *Los Angeles Times,* "not to have a public discussion about it."[152]

Looking back on the previous four years—the wrangling over the Patriot Act, Operation TIPS, TIA, passenger screening, and other programs that were regarded as threats to privacy—it is difficult to dispute the attorney general's premise. Indeed, it appeared to be validated by the reaction to disclosure of the TSP itself. Of course, the premise does not lead to the conclusion that the program should have proceeded as it did. Nevertheless, the fact that the program operated in this way—in intensive secrecy and on the boundaries of the law— was in a perverse way a testament to the power of the checks that ordinarily operated on the executive branch. The Bush administration attempted to skirt restrictions that it was unwilling to confront directly. In this sense, the TSP was a pathological response to the challenge of constituting governmental authority in a moment of crisis.

The administration terminated the TSP in January 2007, replacing it with a modified program approved by the Foreign Intelligence Surveillance Court.[153] This did little to stem controversy over the threat to citizens' rights. The policy question that the TSP provoked—about the proper boundaries of surveillance authority in a moment of emergency—was still unanswered.[154]

## For Aliens, the Gloves Come Off

"We are all Americans," said *Le Monde* on September 12, 2001.[155] This was an admirable expression of solidarity but woefully off the mark as a matter of law and politics, as French citizens imprisoned at Guantánamo Bay Naval Station would soon discover.[156] Of course, every country treats citizens and aliens by different legal standards, and in a crisis there may be a universal tendency to emphasize this distinction more sharply. Nonetheless, the distinction between citizens and aliens proved critically important during the 9/11 crisis. The harm to aliens' rights was substantially more severe than that borne by citizens. While U.S. citizens dealt with distinctly postmillennial concerns such as the corrosion of privacy by advanced technologies, aliens continued to deal with more elemental problems such as protection against arbitrary detention and abuse. This was no accident. The Bush administration pushed hardest against rights where it believed that the institutional and political barriers to the expansion of its authority were likely to be weakest.

The distinction between citizens and foreigners was apparent to alien Muslims living in the United States who were detained on the pretext of immigration violations in the aftermath of 9/11.[157] Foreign nationals were often taken into custody without reasonable evidence of a connection to a terrorist threat and held until authorities were satisfied of their innocence. (One Muslim was detained after an acquaintance reported that he had "made anti-American statements" that did not involve threats. He was held for four months.) Many of them were held long after the FBI was satisfied that they posed no threat. While in custody, detainees were denied access to lawyers and family, kept in harsh conditions, and subjected to physical and verbal abuse.[158] (In

Brooklyn's Metropolitan Detention Center, detainees were repeatedly head-slammed into a wall where the staff had taped a T-shirt with an American flag printed on it, until the wall was covered with blood.)[159] Federal authorities refused requests for information about the number or names of detainees. Many were eventually deported after closed hearings. At least one detainee remained in custody more than five years after the 9/11 attacks.[160]

This was a case of policy improvisation, compounded by bad faith. As we have seen, the United States lacked a law that would authorize the preventive detention of suspected terrorists but also establish rules about the proper use of that power. As a consequence, the federal government developed a makeshift policy of preventive detention, using immigration law as its raw material. Some (but not all) of the missteps of federal authorities could be attributed to the fact that they were inventing the rules of the game as they proceeded. Only aliens, of course, would suffer the consequences of such improvisation.

The Bush administration understood that it was unlikely to encounter substantial roadblocks so long as it concentrated its efforts in this way. A federal court conceded this much in 2006, when it dismissed elements of a class-action lawsuit brought by several of the post-9/11 detainees. The steps taken after 9/11 may have been "crude," agreed Judge John Gleeson, but the government was free to treat aliens in ways that would be unacceptable for U.S. citizens.[161]

As the U.S. military began to collect prisoners in its Global War on Terrorism, the Bush administration took steps to ensure that these prisoners, too, would remain outside the law. In December 2001, the Justice Department assured defense officials that prisoners held at the U.S. naval base at Guantánamo Bay would be unable to appeal to American courts about their detention. "The great weight of legal authority," Justice officials told the White House, "indicates that a federal court could not properly exercise habeas jurisdiction" over prisoners at Guantánamo.[162] This effort to evade the writ of habeas corpus was effective only for aliens; it is settled law that U.S. citizens have this legal remedy wherever they are held. As a British judge observed in November 2002, contrasting the predicament of British detainees with that of U.S. citizen Yaser Hamdi, also captured in Afghanistan and briefly held at Guantánamo,

The United States has chosen to place non-U.S. citizens in a different position from U.S. citizens. . . . [U.S. citizens] have access to the courts in the United States. Non-U.S. citizens are detained in a place over which the United States has de facto control, but from which the detainee has no ability to test the legality of his detention. He is in a legal black hole.[163]

The administration took further steps to deny remedies for unjust imprisonment. As detainees arrived at Guantánamo, Defense Secretary Rumsfeld announced that they were not protected by the Geneva Conventions.[164] As a result, the prisoners would not have the right to have their detention reviewed under procedures required by the Geneva Conventions. Again, the administration believed itself to be on defensible ground: precedent suggested that even if the Guantánamo prisoners gained a hearing in U.S. courts, judges would conclude that they could not demand enforcement of the Geneva Conventions. Detainees also became liable to prosecution for war crimes under new procedures issued by President Bush in 2001 that applied only to "any individual who is not a United States citizen."[165] Rules on the operation of these war-crimes commissions compromised the detainees' rights in ways that would have been unacceptable in cases involving citizens.[166]

The Bush administration did not incur a significant political price for these decisions. Much of the American public accepted White House assurances that Guantánamo held "the worst of a very bad lot . . . devoted to killing millions of Americans."[167] In a 2002 Gallup poll, only 4 percent of Americans disapproved of the treatment of the Guantánamo detainees.[168]

To the surprise of the Bush administration, it was the Supreme Court that upset plans for Guantánamo. In June 2004, the Court ruled that the detainees were entitled to challenge in U.S. courts the procedures that led to their imprisonment.[169] The administration responded by hastily establishing tribunals to determine whether the detainees were properly held as enemy combatants. The reviews revealed that the detainees were not, in fact, "the worst of a very bad lot." U.S. forces had often received prisoners from Afghan bounty hunters and consequently had no direct knowledge of the circumstances under which they had been captured.[170] Most detainees had not committed any hostile acts against the United States or its allies. Less than one-tenth were al Qaeda fighters.[171]

There were still serious defects with this review process: detainees were not allowed to choose counsel or see classified evidence against them; they were presumed to be enemy combatants until proved otherwise; and in over 90 percent of the cases, tribunals ruled in favor of continued detention.[172] Detainees continued to seek remedies in U.S. courts for problems with the tribunals, as well as with military commissions, as the U.S. military began prosecuting war crimes.

Congress was not sympathetic to these complaints. The Detainee Treatment Act of 2005 countered the Supreme Court's 2004 decision by limiting the Guantánamo detainees' right to file cases in U.S. courts about tribunals and commissions.[173] One of the bill's sponsors, Senator Lindsey Graham, described it as an effort to limit "frivolous" claims by detainees.[174] Critics decried it as Congress's first attempt to restrict habeas corpus since the Civil War.[175] During the Civil War, however, legal protections were suspended for "all persons" aiding the enemy.[176] The Detainee Treatment Act, by contrast, was explicitly limited to aliens held at Guantánamo.

Uncertainty about the legal status of the Guantánamo prisoners contributed to turmoil within the camp.[177] So, too, did harsh methods of interrogation. In 2004 the Red Cross complained that the U.S. military was using increasingly "refined and repressive" techniques, "tantamount to torture," in an effort to extract intelligence.[178] Internal FBI documents also showed its concern about abusive interrogation tactics at Guantánamo.[179] By 2005, over two dozen prisoners at Guantánamo had begun hunger strikes, and the U.S. military had recorded three dozen suicide attempts and hundreds of other attempts at self-injury.[180]

However, a majority of Americans still favored the continued operation of the facility.[181] A 2006 ABC News/Washington Post poll found that 65 percent of Americans were confident that the U.S. government was adequately protecting the rights of the Guantánamo detainees.[182] Guantánamo had become "one of the more resilient institutions of the Bush administration's fight against terror."[183]

Conditions at Guantánamo were well ordered compared to other detention facilities run by the U.S. military. In Afghanistan, U.S. forces held at least one thousand individuals in detention; as at Guantánamo, there were complaints about the lack of judgment in taking prisoners, the lack of procedures for determining whether detainees were properly held, and the refusal to allow independent inspections or release information about detainees.[184] There were credible allegations of abuse and at least two deaths, which military investigators concluded were caused by beatings.[185] In Iraq, U.S. forces were estimated to have thirteen thousand individuals in custody in 2005. A series of government reports documented horrific abuses at the U.S.-run Abu Ghraib prison.[186] As in Afghanistan, military investigators found that "non-standard interrogation methods" led to the death of Iraqis in U.S. custody.[187]

The Bush administration insisted that errant soldiers were responsible for this abuse. However, the administration had repeatedly insisted on the need to "take the gloves off" with detainees who were believed to have useful information.[188] Rules on interrogation techniques were loosened. Obligations under the Geneva Conventions were "obsolete," White House counsel Alberto Gonzales argued in 2002; the United States was engaged in a "new kind of war" in which it was essential to extract information from prisoners quickly.[189] The Justice Department argued that treaties prohibited "only the most egregious conduct" and that in any case no treaty could limit the president's powers as commander in chief.[190] After these internal documents became public in 2004, Gonzales affirmed the administration's willingness to "follow its treaty obligations" but refused to repudiate the view that the president might be entitled to ignore treaty requirements.[191]

Although revelations about prisoner abuse stirred controversy, the subject rarely posed political risks to the administration equal to those generated by programs that touched citizens directly. A significant proportion of the electorate was unmoved by graphic evidence of wrongdoing at Abu Ghraib: in a 2005 Gallup poll, 36 percent of respondents said that the abuse of Iraqi prisoners bothered them "not much" or "not at all."[192] The subject went largely undiscussed in the 2004 presidential election.[193] In 2007 a federal court ruled that aliens abused by U.S. personnel in Iraq and Afghanistan did not have the right to seek compensation in American courts.[194]

The CIA was given even more leeway than the military in its treatment of captives. Shortly after 9/11, President Bush gave the agency broad authority to kill, capture, and detain terrorists who it believed to be affiliated with al Qaeda. After 2002 the CIA held roughly three dozen "high-value" captives in secret facilities abroad and perhaps another seventy in facilities run jointly by the CIA and cooperating governments.[195] In these facilities, the CIA used "enhanced interrogation techniques" approved by the administration. The list of techniques included waterboarding, a practice in which a prisoner "is bound to an inclined board, feet raised and head slightly below the feet. Cellophane is wrapped over the prisoner's face and water is poured over him. Unavoidably, the gag reflex kicks in and a terrifying fear of drowning leads to almost instant pleas to bring the treatment to a halt."[196] In 2005 the agency's inspector general suggested that some of these techniques might constitute "cruel, inhuman and degrading treatment" prohibited by treaties.[197] At least one detainee held at a CIA facility died from "misapplied" interrogation techniques.[198]

The CIA also expanded the practice of extraordinary rendition, in which U.S. agents kidnapped suspects in other countries and delivered them on CIA-chartered jets to third countries. The Clinton administration had secretly authorized the practice of rendition in 1995 but limited its use to cases in which suspected terrorists were being turned over to third countries for trial. The rendition policy was a product of institutional weakness. The CIA, hard hit by post–Cold War budget cuts and restrictions on its own antiterror activities, was increasingly dependent on the assistance of other nations, often with tainted human-rights records. Rendition was a way of outsourcing its antiterror campaign.[199]

The Bush administration exploited the precedent, relying on rendition more frequently and handing suspects over for interrogation rather than trial. The CIA's Rendition Group followed "a simple but standard procedure. . . . Dressed head to toe in black, including masks, they blindfold and cut the clothes off their new captives, then administer an enema and sleeping drugs . . . [and] outfit detainees in a diaper and jumpsuit."[200] A 2005 report concluded that over 150 individuals were subjected to rendition after 9/11, often transferred to countries known to engage in torture.[201] The CIA sometimes seized individuals who were innocent of any link to terrorism. One abductee, Maher Arar, was beaten by Syrian interrogators and kept in a coffin-like cell for ten months, until he was eventually allowed to return to his home in Canada. A Canadian inquiry later concluded that there was no evidence that Arar posed a security threat.[202]

A *Washington Post* report about secret CIA detention sites stirred only a fraction of the editorial reaction generated by contemporaneous revelations about NSA surveillance.[203] Indeed, a *Washington Post* poll undertaken a few weeks after its exposé found that most respondents approved of the CIA's holding suspects "in secret prisons in foreign countries, where U.S. laws do not apply."[204] Republican leaders in Congress easily blocked calls for legislative inquiries into CIA practices.[205] Nor was there a remedy in U.S. courts for victims of rendition.[206] By contrast, a federal court in 2006 blocked an attempt by the U.S. military to transfer an American citizen held in Iraq to the custody of Iraqi authorities, citing the risk of torture. This was a case, the judge ruled, "that demands particular attention to the rights of the citizen."[207]

There were, however, some constituencies worried by the treatment of U.S. detainees. In 2005 Senator John McCain successfully campaigned for legislation affirming that detainees would be protected against cruel, inhuman, or degrading treatment, "regardless of nationality or physical location."[208] It was prudence, and appreciation of the needs of the widely deployed U.S. military, that led McCain and other Republican senators to push for restrictions on interrogation. "I hold no brief for the prisoners," McCain later said. "Mistreatment of our prisoners endangers U.S. service members who might be captured by the enemy."[209] The White House immediately insisted that the president might have constitutional authority to ignore the law in some circumstances.[210]

In 2006, the Supreme Court delivered another challenge to executive prerogatives on the treatment of detainees. The Detainee Treatment Act of 2005 did not affect cases already in the courts, and in 2006 the Supreme Court again surprised the Bush administration by ruling that its procedures for military commissions did not conform to existing law on war-crimes trials, including Geneva Convention requirements.[211] An implication of the decision was that federal officials might be open to criminal prosecution for using interrogation techniques that violated the Geneva Conventions. The court's decision may have been the motivation for the Bush administration's September 2006 decision to transfer detainees still held in CIA facilities to Guantánamo.[212]

The Bush administration responded to the Court's decision by seeking a new law that would prevent the Court from making independent judgments about what the Geneva Conventions require, either for trials or interrogations.[213] Republican senators with strong connections to the military initially balked at such an open deviation from treaty obligations. Even so, the senators eventually compromised, agreeing on legislation that gives the president broad discretion to interpret treaty obligations and that again blocks attempts by noncitizens to challenge their treatment in U.S. courts.[214] The administration claimed to be satisfied with the outcome. "We kind of take the scenic route," said an administration official, who insisted that executive prerogatives had been broadly affirmed nonetheless.[215]

## The Vicious Cycle

The 9/11 crisis was not a reprise of earlier crises, so far as infringement of citizens' rights was concerned. It was unusual for reasons peculiar to the condition of the United States as a highly advanced liberal state and also as a dominant world power. At home, citizens were largely protected against the crude intrusions on civil liberties that typified earlier security crises. They wrestled instead with threats to privacy posed by new technologies, a problem that could only arise in a society that had developed sophisticated communications and computing technologies, as well as a firm conception of the right to privacy itself. Of course, the fact that government was largely barred from crude violations of citizens' rights also encouraged the displacement of its energies to the exploitation of new technologies, thus aggravating privacy concerns.

The crisis also accentuated the disparity in legal protections for citizens and aliens. There are other first-world nations that would not attempt to stretch the interpretation of international treaties in the same way because, as weaker states, they depend more heavily on the integrity of international law. Some countries face even firmer limitations. The United Kingdom's first attempt at a preventive-detention law, adopted in 2001, was aimed exclusively at noncitizens.[216] However, the United Kingdom's highest court ruled that the 2001 law violated the country's obligations under the European Convention on Human Rights, which allows individuals in the United Kingdom to appeal when laws discriminate in this way.[217] (The second attempt, the Prevention of Terrorism Act of 2005, did not rely on the distinction.) There is no comparable limitation on U.S. legislative power.

The debate over security and rights after 9/11 took place in a field that was, as time passed, strewn with mangled or abandoned policies. The United States needed a coherent policy on preventive detention and did not have one; the same was true for passenger screening, information sharing among law-enforcement agencies, and counterterror investigation and surveillance. Either Congress had refused to give authority to the executive branch or the executive branch had seized authority, ceding legitimacy at the same time; or problems had been fixed through rough improvisation with imperfect tools.

We should not set our standards for rationality and comity in policymaking unrealistically high; but the bar does not need to be set very high to make an unfavorable appraisal of the way in which policy decisions were made after 9/11. In case after case, federal policymakers failed in the attempt to construct legitimate authority: that is, to organize power so that it was effective, properly regulated, and broadly regarded as legitimate. And as we shall see, this was also the case in other parts of the new domain of homeland security.

How do we explain these repeated failures? We can blame overreaching and incompetence by the Bush administration. But we must also acknowledge the reality that the process for negotiating agreement over policies has become more complicated and that the debate over any policy that touches on civil liberties is almost immediately rancorous and hyperbolic. We scramble constantly (or so it seems) on the slippery slope to tyranny. These features—complexity and rancor—were not products of 9/11; they were evident even before the crisis. And it sometimes seemed that these features were reinforced over time. Complexity and rancor encouraged the Bush administration to exploit momentary opportunities or to engage in evasion of the law or to cloak its work in secrecy or to displace its attention to aliens, where the exercise of power seemed less problematic. However, these tactics worked only in the short term. In the longer run, many of these tactics—opportunism, evasion, secretiveness—encouraged deeper distrust of federal authority and consequently greater complexity and rancor. This was a vicious cycle, in which the inability to construct authority led to behavior that compounded the initial difficulty.

# 3

# Home Alone

I kept saying on the air to the U.S. government, "Where are you? Where the hell are you? What the hell is going on?"
—New Orleans broadcaster Garland Robinette, recalling the aftermath of Hurricane Katrina[1]

THERE WAS A fundamental inconsistency in criticism of the Bush administration in the five years after the September 11 attacks. We were often told that the Bush administration was determined to expand the power of the executive branch of the federal government. We were even told that the administration had authoritarian tendencies. And yet the administration was also excoriated for failing to take steps necessary to protect the United States from further attacks. Investments in programs that would protect the nation's borders, or increase its capacity to deal with catastrophe, were often inadequate. Plans to rationalize the work of the federal bureaucracy were foiled by interagency squabbles. Attempts to improve the readiness of state and local governments that would bear the immediate burden of the next disaster seemed half-hearted. These are the hallmarks of a weak government, incapable of imposing its preferences and establishing order, and not a strong one.

How could this inconsistency be explained? One answer might be indifference: perhaps the Bush administration did not really treat homeland security as a top priority and as a result did not seek to expand its influence in all these areas. Another answer is incompetence: perhaps the administration sought to expand its power but lacked the basic qualities of leadership and management skills needed to do it properly.

Neither of these arguments is wholly satisfying. A better explanation must also acknowledge the constraints that continued to shape the development of federal policy after September 11. The Bush administration was, for example, chary about measures that would increase the power of the federal government but incur substantial political costs. For these reasons it persisted with a popular policy of tax cuts and spending restraint. The administration was also confronted with institutional limitations that typify the U.S. form of government: a highly fragmented bureaucracy, state and local governments that defend their jurisdictions carefully, and a Congress that is equally jealous of its prerogatives over matters of domestic policy.

In the realm of domestic preparedness, the Bush administration did not execute an authoritarian project. On the contrary, the administration often declined to act authoritatively or saw its efforts to exercise authority frustrated by formidable obstacles. Indeed, the 9/11 crisis illustrated the challenge of policy innovation even during a period of emergency. Preparedness suffered as a consequence. Hurricane Katrina, which hit the Gulf Coast almost exactly on the fourth anniversary of the September 11 attacks, revealed the persistent vulnerabilities of an advanced liberal state—and the recurrent temptation, in a moment of crisis, to turn to the military for relief.

## Caught in the Vise

Better homeland security often meant increased spending on federal programs. Here, federal policymakers faced three tight constraints. The first of these is Americans' ambivalence about the cost of federal government. Over the past sixty years, federal government revenue— that is, the taxes and charges that pay for federal programs—has averaged about 18.5 percent of GDP. This statistic is remarkably stable— "about as close to a historical constant as one finds in public-sector economics."[2] That this statistic has not varied dramatically is further evidence of the rigidity of the policymaking process at the federal level. Policymakers in the executive branch and Congress confront deeply rooted public resistance to expansion of the federal tax load. For almost all of the past half century, a large majority of Americans have expressed the view that their federal taxes are too high.[3]

Complaints about high taxes have a clear connection to underlying realities. Figure 3.1 shows the relationship between the *actual* federal tax burden—expressed as a share of GDP—and the proportion of Americans who think their taxes are too high, over the past half

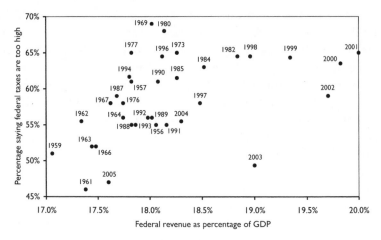

FIG. 3.1. Willingness to pay, 1955–2005.

century. Generally speaking, when federal taxes veer higher than the historical average, concern about taxes also increases. This was the case during the second Clinton administration, when the federal tax burden made its sharpest deviation from the historical average in modern history, and antitax sentiment also grew.[4]

Resistance to increased federal taxes is driven by attitudes and practicalities. According to many surveys, the average American believes that the federal government wastes roughly half the money that it collects in taxes. This held true even after the 9/11 attacks.[5] American households have also committed their income elsewhere, so that tax increases compel awkward adjustments. Two-thirds of U.S. after-tax household income is already committed to housing, transportation, food, and healthcare.[6] A growing proportion of this consumption is financed by long-term borrowing that adds further rigidities into household budgets.[7]

Throughout the 9/11 crisis, the Bush administration pursued a program of tax reductions that returned the overall tax burden to its historical average.[8] Partly because of these tax reductions, the 9/11 crisis became the first security crisis in modern American history in which the tax burden imposed by the federal government actually *declined*. Moreover, these tax reductions had broad support, even after the 9/11 attacks. One month after the attacks, three-quarters of the American public told a Gallup poll that they favored making the first round of tax cuts, introduced in June 2001, effective immediately. Over 60 percent favored additional cuts.[9] A year later, two-thirds of respondents told a Gallup poll that they would support making the 2001 reductions permanent rather than allowing them to expire in 2011.[10] Following the 2003 State of the Union Address, 60 percent of Americans said that President Bush had made a "convincing case" for further cuts.[11] Although support for further reductions softened in the following months, a majority of Americans continued to approve of the overall program of tax cuts in 2003 and 2004.[12] In a Pew poll, 60 percent of respondents said that they would prefer to have increased defense and homeland-security expenditures financed through government borrowing or cuts elsewhere rather than through taxes.[13]

Tax resistance is not the only constraint on federal spending. A second problem is the rising cost of popular entitlements such as Social Security, Medicare, and Medicaid. The cost of these programs is determined by the size of the population over age sixty-five, which will grow substantially for the next thirty years—a phenomenon that the comptroller general has called a "demographic tidal wave."[14] It is estimated that by 2030 these three programs will consume over 15 percent of GDP.[15]

Pressure from entitlement spending arises partly as a consequence of the distinctive features of the American system of governance. If the United States had a universal health-insurance program—covering all Americans, rather than just those over sixty-five—the impact of aging baby-boomers would be less dramatic. But the United States did not adopt a universal program after the Second World War, largely because the U.S. system of government allowed opponents of universal care to subvert the Truman administration's proposals for such a reform.[16] Today, fragmentation of authority makes it equally difficult to restrain escalating entitlement costs. While other countries have taken bolder action to stem the rising cost of pension and healthcare programs, the United States has mainly succeeded in making changes that *increase* long-run costs—such as the addition in 2003 of Medicare Part D, which provides government support for prescription-drug costs of elderly Americans.[17]

A third constraint on the federal budget is the cost of national defense. As we look back on the experience of the past century, it is clear that the United States has become more skilled at performing its defense tasks without drawing heavily on national resources (see

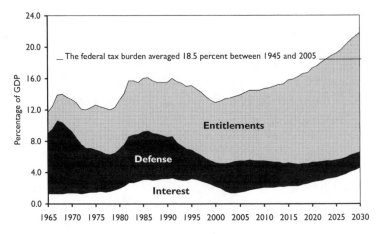

FIG. 3.2. Actual and projected federal spending, 1965–2030. (Congressional Budget Office)

fig. 5.1). In the aftermath of the Cold War, the defense burden dropped further, to only 3 percent of GDP in the final year of the Clinton administration—the lowest level in fifty years. Even before 9/11, a realist who looked at the record of the previous half century might reasonably question whether defense spending was likely to remain at this nadir. In the next four years, defense spending increased to 4 percent of GDP, a significant hike but still one of the lowest levels in modern history.

Figure 3.2 shows the Congressional Budget Office's (CBO) projection of the long-run effect of increased entitlement spending and continuing defense obligations.[18] The CBO makes the very conservative assumption that the share of GDP dedicated to defense will continue to decline, until by 2030 it sinks to 2 percent of GDP, a level not seen since before Pearl Harbor.[19] Even so, the CBO projects that federal expenditures on entitlements, defense, and interest payments on federal debt will exceed 18.5 percent by 2023. To put it another way, these elements *alone* will equal the share of national income taken by federal taxation over the past half century.

At the turn of the millennium, these three constraints—tax resistance, growth in entitlement spending, and the cost of being a superpower—were already putting strain on the federal budget. Committed to a policy of tax reduction, the Bush administration was left with only two tactics to reconcile these pressures. The first was to finance current expenditures through borrowing. The Clinton presidency ended with the federal budget in tenuous balance, but this did not (and could not) last.[20] Throughout the four years of the 9/11 crisis, the federal government annually borrowed an amount roughly equal to 3 percent of GDP. Many conservative critics of the Bush White House criticized this habitual borrowing, arguing that it was unsustainable in the long run and indefensible in principle.[21]

These critics preferred a second tactic: tighter constraints on non-defense, nonentitlement spending. This was the only remaining variable within the federal budget. In fact, this component of federal expenditure grew more slowly than either defense or entitlement spending during the 9/11 crisis.[22] Unfortunately, this category includes federal spending on homeland-security programs. While the Bush administration put a tighter squeeze on other programs within the same category—such as such as environmental protection, education and training, and social services—homeland-security functions also suffered from restraint.[23] "From Day One," says a former inspector general of the Department of Homeland Security, attempts to improve security were compromised by "lack of money."[24]

Ambivalence about the expansion of federal government was vividly illustrated by the troubles of the Transportation Security Administration (TSA). Weaknesses in contractor-run passenger and baggage screening at the four hundred U.S. airports were well-known before the 9/11 attacks. Nevertheless the Clinton administration declined to reform the system, citing opposition from the aviation industry.[25] After the 9/11 attacks, the screening system was quickly federalized: "incompetent" contractors were replaced with employees of the new TSA, which was given tough deadlines for improved screening.[26]

Congress, however, was divided over the wisdom of federalization. (The Bush administration also opposed it.) Fearing bureaucratic expansion, Congress imposed a cap on the number of screeners that could be hired by TSA in 2003.[27] Security chiefs at major airports complained that the cap was based on unrealistic assumptions about the efficiency and flexibility of their new workforce. (Clark Kent Ervin, DHS's inspector general, saw "no rhyme or reason" to the cap.)[28] Congress, unsympathetic, lowered the number again in 2005.[29] Pay and working conditions for screeners were poor. By 2005, the full-time screener workforce had an annual turnover rate of 23 percent, four times higher than the rate for the federal government as whole. The part-time workforce, critical at moments of high demand, had a turnover rate of 50 percent, worse than Wal-Mart. Staff shortages and turnover undercut training efforts, experiments with new screening methods, and deployment of baggage-screening technologies.[30]

In 2005, Ervin concluded that substantial improvements in screening would not be achieved without the adoption of these new screening technologies.[31] However, the Government Accountability Office found that funding shortages were the "primary obstacle" to the deployment of more-efficient systems for detecting explosives in checked baggage. Budget shortfalls also delayed modifications to existing baggage-screening equipment, deployment of puffer machines that could check passengers for explosives residue, and testing of screening practices.[32]

In August 2006, British counterterrorist agencies foiled an ambitious plan to destroy ten cross-Atlantic flights using liquid explosives that cannot be detected by existing screening technologies. The threat was well-known: a failed 1995 plot to destroy U.S. jets would have used the same material. Aware of the limitations of its equipment, TSA announced in 2002 a research-and-development program to achieve "revolutionary" improvements in screening methods, including the capacity to detect liquid explosives. (One of its initiatives was coined Manhattan II, after the massive crash project that led to the development of the nuclear bomb in the Second World War.) Unfortunately, this program quickly fell foul of "competing priorities in a tight budget environment": in 2003, TSA cut its research-and-development budget by half to meet shortfalls elsewhere in the agency.[33] In 2006, DHS attempted another cut in research and development, this time to cover the cost of guarding federal buildings.[34]

(The invocation of "competing priorities," along with its fellow traveler "tough choices," was a reliable marker of an attempt to reduce spending on critical initiatives. The Department of Health and Human Services mounted the same defense of its effort to limit spending on programs to improve the healthcare system's readiness for bioterror attacks.[35] Public-health professionals protested that the commitment to improving the nation's public-health infrastructure was fading with the memories of September 11.)[36]

Despite these difficulties, the aviation industry was still advantaged in comparison to other sectors. While the federal government spent $4.6 billion on aviation security in 2005, it spent only $108 million to secure the nation's more heavily used mass-transit systems, vulnerable to attacks such as those in London and Madrid.[37] Between 2001 and 2005, Congress allocated $500 million for grants to improve security at U.S. ports, a substantial amount in absolute terms but still only a fraction of the $7.3 billion that was initially estimated to be necessary to secure maritime facilities.[38]

The U.S. Coast Guard, whose fleet of cutters and aircraft protect the ninety-five thousand miles of U.S. shoreline, was also checked by budget constraints. Although the mission of the Coast Guard had expanded over the decades—through the expansion of U.S. territorial waters, the addition of new missions such as drug interdiction, and the tightening of port security after 9/11—it continued to operate with the same size workforce as in 1967.[39] More problematic was the aging fleet itself, acquired in the 1960s and 1970s, poorly maintained because of cutbacks in the 1990s, and now obsolete and prone to failures.[40]

Throughout the 1990s, the Coast Guard struggled to develop a plan for modernizing its fleet despite severe budget constraints.[41] In 1997 the Coast Guard developed a scheme, the Integrated Deepwater System, by which it would make payments of $17 billion over twenty years to private industry for replacement of ships and aircraft. In key respects, the Deepwater System was the product of an era of fiscal restraint. This was catch-up modernization on the installment plan, avoiding large upfront capital expenditures. (The plan was later extended to a quarter century.) The Coast Guard also gave contractors an unusual degree of discretion over the management of the project. This was a tacit admission of the limitations of the Coast Guard's own administrative capacities, weakened by years of budget cuts.[42] It was also consistent with the Clinton administration's belief that excessive oversight of contractors raised costs. The Clinton administration trumpeted Deepwater as a project that would generate "maximum efficiency and savings" by giving contractors more flexibility to determine how the Coast Guard's needs should be met.[43]

However, the Deepwater project stumbled badly. Conservatives in Congress were hostile to the plan and repeatedly challenged the Coast Guard's statements about the deterioration of its fleet.[44] Deepwater was finally launched in 2002, but in following years Congress failed to appropriate the funds required by the initial plan.[45] The shortfalls led to project delays.[46] The project also suffered from significant cost overruns and technical failures that were attributed to the lack of an adequate workforce within the Coast Guard to monitor the work and to undue deference to its contractors.[47] These were, of course, the risks accentuated by the initial scheme; essentially, a cash-strapped government had gambled that these risks would not materialize, and lost. (Deepwater's main problem, Coast Guard commandant Thad Allen finally said in April 2007, was that the government had "relied too much on contractors to do the work of government as a result of tightening budgets.")[48] Almost a decade after Deepwater was first proposed, the Coast Guard fleet continued to suffer from declining fleet readiness.[49]

The U.S. Border Patrol faced similar difficulties. In 2001 the Border Patrol had ten thousand agents, responsible for patrolling eight thousand miles of the U.S. border. Congress had increased the number of agents in the 1990s, but this was driven largely by concern about illegal immigration, and new agents were allocated to the U.S.-Mexico border. Even so, it remained clear that the southwest border could not be secured without substantial additional spending.[50] The U.S.-Canada border, meanwhile, remained woefully understaffed, with only 324 agents assigned to its four-thousand-mile span. A 2000 Justice Department study found that the Border Patrol was unable to respond adequately to illegal activity on the northern border because of lack of staff and equipment. A follow-up report in 2002 found "minimal" improvements following 9/11.[51]

The 9/11 Commission criticized weaknesses in the Border Patrol's capabilities, but budget pressures checked its growth after 9/11.[52] Indeed, the Border Patrol's 2004 budget was essentially unchanged from 2000, after adjusting for inflation.[53] In 2004, Congress set a target of adding eight thousand new agents over the following four years, but President Bush's next budget promised only two hundred new officers.[54] Acting Homeland Security secretary James Loy told journalists that he had been warned to "think carefully about spending restraint."[55] In May 2006, as public attention turned from terrorism to illegal immigration, President Bush finally promised "dramatic improvements" in the Border Patrol. But these were promises of future action, aimed principally at the U.S.-Mexico border.[56]

Of all threats facing the United States after 9/11, the most ominous was the prospect of attack with a nuclear weapon or "dirty bomb" containing radioactive material. For this reason the 9/11 Commission said that limiting access to material held in poorly secured locations overseas was its foremost concern.[57] The federal government's effort, the commissioners complained in 2005, was not equal to the threat. The Bush administration attempted to cut funding for securing nuclear stockpiles during its first term but was countered by Congress, with the result that the budget was essentially unchanged from the last year of the Clinton administration.[58] The pattern was reprised during Bush's second term. Opportunities to restrict access to nuclear materials, an expert said in 2006, were "going begging for lack of funds."[59]

## Turf Wars

The federal homeland-security apparatus was not only short of money. It was compromised by divided and overlapping responsibilities. The problem of bureaucratic fragmentation is vividly illustrated by a chart that circulated in Washington in fall 2001 (fig. 3.3). Disarray within the executive branch became a popular (and politically expedient) explanation for the failure to deter or respond adequately to terror attacks. The remedy was reorganization. As the Hart-Rudman Commission on National Security said in its 2001 report, the federal government needed to reshape its homeland-security bureaucracy so that it was "coherent and integrated." This was again a problem of authority: reorganization was essential so that it would be possible, in a moment of crisis, to say "quickly and surely who is in charge."[60]

The largest of the post-9/11 reorganization projects was the creation of the Department of Homeland Security (DHS), authorized by the Homeland Security Act in 2002[61] and formally established in March 2003, which combined twenty-two organizations culled from eight federal departments and agencies.[62] The Bush administration initially opposed the creation of DHS, but not because it was averse in principle to coordination or reorganization. A week after the 9/11 attacks, President Bush established a new Office of Homeland Security led by Pennsylvania governor Tom Ridge to "coordinate a comprehensive strategy to safeguard our country." It was, Bush told the American public, "a Cabinet-level position, reporting directly to me."[63]

The administration was finally moved to support the establishment of a new Homeland Security department by two considerations,

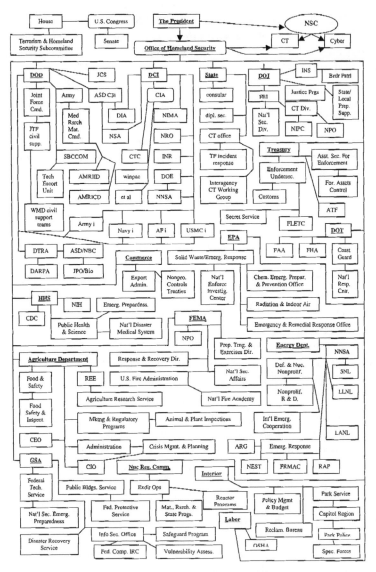

FIG. 3.3. Prepared by staff of the House Subcommittee on Terrorism and Homeland Security, this chart shows federal agencies with functions relating to homeland security. It was circulated by the White House in fall 2001 to illustrate the challenge of creating a new Department of Homeland Security. (From Alison Mitchell, "Disputes Erupt on Ridge's Needs for His Job," *New York Times*, November 4, 2001, B7)

both testaments to the practical limits on presidential power. The first was Ridge's inability, despite his stature and access to the president, to secure the cooperation of departments and agencies.[64] His December 2001 plan to merge Customs, Border Patrol, and Coast Guard activities into a new Federal Border Administration "set off a storm" within the administration and was quickly scuttled.[65] The second consideration was the realization that Congress would likely adopt a reorganization bill even without the administration's endorsement. "The White House legislative affairs office began to take a head count on Capitol Hill," said adviser Richard Clarke, and it concluded that if the president did not act, he would be compelled to sign a law named after the running mate of his opponent in the 2000 election.[66]

If the point of reorganization was to break down "old categories, old jurisdictions, and old turf," then it was a failure.[67] A 2004 analysis complained that DHS had proved to be "rife with turf warfare."[68] "Civil wars" within the department delayed several initiatives, including efforts to tighten security on the transportation of hazardous chemicals and development of technologies to improve border control.[69] The most notorious case of infighting was a battle in which the Bureau of Immigration and Customs Enforcement (ICE), responsible for compliance to immigration and customs laws within the United States, fought for hundreds of millions of dollars that it said should have been transferred from the Bureau of Customs and Border Protection (CBP), responsible for enforcement at the border itself. ICE eventually won its resources, but only after a three-year struggle during which it was compelled to impose a hiring freeze and release illegal aliens with criminal convictions whom it could no longer afford to detain.[70]

DHS had equal difficulty in integrating agency systems for managing money, information, and contracts.[71] Attempts to develop new personnel rules for the department also stumbled. Part of the difficulty was the inherent complexity of the task: workers in DHS were represented by seventeen unions, laboring under twenty-seven different pay systems.[72] However, personnel reform also became the forum for another ugly tussle over executive prerogatives.[73] After it acceded to the idea of a new department, the Bush administration insisted on broad flexibility in crafting rules for managing its employees.

The administration's tactic was not novel: the Clinton administration also tried to free several federal agencies from civil-service laws.

However, the Clinton administration was careful to preserve the negotiating rights of unions, whereas the Bush administration was determined to challenge "power sharing" with unions directly.[74] The Bush proposal for flexibility on personnel issues was fiercely resisted by unions and Democrats in Congress. Despite claims that the final bill gave President Bush "nearly carte blanche authority to bypass civil service rules," the Homeland Security Act actually retained some critical restrictions on the executive's power to revise personnel policy without union agreement.[75] Its authority to draft new rules would expire in five years.

After the failure of discussions with unions over the content of new rules, DHS issued a policy in 2005 that restated the administration's expansive view of management rights. At this point, the Bush administration ran headlong into the restrictions contained within the Homeland Security Act. Federal unions promptly sued, and a federal court struck down DHS's proposed scheme, ruling that it failed to respect bargaining rights or preserve fair grievance procedures as the law required.[76] DHS challenged the decision but was firmly rebuffed by an appeals court in 2006.[77] In 2007, DHS retreated from its broad plan to overhaul personnel rules, proposing a smaller-scale pilot project for 2008.[78]

An immediate consequence of the muddle in DHS reorganization was plummeting morale. A 2005 study found that DHS had the worst working conditions of any federal department.[79] In a 2006 survey of federal workers, DHS ranked last among major federal agencies on key measures of organizational health.[80]

Ineffectual leadership contributed to DHS's woes. This was a structural problem and not simply one of personalities. Former inspector general Clarke Ervin complained that senior administrators within DHS often lacked the authority to induce cooperation from their lower-level counterparts.[81] The department also suffered from the inexperience and massive turnover of political appointees charged with guiding the merger.[82] By 2005, DHS had lost its secretary, its deputy secretary, three under secretaries, and six assistant secretaries; its chief security officer; its chief information officer and his deputy; its cybersecurity director and his deputy; and dozens of other key personnel.[83] By 2006, two-thirds of DHS's senior executives had departed, often taking more-lucrative positions as lobbyists for homeland-security contractors.[84]

In 2007 the Bush administration was still developing a "leadership model" for the department. A January 2007 report commissioned by DHS recommended that it hire contractors to refine its "vision and strategic goals" and "expedite the culture development process" within the department. The study criticized the DHS's reliance on political appointees and urged the Bush administration to begin "supplementing" the department's leadership with career employees to prevent a "possible Homeland Security 'meltdown'" following the 2008 presidential election.[85]

Reorganization was also hampered by Congress's inability to put its own two houses in order. Twenty-six committees and sixty subcommittees in the House of Representatives and Senate shared jurisdiction over homeland-security matters, and they did not respond well to the suggestion that agency rationalization should be accompanied by a comparable clarification of committee responsibilities.[86] "It is an issue of power," said 9/11 Commission co-chairman Lee Hamilton, who complained in 2003 that fractured congressional oversight "sowed confusion" within the executive branch.[87] Only after the 9/11 Commission criticized its inaction did the House of Representatives create a new standing committee on homeland security, still with limited authority.[88] The Senate took similarly halting steps to reform oversight. The committee changes, specialists Thomas Mann and Norman Orenstein conclude, were "limp and inadequate."[89]

A second reorganization, intended to improve coordination within the network of intelligence agencies, encountered difficulties similar to those that plagued DHS. The federal intelligence community is highly fragmented, with responsibilities for collection and analysis of intelligence shared by seventeen agencies.[90] Attempts to integrate the work of that community before 9/11 were often stymied by bureaucratic resistance to centralization of control and the reluctance of Congress to rationalize its own oversight mechanisms. (These earlier efforts include the creation of the Central Intelligence Agency itself, which failed in its role as overseer of the intelligence community because of resistance from military intelligence and the FBI, as well as proposals in the 1990s to appoint a powerful director of national intelligence.)[91] Although the Intelligence Reform and Terrorism Prevention Act, passed in December 2004, finally established the post of national intelligence director, the powers of the position are still constrained, both formally and by the bureaucratic and political realities that frustrated earlier reforms.[92] The first director, John Negroponte, sought a reassignment after only two years, weary of the "total, ongoing foodfight" among intelligence agencies.[93]

The consequences of reorganization, after five years' work, were not surprising. It is widely recognized that the restructuring of any large government bureaucracy is usually slow, costly, and painful.[94] (The British and Australian governments rejected the idea of a new homeland-security department in part because the exercise seemed likely to be counterproductive.)[95] But there are special reasons why reorganization is particularly difficult within the U.S. system of government. Reorganization is more difficult because the *status quo ante* is so severe. Two centuries of rivalry between the executive and legislative branches has produced a bureaucracy distinguished by its disorder. The executive's capacity to guide reorganization is also more limited. In Westminster democracies, reorganization is a domain in which executive prerogatives are clearly established: legislative assent may be required, but political leaders have broad freedom to move the furniture as they see fit, so that related functions are grouped together and executive control is clearly established.[96] But this has never been the case in the United States.

Executive-legislative rivalry also gives license to bureaucrats who want to fight reorganization. All bureaucrats may have an "instinct for autonomy,"[97] but the U.S. system gives more freedom for this impulse to be pursued.[98] Also, the U.S. federal government does not have a unified cadre of senior civil servants, trained to take a broader view of the executive branch, that is able to check the fissiparous impulses of the lower parts of the bureaucracy.[99] Moreover, rapid turnover among political appointees is not unusual. The tenure of political appointees has been on the decline for decades: in the post-Nixon era, average length of service sank to a low not seen since the Jacksonian era.[100]

As the tenure statistic suggests, reorganization is not only more difficult than in other countries; it is arguably more difficult than in earlier years. The creation of DHS was often compared to the merger of the War and Navy Departments into a new defense establishment, a change authorized by the National Security Act of 1947. The Bush administration itself described the DHS amalgamation as "the biggest governmental reorganization in sixty years."[101] Indeed, the administration asserted a close parallel between the two reforms: just as the advent of the Cold War required "new organizational structures" in 1947, so did the Global War on Terror in 2002.[102]

Nonetheless, there were critical differences between the reforms of 1947 and the post-9/11 reforms. The post-9/11 reforms required the integration of organizations that were more numerous, larger, and better established. Contemporary organizations are also more complex, both in their internal structure and relationship to the outside world. The internal administrative systems of federal agencies in 1947 were, by today's standards, relatively primitive. In part this is a product of technological change: sixty years ago, no chief information officer could be tasked with devising a department-wide enterprise architecture. Policies on financial and personnel management have also become more detailed. For example, antidiscrimination rules (and new offices to enforce those rules) were added as a consequence of the "rights revolution" of the 1960s and 1970s.[103] The case law that interprets these rules has become more extensive. Unionization in the federal government had been "going nowhere" before 1962; today the federal government is the most highly unionized sector of the American economy, and unions play a critical role in negotiations over changes to the federal bureaucracy.[104]

The accompanying problem of rationalizing congressional oversight was also simpler in 1947. The Legislative Reorganization Act, passed in 1946, simplified Congress's committee system and actually anticipated the consolidation of defense agencies.[105] Over succeeding decades, however, it became more difficult for Congress to reorganize itself. The number of standing subcommittees in the House of Representatives almost doubled, the number of committee staff increased eightfold, and the amount of time and money invested in committee work soared. "Jurisdictional clarity" among House and Senate committees steadily declined.[106] The congressional committee system is more complex, more deeply entrenched, and more resistant to reform than at any other point in modern history.[107]

## Governing by Proxy

The task of persuading agencies within the federal government to work together—a problem of *intra*governmental collaboration—was matched by the challenge of *inter*governmental coordination, that is, grappling with the division of authority within a federal system of government.

The federal government's ability to command state and local co-operation has significant limits. Although it was fashionable to lament the "colossal expansion of federal government" in the waning decades of the twentieth century, the reality was more complex.[108] State and local governments expanded more rapidly over the past half century. In 1948 there were roughly five state and local workers for each federal worker; fifty years later, the ratio was sixteen to one.[109] State and local spending dwarfed the federal government's own spending on domestic operations.[110]

Over the twentieth century the federal government developed an array of techniques for influencing state and local policies. These techniques varied substantially in their effectiveness.[111] In the 1980s and 1990s there was a broad backlash against federal attempts to mandate state and local cooperation, encouraged by the slump in public esteem for federal government and the rising strength of state and local lobbies in Washington.[112] The federal government has continued to rely heavily on softer inducements, such as conditional grants, but these are notoriously weak instruments for shaping state and local behavior.[113]

The usual politics of intergovernmental cooperation continued to operate even after the 9/11 attacks. This was evident in the debate over reform of standards for issuing driver's licenses. Before 9/11, state legislators protested that federal regulation of licensing would violate "basic federalism principles."[114] Although the Bush administration conceded that a lack of standards created a vulnerability that had been exploited by the 9/11 hijackers and could be exploited by other terrorists—thirteen hijackers had licenses from Florida, which required no proof of residence[115]—it insisted in 2002 that the subject "falls squarely within the powers of the states" and offered only "suggestions, not mandates" for reform.[116]

In 2004, the 9/11 Commission urged the federal government to take the initiative and set licensing requirements.[117] Even so, the Bush administration refused to endorse legislation passed by the House of Representatives that would impose standards, insisting that "additional consultation with the States" was needed to address their concerns.[118] Congress compromised in December 2004 by giving the administration a two-year period to negotiate with states over licensing standards.[119] When Republican leaders in the House reintroduced legislation to impose standards two months later, the Bush administration reluctantly reversed itself, as a concession to build support among conservative legislators for the president's controversial immigration-reform plan.[120]

Federal grants continued to be the principal, and still imperfect, tool for influencing state and local decision making. These were aimed primarily at improving the capabilities of police, firefighters, and public-health workers, the "first responders" to domestic crises. Studies of the 9/11 attacks revealed weaknesses in first-responder capacity that proved to be pervasive: inadequate equipment, poorly functioning communications systems, and lack of training.[121] First responders, a 2003 study concluded, were "dangerously unprepared."[122] If local governments had plans for emergency response, they were developed in isolation from other governments and prone to breakdown in actual crisis.[123]

Between 2002 and 2006 the federal government spent about $15 billion on grants for first responders.[124] It was unclear what good the money had done. One federal audit found that Indiana state officials had ignored their own plan for disbursing federal money and failed to check on how it was spent by local authorities; as a result, there were "no assurances of the efficiency or effectiveness of Indiana's progress in preparing for terrorist incidents."[125] An audit of grants to Virginia reached similar conclusions. Congressional inquiries highlighted stories of rural counties that had purchased sophisticated equipment that they were unlikely ever to use or of cash-strapped emergency services that had diverted money to problems that seemed more urgent. State and local leaders complained about lack of direction on what they were to do with the money they received.[126]

Financial control is inherently difficult when federal funds are broadly disbursed, but much of the difficulty with homeland-security grants arose from confusion within the federal government itself. DHS did not provide clear standards about the aims of its grant programs until 2005.[127] There were also reasonable grounds for believing that the real purpose of the grant programs was simply to redistribute federal revenue. The formula for distribution of homeland-security grants stipulated that 40 percent should be divided equally among the fifty states; the remaining 60 percent was divided among the states according to population. No consideration was given to the actual risk of terrorist attack in each of the states. This produced odd results: on a per capita basis, Wyoming and Vermont received grants that were six times higher than those for New York.[128] Many states replicated the federal formula as they redistributed grants to local governments, aggravating the disconnect between money and risk. In Kentucky, the city of Louisville received only one-fiftieth of the state's allotment of federal grants, even though it was home to one-quarter of the state's population.[129]

Congress bore most of the criticism for the failure to send money where it was most urgently needed. "In a free-for-all over money," the 9/11 Commission said, "it is understandable that representatives will work to protect the interests of their home states or districts." Nonetheless, the commission said, "Hard choices must be made."[130] Despite the caution, legislators from small and rural states continued to obstruct attempts to revise the formula for dispersing grants. Senator Patrick Leahy of Vermont protested that any alteration would "shortchange rural states."[131] The Senate rejected attempts to remove guarantees on equal funding for states in 2005. "The bottom line," Senator Joseph Lieberman of Connecticut told his colleagues in 2005, "is more states have more to gain" from the status quo.[132]

Although the Bush administration was sometimes cast as a proponent of risk-based distribution of grants, it was also ambivalent about making politically awkward choices on the allocation of money. There was no *legislative* requirement that the remaining 60 percent of homeland-security grants should be distributed by population; this guideline was set by the executive branch.[133] The administration had more leeway in dispensing grants for port security but again bent to political pressures: a 2005 audit concluded that grant decisions had been made with the intent of "spreading funds to as many applicants as possible."[134] Another program for high-risk urban areas was watered down as DHS responded to city leaders who felt they had been unfairly excluded.[135]

The administration had good reason to be wary about attempts to exercise discretion in allocating grants. In 2006, DHS secretary Michael Chertoff announced that the agency would develop new procedures for grant allocations that would benefit communities "demonstrating the greatest need."[136] The department developed a procedure in which one hundred peer reviewers rated proposals according to a complex formula.[137] The process, Chertoff said, took decisions "out of the hands of the politicians."[138] However, the rating exercise was savaged in the media and in Congress when its first round of decisions resulted in a reduction of grants to New York and Washington, DC. "The Department of Homeland Security," said Representative Pete King of New York, chair of the House Homeland Security Committee, "has declared war on New York."[139]

## Storm Warning

The federal government spent four years preparing itself for another calamity like the 9/11 attacks. On August 29, 2005, Hurricane Katrina hit New Orleans and the U.S. Gulf Coast, causing the most severe natural disaster to hit the nation in a century.[140] Katrina was not a terrorist-induced event; however, the Bush administration had made clear that the steps it was taking to prepare for terror attacks would enhance government's ability to deal with natural disasters as well.[141]

Unlike a terrorist attack, the federal government had ample warning about the hurricane threat to New Orleans. The city, said *Scientific American* in 2001, "is a disaster waiting to happen."[142] In 2004, the Federal Emergency Management Agency (FEMA) actually organized a simulation, labeled Hurricane Pam, in which a hurricane of comparable strength destroyed a half-million buildings and required evacuation of one million people in the New Orleans area. The National Hurricane Center warned about Katrina's strength two full days before it hit the Gulf Coast. And yet the governmental response to the devastation caused by the hurricane was shockingly inept.[143] Katrina, said DHS's former inspector general, showed that the United States is "still dangerously unprepared for disasters."[144]

The debacle provided a horrific illustration of the vulnerabilities of the U.S. system of governance. The most popular explanation for the post-Katrina debacle was political cronyism.[145] President Bush's first choice as FEMA head, Joe Allbaugh, was his 2000 campaign manager and had no training in emergency management. (Allbaugh resigned in 2003 to head a consulting business that would "take advantage of business opportunities in the Middle East following the conclusion of the U.S.-led war in Iraq.")[146] His successor, Michael Brown, came to FEMA from a post at the International Arabian Horse Association. Other key appointees within FEMA were equally inexperienced.[147]

Of course, cronyism is not unique to FEMA; rather, it is a chronic problem within the U.S. government, where the idea of a thoroughly professionalized bureaucracy has always been anathema.[148] Political appointees, rather than career public servants, are chosen to lead federal agencies because they are expected to serve as checks on bureaucratic power. But appointees often have two significant liabilities: limited competence and weak ties to leaders in other agencies. This can lead to a *diminution* of executive control, as we saw after Katrina: the limbs of government did not move as the president might have wished them to.

There were other systemic problems whose effects were manifested after Katrina. One of these was the uncertainty about the proper role of the federal government in responding to disasters. For most of U.S. history, the federal government had a secondary role in disaster management. ("Not a single federal dollar" was spent on relief on the cataclysmic 1927 Mississippi flood.)[149] The federal role was slowly consolidated in the 1970s, with the passage of the Disaster Relief Act of 1974 and the creation of FEMA itself in 1978. However, FEMA was preoccupied with another mission—civil defense against nuclear attacks—throughout the 1980s.[150]

It was the Clinton administration that gave FEMA a higher profile in responding to natural disasters—although even then it was careful not to intervene without the consent of governors. The agency was never intended to hold a "command position" in emergency response.[151] Even so, FEMA's role provoked controversy. Critics complained that the Clinton administration had perfected a policy of "disaster Keynesianism"—a politically popular formula of generous payments for postdisaster assistance. In 1998 the U.S. General Accounting Office reported a substantial growth in disaster-assistance costs in the 1990s, caused by an increase in the number of presidential disaster declarations and the loosening of eligibility for assistance.[152] Disasters were more likely to be declared in states that were politically important to the president.[153] Along with increased spending came complaints about lack of controls to assure that aid was used properly.[154]

FEMA Director Allbaugh had these criticisms in mind when he told Congress in May 2001 that the federal role in disaster management "may have ballooned beyond what is an appropriate level." Disaster assistance, Allbaugh said, had evolved into an oversized entitlement program. He promised that FEMA would "restore the predominant role of state and local response to most disasters." Allbaugh conceded that this would not be an easy task.[155]

Hurricane Katrina showed one of the difficulties. In a moment of crisis, nuanced debate about the boundaries of federal responsibility is overwhelmed by the realities of a radically changed media environment. Like 9/11 itself, Katrina was an information-age crisis. *MediaWeek* reported that the cable news networks "racked up stunning ratings" for their nonstop coverage of the disaster.[156] As on 9/11, Americans were "drawn together," says historian Douglas Brinkley, "by the shared response of living together through a searing event, moment by moment."[157]

This intense coverage had the effect of drawing the federal government into the eye of the storm, whether it wished to be there or not. CNN anchor Anderson Cooper was lauded when he chastised Republican Senator Mary Landrieu for defending the federal response to Katrina. "A man came up to me . . . today," Cooper reported, "and said, . . . 'Don't we pay taxes for the federal government to be protecting us?' "[158] By the end of the week, this was a widely shared complaint. Most Americans believed that the federal government should have been better prepared for Katrina. Many held it, rather than state and local governments, primarily responsible for the failure to respond effectively.[159]

FEMA was not built to handle this job. "If you want big capability," a FEMA official told a Senate inquiry in 2006, "you got to make a big investment."[160] But even the Clinton administration had declined to do this: with three thousand employees, FEMA was about one-sixth the size of the New York City Fire Department. Under the Bush administration, fiscal pressures further corroded its capacity. FEMA reduced the number of its emergency-response and medical-assistance teams and eliminated funding for training. The response team mobilized for New Orleans was, at the moment of Katrina's landfall, "theoretical": it had never worked together as a unit. FEMA's urban search-and-rescue teams also operated on a shoestring budget, a Senate investigation later found, using hand-me-down equipment. Funding shortfalls delayed the development of FEMA's plans for the 2005 hurricane season.[161]

The absorption of FEMA into the Department of Homeland Security, pitched as a way of bolstering its capabilities, largely backfired. "FEMA is really now FEMA on steroids," Michael Brown had said in June 2003. "That's the best way to describe us."[162] In reality, FEMA staff complained, DHS treated FEMA as an "organ donor," extracting money to pay for central functions not funded by Congress.[163] Key functions were moved elsewhere in the department. Morale plummeted. In a 2004 survey, a majority of FEMA's career officials said that the agency had deteriorated since its absorption into DHS and that they would prefer to move to jobs elsewhere if possible.[164]

Limited in its own capacities, FEMA's success hinged largely on its ability to coordinate the deployment of resources held by other federal agencies. Within a sprawling bureaucracy, this was no easy task. In 2002, the Bush administration began to develop a National Response Plan that explained how federal efforts would be synchronized in a moment of crisis. In January 2005, DHS secretary Tom Ridge announced that the plan had been finalized, calling it a "bold step forward in bringing unity in our response to disasters and terrorist threats."[165] "The end result," Ridge promised, "is vastly improved coordination . . . to help save lives and protect America's communities."[166]

This, a White House adviser later conceded, was "false advertising."[167] The National Response Plan conveyed the impression of rationality in crisis response, but the tendency toward disarray could not be easily suppressed. A training exercise undertaken in April 2005 revealed "confusion at all levels" and "a fundamental lack of understanding" about procedures contained in the plan. Indeed, key components of the plan were still incomplete when Katrina hit the Gulf Coast five months later. DHS itself did not activate key procedures within the plan for four days after the National Hurricane Center's warning of Katrina's path and devastating power.[168]

There was other evidence of the difficulty in meshing the work of different levels of government. At its conclusion in July 2004, FEMA announced that the Hurricane Pam simulation had allowed FEMA and other agencies to make "great progress in our preparedness efforts."[169] In fact, the exercise revealed serious gaps in preparedness. The City of New Orleans, which had received $18 million from the federal government since 2002 to improve its response capabilities, reported that it still had no plan for evacuation of poor or disabled citizens. The exercise "reinforced the importance of coordination," the Senate investigation found, but this was hampered by the unwillingness of agencies to pay for follow-up planning. Critical components of a response plan for New Orleans were incomplete a year later.[170]

In a moment of crisis, response experts say, it is important to establish *unified command*, a voluntary arrangement in which agencies coordinate their actions. (The contrast is to *unity of command*, in which a single head has complete formal authority, an outcome that is often unattainable in a federalized system.)[171] After Katrina, efforts to establish a unified command largely collapsed, a consequence of confusion about procedures, lack of experience among political leaders, distrust, and political antagonisms.[172] Indeed, the policies laid out in the National Response Plan were not well-suited to high-profile crises in which political leaders face strong incentives to assert command or shift blame.[173] Five days after Katrina's landfall, Mayor Ray Nagin said, there were still too many chiefs calling the shots.[174]

## Declaring War on Katrina

Despairing over the inability of civilian authorities to provide relief, many of Katrina's victims turned to the military for help. Thirteen years earlier, an exasperated local official in Florida, coping with the damage caused by Hurricane Andrew, had asked, "Where in hell is the Cavalry?"[175] This, of course, was an evocation of the familiar scene from the Western movie in which the U.S. Cavalry rides over the hilltop to rescue a besieged settler family. In Florida, and later in the Gulf Coast, it captured the popular sentiment that, whatever the fine points of constitutional responsibilities might be, the federal government had a duty to respond quickly to disaster. "The Cavalry didn't show up," said a New Orleans official. "I was mad as I could be."[176]

Five days after Katrina's landfall, residents meant this call for military assistance literally as well: they wanted troops to restore order and organize aid. On September 3, President Bush ordered the deployment of seven thousand troops to New Orleans—including, coincidentally, elements of the First Cavalry Division. "Basically," said a disaster-response expert, "We declared war on Hurricane Katrina."[177]

The relief was palpable. "Thank you, Mr. Army!" a little girl shouted as troops entered the city.[178] The U.S. military appeared to offer something more reliable than the promise of "unified command": actual unity of command, backed by robust capacity. The desire for clear authority was evidenced in the praise given to Lt. General Russell Honoré, commander of the military task force. Honoré, CNN reported, was a "cigar-chewing, stomping, cussing general" who nonetheless stooped "to pick up babies on the street and take them to safety."[179] Mayor Nagin lauded Honoré as a "John Wayne dude who can get some stuff done."[180]

In fact, the mobilization of troops suffered from its own complications. The Posse Comitatus Act, adopted shortly after the Civil War, generally prevents federal troops from enforcing law within U.S. borders. Deployment of federal forces also had to be coordinated with the use of National Guard troops controlled by the State of Louisiana, which did have law-enforcement powers. President Bush could have relied on another postbellum law, the Insurrection Act, to justify the use of federal troops in restoring order, but the administration was reluctant to bear the risk of political controversy from exercising that authority.[181] "Can you imagine how it would have been perceived," a senior administration official said, "if a president of the United States of one party had pre-emptively taken from the female governor of another party the command and control of her forces?"[182]

Bush and Louisiana governor Kathleen Babineaux Blanco negotiated for four days but failed to reach agreement on a command structure that would comprise federal and National Guard troops.[183] The antagonism between Bush and Blanco was offset by the longtime friendship between two career officials—Honoré and Major General Bennett Landreneau, commander of the Louisiana National Guard—who worked out problems of coordination informally.[184]

"The Department of Defense saved the day," a federal official said later.[185] Given the weakness of civilian agencies, and the continued unwillingness of the public to countenance tax increases that would pay for improved emergency response, the Bush administration began to push for an expanded military role in domestic crisis response.[186] It was clear, the president said, "that a challenge on this scale requires . . . a broader role for the armed forces—the institution of our government most capable of massive logistical operations on a moment's notice."[187] Bush suggested that the Defense Department—the only federal organization with the capacity to "marshal resources and deploy them quickly"—might become the lead agency for response to major disasters.[188] The administration asked Congress to amend legislation that limited the domestic role of federal forces and directed military commanders to develop plans for rapid response to disasters.[189] In October 2006, Congress changed the law so that federal troops could be used to restore order after a natural disaster, epidemic, or terrorist attack.[190] This response to Katrina, with its turn to the military, echoed the administration's response to the 9/11 attacks.

# 4

# Soothing the Market

The most important thing, war or no war, is for the economy to grow.
—White House press secretary Ari Fleischer,
March 2003[1]

THE U.S. GOVERNMENT wrestled with at least three challenges in governance in the aftermath of 9/11: first, how to manage the tension between extension of law-enforcement powers and sensitivity on civil liberties; second, how to put its bureaucracy in order, through reorganization and improvement of the capabilities of federal agencies; and third, how to manage the market in a moment of crisis. The Bush administration's record on this third challenge was clear. It served the market; it did not govern it. In the immediate aftermath of the attacks, the federal government moved swiftly to ensure that the market's tempo was not interrupted. After the first few months of crisis, when it was clear that the market had regained its footing, the federal government still moved cautiously, avoiding firm assertions of regulatory power.

We might say that deference to the market is precisely what should be expected from a Republican administration and Republican Congress. In saying this, however, we would concede that in at least one area the administration's policy was *not* distinguished by the forceful assertion of authority. In any case, it is too easy to attribute the behavior of the Bush administration simply to its ideological predispositions. There are strong continuities between many Bush policies and those of the Clinton administration. Democratic or Republican, federal policymakers now confront a range of political, technical, and legal considerations that largely prevent a forceful extension of federal power over the market. The result, instead, is careful attention to the needs of the market, as well as cautious and sometimes incomplete regulation, even in a moment of crisis.

## The New Realities of Market Governance

Three critical realities tempered the exercise of federal authority over the market in the new millennium. The first is that the market is broader, more complex, and more vulnerable to disruption than ever before. This is sometimes treated as a result of economic globalization, which has linked national markets so tightly that unexpected events in one corner of the world can quickly reverberate in another. Indeed, a former senior official of the International Monetary Fund *defines* economic globalization as "a phenomenon by which economic agents in any given part of the world are much more affected by events elsewhere in the world."[2] Throughout the 1990s the world was given repeated demonstrations of this interdependence, as financial crises in Mexico, Thailand, and Russia rippled around the globe. Interdependence is not limited to financial markets. As Barry Lynn says, production systems are also "more interactively complex and tightly coupled."[3] The 9/11 attacks showed how easily globalized production systems could be upset by restrictions on air travel and controls on the traffic of goods and people through U.S. borders.

However, this growing interdependence is not strictly a result of globalization. It is symptomatic of a much longer process of market expansion, of which globalization is only the most recent phase. Globalization was preceded by a period in which new modes of communication and transportation led to the growth of interregional commerce within the United States and the emergence of a truly national economy.[4] This process continues today—for example, through the integration of regional power grids. Integration within national borders also creates interdependencies—evidenced by the 2003 blackout, in which an errant tree branch in Ohio triggered a series of events that caused $6 billion in damage throughout the northeastern U.S. and Canada; recurrent crises over contamination of pharmaceuticals and food products; and Hurricane Katrina, which interrupted oil and gas production in the Gulf of Mexico and caused a nationwide energy shock.[5]

Market expansion generates wealth. At the same time, however, it generates interdependencies that can be exploited by terrorists. It is increasingly difficult to protect against these vulnerabilities for technical, legal, and political reasons. This is the second critical reality of postmillennial market governance. From a *technical* point of view, it may be difficult to anticipate the many ways in which a highly complex system might be prone to attack. Indeed, there may be no single organization that has a coherent overall view of the operation of the market in which it works.[6] Government agencies, standing outside the market, may be even more disadvantaged in their attempts to understand these complex systems. The *legal* predicament has to do with jurisdiction: a growing market may soon grow beyond the limits of any single government's authority. Regulatory action is then complicated by the need for coordination among national and subnational governments.

The *political* checks on government action to correct market vulnerabilities are twofold. First, government is confronted with increasingly powerful industry lobbies. The perception that Washington's lobbyist industry had exploded in the past decade is widespread, if slightly askew. In 2006, during the scandal over abuses by lobbyist Jack Abramoff, it was often reported that the number of lobbyists operating in the capital had doubled over the preceding five years. Conservatives, and many journalists, attributed the explosion to the rapid growth of government itself. As spending has increased, the argument went, so too has the community of interest groups seeking to influence the distribution of federal largesse.[7]

This logic is mistaken on two counts. First, there has not been a commensurate increase in spending; indeed, federal spending as a share of GDP was lower in 2001–2005 than in the preceding quarter century.[8] Second, the data on the number of federal lobbyists is itself flawed. Paradoxically, this is the consequence of reform—specifically, the 1995 Lobbying Disclosure Act, which requires lobbyists to register and make disclosures about their activities. It has become routine to report on the number of lobbyist registrations contained in the database created by the law. But the database provides a historical record of *all* lobbyist registrations filed since 1997; lobbyists who are no longer active are not removed. It is inevitable, therefore, that this number will increase over time.[9]

Although the pace may be overstated, it is nonetheless true that that the lobbying in Washington has grown steadily throughout the modern era, including the past decade.[10] For example, the amount of money spent on lobbying activities increased by about 50 percent between 1997 and 2004 (fig. 4.1). The number of "big lobbyists"—those who reported spending more than $1 million in a six-month period—

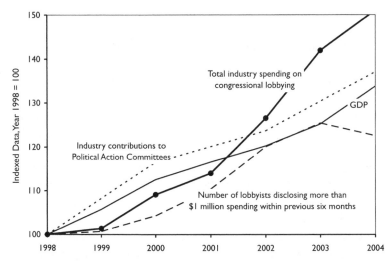

FIG. 4.1. Growth in lobbyist activity, 1998–2004. All data indexed so that 1998 = 100. (PoliticalMoneyLine.com; Center for Responsive Politics; Senate Office of Public Records; U.S. Budget Historical Tables)

increased by roughly one-third over the same seven years, as did the amount of money contributed by business to political action committees. ("The town," said Norman Ornstein in early 2007, is "virtually awash in money.")[11] There may be a straightforward explanation for these trends. The economy also grew by roughly 35 percent in these seven years. As income grows, so too does spending on many goods and services. There is no obvious reason why spending on political influence should be an exception to this general rule.[12]

Nonetheless, there is a worrying interdependence between growing lobbyist largesse and the financial needs of presidential and congressional incumbents and challengers. In 2004, a winning campaign in the House of Representatives spent $1 million; a winning Senate campaign, $7 million; the winning presidential bid, $345 million.[13] A combination of factors contribute to escalating campaign costs. One is the absence of statutory limits on campaign spending, following the Supreme Court's 1976 decision that such limits violate the First Amendment guarantee of freedom of speech.[14] Another factor is the market price of advertising in the broadcast media, the dominant component of campaign budgets.[15]

It is reasonable to assume that the private sector expects to reap benefits from its expanding investment in political influence. It is difficult to substantiate whether this expectation is realized.[16] Some research supports the commonsense supposition that legislators who rely extensively on business campaign contributions are likely to support certain kinds of pro-business legislation.[17] A larger body of research bolsters a different, although still troublesome, conclusion: that the growth of lobbying simply makes the process of policymaking more complicated and lengthens the time required to negotiate legislation.[18] This implies that the cumulative product of investments in lobbying and political campaigns is not necessarily a pro-business policy shift but stasis.[19]

There is a second political constraint on market governance: an acute awareness on the part of political leaders of the electoral backlash that will follow if government takes steps that are believed to undercut economic growth. By 2001 it was taken as axiomatic that voters respond to economic slowdowns by withdrawing support from incumbent presidents and members of Congress. Research validates this view.[20] This has been especially true in the half century following the Second World War.[21]

The decade preceding the 2001 attacks affirmed the connection between economic growth and political survival. President Bush's father, George H. W. Bush, was credited with a diplomatic and military triumph in the Gulf War, but this was outweighed by an economic slowdown at home and plummeting consumer confidence. The shift in economic conditions was not dramatic: in real terms, the economy continued to grow in 1990–92. Nonetheless, the Clinton campaign exploited the elder Bush's weakness. Clinton's chief strategist, James Carville, posted a caution in the campaign's Little Rock headquarters: "The Economy, Stupid." By the 1992 election, public confidence in Bush's leadership had collapsed.[22]

Clinton heeded Carville's advice even after the election. Like the younger Bush, Clinton began his presidency without a strong electoral mandate.[23] Unlike the elder Bush, Clinton gave the economy conspicuous attention, carefully trimming policies so that they would not jeopardize a recovery.[24] The quick resurgence of the economy benefited Clinton, to the deep frustration of his opponents. Throughout the Lewinsky scandal and the Republican campaign for impeachment, public support for Clinton remained buoyant, even though most Americans questioned his integrity.[25]

On the eve of the September 11 attacks, George W. Bush was preoccupied with the political dangers that would follow an economic slowdown. The economy stagnated in the first three quarters of 2001, and consumer confidence slid sharply.[26] Public opinion about Bush's competence in managing the economy, and approval of his overall performance, was softening.[27] There were uncomfortable parallels to 1990–92. Bush, the *New York Times* reported on September 9, 2001, was "determined not to repeat the mistake his father made" by failing to respond quickly to signs of economic reversal.[28]

## Get Down to Disney World

Key economic indicators may have been unpromising before the 9/11 attacks, but immediately afterward it was clear that these indicators were blinking red. Consumer confidence dropped to its lowest level since 1993.[29] Mass layoffs, already at a level not seen in several years, increased further.[30] The unemployment rate rose to 5.3 percent in October, the highest rate in four years. The travel and airline industries were hit especially hard. Analysts later estimated that the airline industry experienced an immediate 30 percent drop in demand.[31] Two major airlines teetered on insolvency.[32]

The federal government responded to these signals with unusual alacrity. In the space of four days, Congress provided $40 billion in emergency appropriations for security and recovery.[33] Within the span of only one day, Congress passed, and the president signed, an additional $15 billion aid package for the airline industry.[34] Al Qaeda had "targeted our economy," Bush told the nation on September 22, promising he would persist with tax cuts to counter the economic shock caused by the attacks.[35] "There ought to be more" tax cuts, Bush said later, "to make sure that the consumer has got money to spend, money to spend in the short term."[36] Three times in the remainder of 2001, the independent Federal Reserve signaled its goal of reducing interest rates in an effort to encourage business and household spending. A few months later, Congress approved another $50 billion in tax breaks and direct aid for economic recovery.[37]

The Bush administration also provided intangible aid by launching a "pro-consumption publicity blitz" on behalf of the travel industry.[38] At a rally at Chicago's O'Hare Airport two weeks after the attacks, Bush encouraged the American public to start traveling again. "One of the great goals of this nation's war is to restore public confidence in the airline industry," said the president. "Fly and enjoy America's great destination spots. Get down to Disney World in Florida. Take your families and enjoy life, the way it's meant to be enjoyed."[39]

At the urging of J. W. Marriott Jr., chairman of the Marriott hotel chain and a long-time Republican, Bush also participated in a $20 million advertising campaign launched by the Travel Industry Association of America (TIA). Designed to "link travel to patriotic duty," the campaign told Americans that the terrorists had intended to strike at one of their "fundamental freedoms," the right to travel.[40] Seventy percent of Americans reported that they saw Bush's advertisement for TIA during its four-week run. An industry survey found that most Americans understood it as an appeal to travel and spend more money to boost the economy.[41]

Many Americans appreciated that there was something strangely out of kilter about the president's prominent role in boosting consumption in a moment of crisis. There was nothing inappropriate about presidential sympathy for the plight of the market; it was Calvin Coolidge, after all, who first asserted that the chief business of the American people is business. But Coolidge also said, in the same 1925 speech, that business

> is not the main element which appeals to the American people. We make no concealment of the fact that we want wealth, but there are many other things that we want very much more. We want peace and honor, and that charity which is so strong an element of all civilization. The chief ideal of the American people is idealism.[42]

Throughout the twentieth century, popular conventions about the role of the president were premised on the notion that he should use the bully pulpit to appeal to these higher ideals. The president cared about the market but stood above it. This was particularly true in crises, when the role of the president was to emphasize the unusual quality of the moment and shake the nation free of commercial preoccupations, as Franklin Roosevelt did a year *before* Pearl Harbor:

No one can tell the exact character of the emergency situations that we may be called upon to meet. We must prepare to make the sacrifices that the emergency—almost as serious as war itself—demands. A free nation has the right to expect full cooperation from all groups. A free nation has the right to look to the leaders of business, of labor and agriculture to take the lead in stimulating effort, not among other groups but within their own groups. The best way of dealing with the few slackers or troublemakers in our midst is, first, to shame them by patriotic example, and if that fails, to use the sovereignty of government to save government.[43]

Indeed, President Bush sometimes tried to fulfill the role dictated by convention. "A time of war," he told the nation in 2005, "is a time of sacrifice."[44] The nation and its values would triumph, he said in 2006, "with sacrifice and determination."[45] However, these appeals were undercut by the more pressing need to maintain consumer demand. Three weeks after the attacks, Bush was asked whether the federal government would ask average Americans to do anything other than spending to help in the crisis. Bush replied,

Well, I think the average American must not be afraid to travel. We opened Reagan Airport yesterday for a reason—we think it's safe, and that people ought to feel comfortable about traveling around our country. They ought to take their kids on vacations. They ought to go to ball games. . . . Americans ought to go about their business.[46]

The political risks associated with an economic downturn were too high to permit a consistent appeal for sacrifice. Bush lacked the standing to do it. The duty of the contemporary president was to use the sovereignty of government to save the market, even if it meant that the president himself was required to make speeches and advertisements in which he praised the in-flight service of United Airlines and encouraged vacations in Orlando.

Bush was not the only leader to be caught in this confusion of rhetoric. In December 2001, Congress directed the U.S. Treasury to begin selling small-denomination Patriot Bonds to the American public. The intention was to evoke memories of War Bonds issued during the Second World War and to provide "a way for patriotic Americans to contribute directly" to the defense of the homeland.[47] The comparison, however, was unsustainable. War Bonds financed one-fifth of total defense expenditures during the Second World War. By contrast, the sale of Patriot Bonds in 2002 did not even cover the cost of the airlines bailout.[48] The difficulty lay with the premise. Patriot Bonds were a device for saving, and this was not what patriotic Americans were enjoined to do in the wake of the 9/11 attacks. The proper response to the crisis, said New York mayor Rudolph Giuliani, was "spend, spend, spend."[49] Within two years, U.S. net savings sank to the lowest level in a half century.[50] At the same time, however, the economy bounced back—a tribute, the International Monetary Fund concluded, to the "remarkable resilience" of consumer spending.[51]

## Chemical Facilities

The new politics of market governance was also at work on another issue: the security of chemical facilities. In this case, however, the result was anything but a forceful assertion of federal authority.

The chemical industry has been called "the central industry of modern civilization," and with good reason: many other critical sectors of an advanced market economy depend on a steady and massive supply of sometimes dangerous chemicals.[52] A highly developed economy will have large facilities for manufacturing chemicals, the means of transporting chemicals by road or rail, and many plants that maintain a large inventory of chemicals used in production.

As with many other aspects of an advanced economy, this infrastructure generates both wealth and danger. Chemical plants, or businesses that stockpile chemicals, are often located close to major cities, creating a risk of death or injury through accidental release. In 1984, the accidental release of toxic gases from a pesticide plant in Bhopal, India, caused fifteen thousand deaths, leading American authorities to gauge the risk of similar accidents in the United States. In the 1990s, the Environmental Protection Agency found seven hundred locations where an accidental release of chemicals might threaten at least one hundred thousand people. Thousands of other facilities posed a worst-case threat to lesser numbers.[53]

Even before 9/11, there was concern that terrorists could cause mass casualties by attacking U.S. chemical facilities. A 1999 federal report found that security at chemical plants "ranged from fair to very poor"; security for chemical shipments was "poor to non-existent."[54] A few months later another federally funded study concluded that an attack on chemical facilities would be one of the simplest ways for terrorists to harm large numbers of people.[55] A 2000 Justice Department report also concluded that the risk that terrorists would attempt to cause an industrial chemical release was "real and credible."[56] Congress actually directed the Justice Department to complete a further report on the vulnerability of chemical plants to criminal and terrorist attacks, but the Clinton administration, citing funding shortfalls, failed to do it.[57]

After 9/11, concern about assaults on chemical plants mounted. Weeks after the attacks, the Army's surgeon general estimated that an assault on a chemical plant in a densely populated area might kill or injure as many as 2.4 million people, a figure far higher than earlier calculations.[58] CIA head George Tenet told Congress in February 2002 that one of the agency's "highest concerns" was that terrorists might attack the chemical industry.[59] Plant security, homeland-security officials later said, was "vitally important" and "a very high priority" for the administration.[60]

And yet this was another instance in which the Bush administration, far from grasping at power, refused to test its limits. The EPA already had a mandate under the Clean Air Act of 1990 to compel chemical facilities to prepare plans for Bhopal-style accidents, and environmental groups argued that this power could be used to anticipate terrorist attacks as well. The agency itself conceded that existing law might be interpreted more broadly.[61] However, the EPA was unloved within the Republican majority in Congress, some of whose members viewed the agency as a "Gestapo bureaucracy."[62] (There was no unanimity on this point; others asserted that the Occupational Safety and Health Administration was the true "Gestapo of federal government.")[63] Republican leaders and industry spokesmen made clear that they opposed an expansion of EPA responsibilities.[64] Citing the risk of litigation, the agency decided in October 2002 that it would not "push the envelope" in interpreting the Clean Air Act.[65]

Instead, the Bush administration chose to encourage a voluntary effort by the chemical industry to improve security. The main industry association, the American Chemistry Council, developed a code that required its member companies to make an assessment of risks and take precautions to improve security. Smaller industry groups devised similar guidelines.[66] The Department of Homeland Security, which assumed the EPA's oversight responsibilities in 2003, provided technical advice on security and supported the development of an industry-wide Chemical Sector Coordinating Council, as well as a network to share information about potential threats.[67]

This emphasis on industry voluntarism had its merits and widely recognized political advantages. Crafting a sensible policy to security required answers to difficult questions—about the range of businesses that should be required to take precautions, about the most sensible precautions in each distinct case, and about the priority of terrorist threats compared to other dangers, such as workplace accidents. Arguably the industry had better knowledge than a small group of government regulators on these issues. Moreover, voluntarism avoided political controversy over expansion of federal regulation. (For this reason, the Clinton administration had widely advertised its emphasis on "non-coercive partnerships" between the EPA and the private sector. This approach, Vice President Al Gore said in 1996, was the administration's "mainstream strategy" for federal regulatory agencies.)[68]

Nonetheless, voluntarism had its limits. Many voluntary guidelines were vague, and industry associations often lacked procedures to verify whether businesses actually followed their own security plans. Industry guidelines did not require businesses to consider effective but more costly improvements in security, such as the redesign of manufacturing processes to eliminate the need for hazardous chemicals.[69] And a large number of hazardous-chemical facilities were not covered by any voluntary security code at all.[70] A series of reports by federal auditors concluded that it was difficult to gauge how effective the industry had been in dealing with security threats.[71] Industry watchdogs complained that restrictions on disclosure of EPA information about industry hazards, also justified on security grounds, undercut their ability to track security improvements.

The Bush administration appeared to concede that the voluntary approach was not completely satisfactory. In October 2002, Homeland Security Advisor Tom Ridge and EPA administrator Christie Whitman promised that they would work with Congress to obtain legislation supported by both parties.[72] Critics dismissed this as stalling. Republicans and Democrats in Congress had been deadlocked for months over legislation to create a new department of homeland security, and partisan rancor had mounted as the 2002 midterm election neared.

Bush himself had just attacked Democratic senators who opposed his proposals for DHS for being "more interested in special interests [than] protecting the American people."[73] After the 2002 election, the administration remained silent on the question of what new legislation should contain. Its *National Strategy for Physical Protection of Critical Infrastructure,* released in 2003, restated a vague commitment to "work with Congress to enact legislation."[74]

Congress, however, proved incapable of formulating a law to secure chemical facilities. Intensive lobbying by the chemical industry contributed to legislative paralysis. After a Senate committee approved a bill sponsored by Senator Jon Corzine of New Jersey in July 2002, the chemical industry launched an aggressive campaign that "crushed" the proposed legislation.[75] Corzine's attempt to revive his bill in the 108th Congress was also foiled by concerted industry opposition. In 2003, the American Chemistry Council launched a multi-million-dollar campaign to counter negative news coverage about the risks of chemical production.[76] Other factors contributed to stalemate. In the House of Representatives, committees competed for jurisdiction over new legislation.[77] Partisan divisions also mounted as the 2004 election neared.[78] By the end of 2005, Congress had done nothing more than approve statements affirming, in general terms, the need for legislation.[79]

The Bush administration, meanwhile, played no constructive role in building agreement on a new law. A former White House adviser on homeland security conceded in April 2005 that many of his former colleagues actually believed "that their only options for improving the security of chemical facilities . . . are voluntary measures conducted in cooperation with the chemical industry."[80] In June 2005, a senior DHS official told a Senate committee that the administration was still "not quite ready to propose or approve of any particular legislative provisions" on chemical-plant security.[81] In March 2006, Homeland Security Secretary Chertoff challenged Congress to pass legislation by the end of the year but refused to detail what the law should contain.[82] Chertoff balked at endorsing the most prominent bill, introduced by Senators Collins and Lieberman earlier in the year. Industry continued to press for weak legislation. By 2006 it also lobbied for an assurance that federal legislation would override stronger state and local law—a demand given added urgency, ironically, by New Jersey regulations enthusiastically endorsed by newly elected Governor Corzine.[83]

Congress appeared finally to act on chemical-plant security five years after the 9/11 attacks. In the waning days of the 109th Congress, House and Senate negotiators agreed to insert brief language in the homeland-security appropriations bill that would require the regulation of chemical facilities.[84] This was hailed by legislators as bold action, but these seven hundred words were better understood as a sad testament to the inability to construct a meaningful policy. The Department of Homeland Security was given broad discretion to decide which facilities would be regulated, whether compliance with existing industry codes could satisfy federal requirements, and whether regulations should compel the use of less-dangerous technologies. Congress had scarcely legislated at all. Rather, it conceded its inability to agree on legislation and invited the executive branch to improvise a placeholder. It admitted as much by stating that its grant of regulatory authority would expire in 2009—a proviso added, its sponsors conceded, so that Congress would be prodded to consider more-complete legislation. In December 2006, the Homeland Security Department issued draft rules—"heavily influenced by the chemical industry," as the *Wall Street Journal* observed—that give the sector substantial freedom to decide how safety should be promoted.[85]

## Protecting the Grid

The federal government's measures to improve security within the electric power system were also restrained, again because of considerations typical of postmillennial market governance.

The electric power system of the United States has been described as "the most complex machine ever invented."[86] But strictly speaking it is not an invention. It is an evolving system that now comprises more than three thousand firms, sixteen thousand generating units, and 160,000 miles of transmission lines.[87] Moreover, it is now critical to modern life—the "fundamental infrastructure" of an advanced economy, without which a host of other systems would collapse.[88] Americans are accustomed to a high level of reliability, with outages that strike less than 0.02 percent of the time.[89] The complexity of the system, and our dependence on it, could make the power system a prime target for terrorist attacks. In 1990 a study by the federal Office of Technology Assessment concluded that terrorist groups might attack critical components of the system and cause "enormous disruption and expense for society."[90]

Even in the short span since 1990, circumstances have changed dramatically, potentially increasing vulnerabilities. On one side, dependence has increased. Consumption of electricity in the United States grew by 40 percent between 1990 and 2005.[91] Some of this change was caused by the explosion of power-hungry information and communication technologies. These technologies are now central to the operation of other sectors, such as banking and finance. Technological change has also heightened our expectations about reliability. "A silicon-based economy," says one analyst, "is extremely sensitive to power outages even of very short duration."[92]

The internal structure of the power system has also become more complex since 1990, largely as a consequence of liberalization. The electricity industry was once dominated by monopolies that generated and sold power within separate territories. Over time, local transmission systems have become more tightly connected, and monopolies have been replaced by markets in which power generators compete to serve industrial and retail clients. Liberalization has been the product of political and technological shifts. A growing lobby of independent power producers and electricity traders—including, most notoriously, the now-bankrupt Enron—have prodded U.S. governments to liberalize.[93] More-sophisticated systems for monitoring and channeling power flows also make it feasible to replace stable monopolies with fast-moving markets.[94] By 2006, the U.S. electricity system could be described as containing "vast pools of energy moving in interstate commerce," bought and sold by a growing number of players executing a burgeoning volume of transactions.[95]

The very complexity of the liberalized power system makes it difficult for actors within it to gauge the extent of its vulnerabilities.[96] There is a case to be made that the system confronts serious dangers. Most of the physical components of the system—its vast network transmission lines and substations—cannot be protected from a determined attacker.[97] The electronic control systems that are used to govern power grids are also vulnerable—largely because businesses have abandoned proprietary software and closed communications channels to use more broadly accessible software that rely on communications networks shared with many other users.[98] The risk of a "cyberattack" on these systems is not hypothetical: in 2003, the Slammer virus weakened controls within U.S. utilities but fell short of causing blackouts.[99] Specialists have warned that a carefully planned cyberattack by terrorist groups or enemy states could have a devastating effect on U.S. power grids.[100]

These risks may be compounded by the frailty of the power system after a decade of growth and restructuring. Transmission capacity has not kept pace with power flows, reducing the grid's ability to deal with disruptions. Businesses facing new market pressures have also reduced investment in measures to assure security and reliability.[101] There is evidence that power outages became more frequent and more severe throughout the 1990s.[102] A series of major events—two 1996 blackouts in the western United States, the 2000–2001 California power crisis, and the 2003 northeastern U.S. blackout—suggest that tightly integrated grids are more susceptible to cascading failures.

This is a dire view of the power system's vulnerability, but it is not universally held. Some specialists argue that the threat of cyberterrorism is vastly exaggerated. This outlook is driven by skepticism about enemy capabilities—and also by an optimistic view of the power system's capacity to absorb disruptions caused by cyber- or physical assaults. "It would take the efforts of a well-coordinated paramilitary organization," says industry veteran Jack Feinstein, to cause the damage necessary to assure a large-scale blackout.[103] And it is not clear that the power system is an appealing target for terrorists. Although the 2003 blackout caused substantial economic losses, it did not lead to many of the results that terrorists value, such mass panic, deaths, or collapse in public order.[104] Uncertainties such as these, aggravated by the growing complexity of the industry's structure, have complicated debates about the best way of improving security within the electric power system.

Another complication is the growing mismatch between the breadth of the system and the authority of regulators. Historically, state regulatory commissions have carried much of the responsibility for overseeing the electricity industry. As the industry has grown and developed interdependencies that cross state borders, the capacity of state regulators to assure reliability has declined. In 1998, a federal task force said that the failure to address the need for new regulatory structures would expose "substantial parts of North America . . . to unacceptable risk." There was, it said, an "urgent need" for reform.[105]

Nevertheless, the federal government stepped carefully as it attempted to address the growing regulatory mismatch. Throughout the Clinton administration, the Federal Energy Regulatory Commission (FERC) encouraged businesses within the industry to establish regional groups that would oversee the transmission of power and also address reliability issues. But FERC was wary about using its authority to compel the creation of regional groups, fearing that this would lead to litigation.[106] In fact, a 1996 FERC order encouraging liberalization (but still taking a voluntary approach to the creation of regional groups) *was* challenged by nine states, which thought it went too far in undercutting their regulatory powers, and by Enron, which thought it did not go far enough. The U.S. Supreme Court eventually upheld FERC's order six years later.[107]

The Clinton administration also encouraged a nongovernmental body, the North American Electric Reliability Council (NERC), to toughen its guidelines on the measures that businesses within the sector should take to assure reliable supply of electricity. NERC is an industry group initially set up to forestall federal legislation on reliability standards following the 1965 Northeast blackout.[108] But compliance with NERC standards was once again voluntary and relied heavily on peer pressure. These informal enforcement mechanisms began to collapse in the 1990s as more firms entered the industry and competitive pressures intensified.[109]

Federal legislation could have clarified FERC's authority to establish regional groups with responsibility for managing the emerging electricity markets and could have given teeth to reliability standards for firms in the industry. The Clinton administration eventually included both measures in a plan for "comprehensive reform" of the electricity industry sent to Congress in 1999. But Congress proved unwilling to endorse the Clinton plan and incapable of agreeing on any alternative.[110] Twenty bills that would have established mandatory reliability standards died in the 106th Congress. Meanwhile, the reliance on voluntarism meant that the process of creating regional groups proceeded slowly. As a federal study later said, "aligning and harmonizing the incentives" of companies and agencies within the industry was not an easy task.[111]

In 2002, the Bush administration—firmly committed to liberalization, closely tied to Enron, and buoyed by the Supreme Court's affirmation of FERC authority—made its own effort to rationalize the governance of the electricity industry. In July 2002, FERC proposed a "standard market design" that it would apply to regional markets across the nation. The design included measures to accelerate the creation of regional groups and a proposal for security standards that would be imposed by FERC on all firms participating in the electricity industry. FERC wanted to make the security rules effective within eighteen months.[112]

However, FERC's market-reform plan encountered opposition from state governments and their allies in Congress, and FERC began a retreat. In February 2003, it announced a delay in the scheduled implementation of security standards. In April 2003, it announced a larger revision of its plan to accommodate state complaints.[113] Still not mollified, Congress threatened legislative action to delay adoption of the plan for another three years.[114] By 2005, the reform project was "six feet under," according to Commissioner Nora Mead Brownell.[115] FERC finally conceded defeat and issued an order terminating its process for formulating a standard market design.

Meanwhile, evidence continued to mount of the weaknesses in existing regulatory structures. In 2004, the task force responsible for examining the northeastern U.S. blackout found that it was partly caused by the failure to create an effective regional organization to govern power transmission and by industry inattention to NERC's reliability standards. Its "single most important" recommendation was for federal legislation to improve compliance with the standards.[116] The Bush administration endorsed the proposal.[117]

Congress finally provided legislative authority for enforceable reliability standards in the 2005 energy bill.[118] Still, this assertion of federal authority was carefully hedged. Strictly speaking, it is the industry group NERC that is given the power to make and enforce reliability standards. Although FERC formally approves the standards, it is obliged to defer to NERC's judgment on the appropriateness of the rules.[119] NERC itself is also required to delegate its authority to regional reliability organizations in order to meet state governments' fear of "one-size-fits-all" requirements.[120] State regulators also preserve their ability to impose additional safety requirements within their state.

## Container Security

The political, technical, and jurisdictional problems raised by expanding electricity markets were substantial. But the markets themselves were, at least, largely contained within U.S. borders; the appropriate role of federal and state governments might be contested, but at least there was no question that between them, there was jurisdiction to address security threats.[121] The situation was more complex as federal authorities wrestled with the problem of security in containerized shipping.

At the center of the problem is a technical innovation that has revolutionized international trade: the shipping container, a steel box forty feet in length that is capable of holding three thousand cubic feet of cargo.[122] Introduced in the late 1950s, containers have radically reduced the cost of shipping goods over long distances. This technical innovation, combined with a shift toward more-liberal trade policies, led to a boom in importation of goods into the United States in the last quarter of the twentieth century.

The total value of goods imported into the United States multiplied three times in inflation-adjusted dollars between 1978 and 2000.[123] The number of shipping containers passing through major U.S. ports increased by 50 percent between 1995 and 2000 (fig. 4.2). Moreover, the market continued to expand *after* 9/11, with blithe disregard for new concerns about security and encouraged by federal

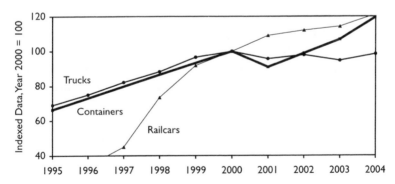

FIG. 4.2. The consequences of liberalization: growth in container traffic at U.S. ports and in number of trucks and railcars crossing U.S. land borders, 1995–2004. Data indexed so that 2000 = 100. (U.S. Bureau of Transportation Statistics)

policies intended to prop up consumption; by 2004, the total number of shipping containers handled by major North American ports was almost double the 1995 figure. There was comparably explosive growth in trade over land borders, whether by truck or by rail.

This massive growth in containerized shipping creates substantial security concerns because of the difficulty of detecting precisely what is held in each container. Containerization, says Marc Levinson,

> is a blessing for exporters and importers, but it has become a curse for customs inspectors and security officials. Each container is accompanied by a manifest listing its contents, but neither ship lines nor ports can vouch that what is on the manifest corresponds to what is inside. Nor is there any easy way to check: opening the doors at the end of the box normally reveals only a wall of paperboard cartons. With a single ship able to disgorge 3,000 40-foot-long containers in a matter of hours, and with a port such as Long Beach or Tokyo handling perhaps 10,000 loaded containers on the average workday, and with each container itself holding row after row of boxes stacked floor to ceiling, not even the most careful examiners have a remote prospect of inspecting it all. Containers can be just as efficient for smuggling undeclared merchandise, illegal drugs, undocumented immigrants, and terrorist bombs as for moving legitimate cargo.[124]

In October 2001, the discovery in Italy of a stowaway in a container being transported from Egypt to Canada stoked fears about security. Amir Farid Rizk ("Container Boy," as a Canadian cabinet minister nicknamed him) had outfitted his container with a bed, a toilet, a satellite phone, a laptop computer, airport maps, and forged security passes; he was discovered when the ship carrying the container docked en route in the Italian port of Palmi. U.S. officials called Rizk a suspected al Qaeda operative.[125] In fact, the Italians abandoned their prosecution of Rizk within weeks, concluding that it was likely a more clumsy attempt to flee personal and legal problems in Egypt.[126]

More disturbing was a 2004 attack on the port of Ashdod, Israel, launched by suicide bombers smuggled into the port inside a container. Eleven Israelis were killed, but authorities speculated that the real targets were chemical tanks at the port.[127] Security specialists also fear that terrorists might pack containers with ammonium nitrate to create an explosive that could devastate a major U.S. harbor or that they might load a container with a nuclear or biological weapon.[128] A 2006 Rand study concluded that a nuclear device detonated inside a container at Long Beach would kill sixty thousand people instantly and cause damage equal to one-tenth of U.S. GDP.[129]

Improving container security is a daunting task. The millions of containers that reach U.S. shores each year trace paths that often begin in poor countries, in which neither business nor government have resources to invest in security measures and in which corruption is commonplace. The U.S. government could, in theory, insist on inspecting every container that arrived at U.S. ports, but this would require a threefold increase in customs personnel, disrupt trade, and perhaps come too late to prevent devastation by a weapon of mass destruction. The United States could insist that containers delivered to its ports be retrofitted with new high-tech security features or that trading partners adopt their own policies to improve security, but these steps might also cause economic and diplomatic turmoil.[130]

After 9/11 the United States attempted to develop a system for assuring container security that accommodated such constraints. One component was the Container Security Initiative, pitched as a project to "push the United States' zone of security beyond its physical borders" by locating U.S. customs inspectors at major overseas ports. As a DHS official said in 2005, this required "leveraging the authority of foreign governments through diplomacy."[131] By 2006, DHS had staff at foreign seaports handling 73 percent of container traffic heading to the United States.[132] However, many high-risk foreign ports were not included in the program.[133] Some countries placed limits on the number of U.S. officials allowed to work at their ports, and others, unsympathetic to the U.S. antiterror campaign, refused to cooperate at all.[134]

Even in friendly countries, DHS inspectors faced limits on their capacity to maintain security. Budget constraints were one difficulty: in Hong Kong, the world's busiest port, DHS had only eight inspectors.[135] "Sovereignty issues" also prevented the U.S. government from setting minimum requirements on the inspection equipment that should be maintained by foreign ports.[136] As a consequence there was no assurance that containers would be properly checked for weapons of mass destruction even if they had been identified as high-risk by U.S. officials. Indeed, a 2005 audit found that roughly one-quarter of containers flagged by U.S. officials were not actually inspected by their foreign counterparts. In a small proportion of those cases, foreign officials flatly refused to undertake the inspection because they disagreed with the U.S. assessment of risk. The outcome in such cases was telling: the containers were usually loaded on U.S.-bound ships anyway, with a caution that they should be inspected on arrival in the United States.[137]

As a practical matter, U.S. authorities could inspect only a minute percentage of incoming container traffic—seven million containers in 2002, increasing to eleven million by 2005.[138] To decide which containers deserved scrutiny, DHS developed a targeting system in which Virginia-based analysts identify suspicious shipments heading toward the United States. The effectiveness of the system hinges on good intelligence, not only about potential terrorist threats but also about the flow of container traffic. After 2003, DHS insisted that shippers provide cargo manifests at least two days before cargo arrives at a U.S. port. However, there are serious problems with manifests: the forms are often vague or incomplete, sometimes as a deliberate policy to deter theft. Shippers also have the right to alter manifests after containers are unpacked within the United States.[139]

As a complement to its inspection efforts, the federal government also launched the Customs-Trade Partnership Against Terrorism (C-TPAT), a voluntary program in which importers and the shipping industry promise to adopt more-robust security measures in exchange for lowered scrutiny by customs inspectors. Businesses rushed to participate in C-TPAT. One major importer found that the inspection rate dropped from 8 percent of its containers in 2001 to less than 1 percent in 2003, saving it half a million dollars in costs.[140]

However, there were weaknesses in C-TPAT as well. The Homeland Security Department lacked the staff to monitor whether participating businesses had put their promised security measures into place. It quickly abandoned its goal of reviewing each business within three years. By 2006, only one-quarter of the participating firms had been checked by DHS.[141] The government also trod lightly when conducting checks, insisting it did not want "to give the appearance of conducting an audit." The scope of the reviews, a 2005 study found, were agreed on with the company. DHS itself had no guidelines for judging whether a business's measures were adequate.[142]

Federal officials had good reason to manage C-TPAT carefully. In the 1990s, the Clinton administration used a similar technique to improve workplace safety within the United States. The Occupational

Safety and Health Administration (OSHA) told employers that they could reduce the risk of inspections if they developed their own safety systems, including precautions not actually required by federal law. OSHA's "cooperative compliance program" was touted by Clinton officials as evidence that the federal government would not apply a "command and control paradigm" in dealing with the business community.[143] (OSHA, remember, was another of the federal government's "Gestapo" agencies.) Even so, the National Association of Manufacturers attacked the administration's "Soviet-style" behavior.[144] In 1999, a federal appeals court struck down the OSHA program, ruling that the Clinton administration had improperly used the threat of enforcement to impose new rules on business.[145]

Had C-TPAT been applied vigorously, it might have been vulnerable to similar attacks by disgruntled businesses.[146] The solution was statutory authorization of the program. However, the U.S. Chamber of Commerce (which had previously joined in the litigation against OSHA) opposed a new law, insisting that it would impose "the heavy yoke of new regulatory requirements" on American businesses.[147] The White House did not seek authorization, and it was only in 2006 that Congress took the initiative to give C-TPAT a statutory basis.[148] Congress, however, bowed to business pressure not to insist on the installation of high-tech security devices within containers, even within the still-voluntary C-TPAT program. It also retreated from a proposal to consider user fees that would generate revenue to protect ports.

Security continued to prove elusive within the globalized marketplace. An internal DHS study traced the passage of twenty thousand containers and found many opportunities "for unmanifested materials or weapons of mass destruction to be introduced into the supply chain."[149] "It is just a question of time," said maritime-security specialist Stephen Flynn, "before terrorists with potentially more destructive weapons breach the superficial security measures that have been put in place to protect the ports, the ships, and the millions of intermodal containers that link global producers to consumers."[150]

# 5

# Cakewalk

Bush's advisors wondered if they would ever find a way to end the
talking and pull the trigger.
> —Bob Woodward describes the September 15, 2001,
> meeting of key national security advisers[1]

"IT WAS ONLY natural," the *Washington Post* said in 2006, "that the
military would take the lead in fighting terrorism after September
11."[2] This is a simple sentence that is fraught with assumptions about
the dynamics of postmillennial American government. Why is it *only*
*natural* that terrorism is a problem that should be handed to the military? Other countries have dealt with decades-long terrorist threats
and framed the problem in different ways.[3] Some treat it as a problem for intelligence and law-enforcement agencies. Some emphasize
tighter internal security. Few threaten to "take the battle to the enemy," for the obvious reason that they lack the ability to do so. If al
Qaeda had attacked Sydney in September 2001, Australia would not
have invaded Afghanistan.

In the United States, the 9/11 attacks produced a different response. In the immediate aftermath of the attacks, it was clear that the
Bush administration felt impelled to take quick and firm action to assure national security. Impatience permeated its official statements.
How this impatience would be translated into policy outcomes hinged
largely on the capabilities of the federal government. Vice President
Cheney said later that the Bush administration had been "very aggressive defending the nation and using the tools at our disposal to do
that."[4] But the "tools at our disposal" are limited in range. There are a
number of instruments for shaping domestic policy. As we have seen,
many of these are complicated in design, expensive (in terms of budgetary and political costs), and available only with the consent of other
actors, such as Congress or state and local governments.

On the other hand, there is the military—for half a century, the biggest device in the federal toolbox. The military has undergone its own profound changes since the Nixon era. It has pursued a strategy of accommodation to political realities that I earlier described as *neomilitarism*. Technological changes have made it dramatically more efficient in projecting force. It needs fewer people to fight major wars, and it has foresworn coercion (that is, the draft) as a tool for obtaining soldiers. It actively promotes the virtues of military service. These changes have increased the military's autonomy, in the sense of its capacity to wage war without making heavy demands on American society. They have also assured that public respect for the military remains robust, in sharp contrast to other components of the federal bureaucracy. These features of the U.S. military—its increased power, autonomy, and legitimacy—heighten its attractiveness as a policy instrument. Coincident with these changes in the structure and status of the military is a critical geopolitical change: the collapse of the Soviet Union, the rival whose retaliatory capacities had for decades tempered the use of U.S. power.

In short, there were strong incentives for the Bush administration to construe the "terrorism problem" (like other problems on the federal agenda) largely in military terms. It is remarkable how quickly and automatically this was done. At the very moment he was told of the World Trade Center attacks, Bush recalled, "I made up my mind that we were going to war."[5] The War on Terrorism was declared by the president within twelve hours of the attacks.[6] By September 13, Bush had resolved to "hit the Afghans hard."[7] On September 17, Bush instructed the Defense Department to refine its contingency plans for action in Iraq. By November 2001 the military was planning a full-scale invasion of Iraq.[8]

The Bush administration's bellicosity in 2001–2003 led many observers to fear that critical constraints on the exercise of American power had suddenly been tossed aside. The "Bush Doctrine" appeared to lower the bar for military action abroad, allowing the United States to attack other nations before a threat to its national security had become imminent and concrete.[9] Soon after the doctrine's articulation, the United States invaded Iraq, in an apparent demonstration of its commitment to the new doctrine. The invasion was construed as a radical break in U.S. policy. In fact, the Bush administration may simply have stated more openly and forcefully a position toward which the United States had been drifting for many years. It was perhaps the inevitable consequence of internal changes in the structure of the U.S. military and broader geopolitical changes. In any case, Iraq was not a compelling example of radical policy change. Conflict between the two nations had been escalating for a decade; the military was prepared for conflict, and the public was well primed to accept it.

In a larger sense, the usefulness of Iraq as a precedent for a bolder foreign policy was also undone by the inability of the United States to govern the occupied territory properly. The invasion of Iraq was seen to be an abject failure, largely because the United States lacked the administrative capabilities to assure success. In important respects, then, the Bush administration was a prisoner of institutional constraints and policy inertia—both in its decision to go to war against Iraq and in its inability to guide its reconstruction.

## Autonomy

Fifty years of war or threatened war profoundly changed the shape of the U.S. government. In 1950, a federal politician who was asked to name the most powerful man in Washington other than the president had a ready answer: it was the secretary of state.[10] The State Department was "the institutional powerhouse of the U.S. government."[11] By 2001 the center of power had shifted to the Pentagon. "The Department of Defense is a behemoth among federal agencies," the 9/11 Commission said in July 2004. "With an annual budget larger than the gross domestic product of Russia, it is an empire."[12] (The State Department, by contrast, was "a crippled institution," according to the February 2001 report of the Hart-Rudman Commission. "[It] is starved for resources by Congress because of its inadequacies and is thereby weakened further.")[13] The wealth of capabilities held within the defense establishment made it a magnet for high-priority tasks that could not be handled properly by other agencies, such as relief in New Orleans or, later in the Bush administration's second term, the control of illegal immigration on the nation's southern border.

Military leaders were often ambivalent about the accretion of nontraditional functions, which distracted from the core mission of their organizations, waging war. But even with regard to this core mission, there were restraints in the immediate post-Vietnam era. Two considerations weighed against the use of military force overseas. One was the political calculus of military engagement—that is, the tabulation of benefits and costs that any political leader had to make before going to war. "Decisions by a government to use force or to threaten to use force during crises are extremely difficult," said the 1970 Gates Commission, which had been established to consider whether the United States should retain the draft. It listed the considerations that discouraged a quick resort to war: "The high cost of military resources, the moral burden of risking human lives, political costs at home and overseas, and the overshadowing risk of nuclear confrontation."[14]

Omitted from the Gates Commission's calculations was another consideration: the predispositions of the defense establishment itself, which in the post-Vietnam era became chary of indefinite commitments abroad. Caspar Weinberger, defense secretary under President Reagan, argued in 1984 that the United States should not commit forces to combat unless vital interests were at stake and the nation had committed "every ounce of strength necessary . . . to achieve our objectives."[15] Colin Powell, chairman of the Joint Chiefs of Staff from 1989 to 1993, argued that the country should not go to war unless it had resolved to use "overwhelming force quickly and decisively," as it did during the Gulf War.[16]

However, this ethic of restraint in the deployment of U.S. forces was difficult to sustain. Despite Powell's reservations, the George H. W. Bush and Clinton administrations committed thirty thousand troops to Somalia, where clan violence was impeding famine relief. Powell also resisted engagement in the troubled Balkans. Nonetheless, U.S. presence in the region slowly increased. ("What's the point of having this superb military that you're always talking about if we can't use it?" Secretary of State Madeleine Albright asked Colin Powell, during a debate on a Bosnian intervention.)[17] The United States deployed twenty thousand troops as part of a NATO peacekeeping mission to Bosnia in 1995. In 1999 it launched a two-month air campaign against Serbia to compel withdrawal of its forces from Kosovo. Eventually the United States sent six thousand troops to maintain peace in Kosovo.[18]

The Weinberger and Powell doctrines withered because the broader calculus of military engagement that had been roughly described by the Gates Commission in 1970 was changing. A globalizing media had heightened the domestic political pressure to respond to humanitarian crises. The risk of nuclear confrontation was also on the decline. The collapse of the Soviet Union made it easier to contemplate action against Iraq (a nation only 140 miles from the Soviet border and armed with Soviet weaponry) or against Serbia and Afghanistan—one on the border of the Warsaw Pact, the other on the border of the Soviet Union itself.[19]

These were not the only ways in which the calculus of engagement had shifted. Two fundamental changes in the structure of the American military also made it easier to contemplate military action. The first of these was the abandonment, in 1973, of conscription as a method of obtaining fighting forces. This was an understandable reaction by policymakers to the political backlash against the draft during the Vietnam War. There was broad public support for the draft in 1969; within a few years, however, most Americans opposed it. Over the next three decades, antidraft sentiment became more deeply embedded. Throughout the Clinton and George W. Bush administrations, polls found that even larger majorities than in the 1970s and 1980s opposed the return of conscription.[20]

Opposition to the draft was explicitly framed as a classical liberal reform—that is, as a method of resisting the intrusion of state power on the liberties of citizens. Compulsory service, said Milton Friedman in an influential 1967 article, "is basically inconsistent with a free society"—an unacceptable form of social regimentation.[21] Economist Walter Oi argued that the draft represented a form of "implicit taxation," because draftees bore "real and psychic costs" that went uncounted in the federal defense budget.[22] The 1970 Gates Commission, established by President Nixon to consider the case for abolishing the draft, was heavily influenced by such criticisms. (Friedman and fellow economist Alan Greenspan were two of the commission's members.) "Conscription," the commission said flatly, "is a tax." A volunteer military would "minimize government interference with the freedom of the individual to determine his own life in accord with his own values."[23] (A quarter century later, this had become the consensus view: the volunteer military, the editors of the *New York Times* agreed, "is more consistent with the free-choice values of America's market society.")[24]

The decision to abandon the draft and shift to an all-volunteer force was a triumph of liberalization—preceding, but consistent in principle with, reforms that deregulated the American economy in the

1970s and 1980s. The decision also changed the politics of war fighting. It eliminated, for example, the possibility of antidraft demonstrations and draft evasion, and the ensuing prosecution of protesters and evaders, all public acts that have the effect of giving prominence to questions about the legitimacy of conflict itself.[25] In addition, conscientious objection by members of the military became rarer and less likely to draw public sympathy.[26] People in the upper strata of American society are also less likely to have a family member in an all-volunteer military, although the disparity in representation is sometimes exaggerated.[27] Upper-class households are more likely to vote or engage in other kinds of political action; indeed, such households were the backbone of the antiwar movement in the Vietnam era.[28]

A second critical change in the U.S. military was the modernization of its capabilities. Throughout the 1980s and 1990s, the armed services engaged in an aggressive procurement effort aimed at moving from the electromechanical age to the digital age.[29] These new technologies radically improved the ability to collect data from the battlefield, coordinate the movement of troops and equipment, and project force with precision. The Gulf War gave early evidence of the increased lethality of U.S. forces. A 1991 Air Force analysis described allied attacks on the Iraqi power grid:

> The unprecedented accuracy of modern munitions meant that the coalition achieved maximum military effect with minimal force and minimal sorties. One airplane dropping two precision-guided bombs sufficed to destroy a single power generation station's transformer yards. During World War II, by contrast, the Eighth Air Force found it took two full combat wings, a force of 108 B-17 bombers crewed by 1,080 airmen, dropping a total of 648 bombs to guarantee getting just two hits, the minimum necessary to disable a single power generating plant.[30]

There is another way to describe what the U.S. military did between 1981 and 2001: like many businesses, it improved productivity by substituting capital (that is, spending on high-tech weaponry) for labor (that is, spending on soldiers). As S. J. Deitchman observes, the 2003 defense budget was roughly the same as the 1970 budget, even after adjustment for inflation, but the number of personnel was much lower in 2003. The amount spent on equipment for each active-duty

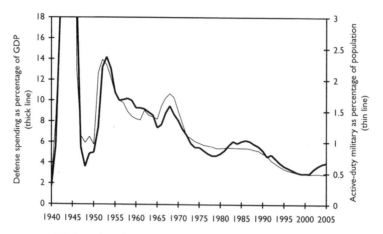

FIG. 5.1. Without breaking a sweat: national defense spending as share of GDP and active-duty military personnel as share of total population. (U.S. Budget Historical Tables; U.S. Census Bureau)

soldier had roughly doubled.[31] It is inevitable that a wealthy, technologically advanced society should develop its military capabilities in this manner.[32] The trend is also encouraged by the rising cost of labor, another consequence of the shift to an all-volunteer force.

However, this trend also changes the calculus of war fighting, as described by the Gates Commission. As the 1991 Air Force report suggested, a technologically advanced force has fewer people engaged in actual combat.[33] In 2002, the proportion of the U.S. population that was employed in the active-duty military was at its lowest point since 1940 (fig. 5.1). Moreover, those who fight also do so, as a 1996 Defense Department report said, "at less risk to themselves."[34] (Even the Iraq War did not overturn the hypothesis that a transformed military could fight with less risk to troops. In 2003–2005, for example, the U.S. military lost 1,692 soldiers a year from all causes, including hostile acts. By contrast, the military lost an average of 2,123 soldiers a year throughout the last decade of the Cold War.)[35] The capacity to minimize the risk to soldiers is important because public support for military engagement is tightly connected to casualty rates, perhaps more so than in the past.[36]

The revolution in productivity also allowed the United States to maintain a powerful military force without straining American pocketbooks. The cost of modern weapon systems may be dramatically higher than that of their forerunners, but the *overall* burden of national defense has declined throughout the modern era (fig. 5.1). Even after the Iraq buildup, defense spending as a share of GDP remains at one of its lowest points since the advent of World War II. As historian David Kennedy says, the United States can deploy history's most deadly military force without breaking a sweat.[37]

## Legitimacy

"The American people," political scientist Frederick Perry Powers said in 1888, "have inherited a deep-seated jealousy of an armed force, and a fear that sometimes seems absurd of the possible use of troops in maintaining a man or clique in power."[38] By the end of the millennium, this understanding of American popular culture was wildly anachronistic. The American military was not feared, even though its power was understood to be awesome. On the contrary, it was the most highly respected component of the federal government.

This is a remarkable fact. The U.S. military had suffered a serious crisis of confidence in the late 1960s and early 1970s. Opinion polls showed that the proportion of Americans who trusted its leadership declined sharply during the Vietnam era. The military was not the only institution to confront a collapse in confidence: the presidency, Congress, the judiciary, and other nongovernmental institutions (such as major churches and the media) all confronted, in varying degrees, a similar decline.

However, the U.S. military became distinctive because of its success in *reestablishing* trust over the following quarter century. By the end of the millennium, the proportion of Americans who expressed confidence in the military was roughly equal to what it had been in the mid-1960s (fig. 5.2). Moreover, there was a large and persistent gap in trust between "the military" and "the executive branch of federal government." (This is an intriguing illustration of the way in which popular opinion can be influenced by the framing of a question, because—as the 9/11 Commission said—the larger part of the executive branch of federal government is the defense establishment.)

The military was not merely trusted. By the turn of the millennium it was also revered as a vessel that contained and protected the

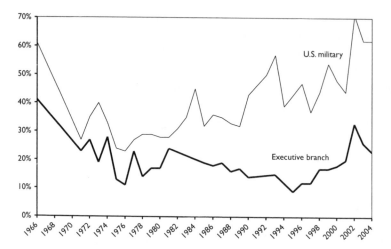

FIG. 5.2. The legitimacy gap: percentage of Americans expressing "a great deal of confidence" in the people in charge of running the U.S. military and the executive branch of the federal government. (Harris Interactive)

nation's core values. Soldiers were praised for their courage, resolution, plain speaking, and religious faith. They were seen to embody an undiluted strain of patriotism and an unreserved willingness to defend the nation against a hostile world. For many social conservatives, the U.S. military was a bulwark against the jaded cosmopolitanism and "yuppie values" of the governing elite.[39] "Many Americans—especially those who dominate the culture—are uncomfortable with military valor," David Brooks wrote in 2005. "This is a culture that knows how to honor the casualties and the dead, but not the strength and prowess of its warriors."[40]

Ironically, though, the entrenchment of this romantic view of the armed services is partly a consequence of the *liberalization* of the military. Abandonment of the "conscription tax" had the consequence (unanticipated by the 1970 Gates Commission) of producing massive government publicity aimed at glamorizing military service. In earlier decades, Congress expressed its intense hostility toward "publicity or propaganda" in support of federal programs.[41] However, Congress eventually acceded to the expansion of military advertising as the armed services struggled to meet recruitment targets in the late 1970s and early 1980s.[42] The U.S. Army's Recruiting Command called on leading marketers to apply business techniques to its outreach efforts, and by the end of the 1980s the advertising firm Young & Rubicam was managing a $100-million-a-year campaign designed "to make the Army cool" among young adults.[43] The trade journal *Advertising Age* rated the Army's effort as one of the most effective advertising campaigns of the twentieth century.[44]

Other branches followed suit. The U.S. Marines developed a sophisticated campaign designed "to sell the intangibles, pride of belonging, honor, [and] courage." One of its 1992 television advertisements featured "armored knights charging at one another with drawn swords, flames and lightning bolts flashing, while a Wagnerian-sounding choir chants 'virtus' and 'potentia' and 'semper fidelis.'"[45] These mass-media campaigns bolstered support for the military even among Americans who never considered joining the forces.[46]

The need to advertise is heightened during periods of economic expansion, when potential enlistees have more options. During the boom of the late 1990s, interest in military service slumped badly. A Defense Department poll showed that 70 percent of young adults probably or definitely would not join the military, a markedly higher proportion than in the immediate post-Vietnam years. The military responded with a substantial expansion of its advertising campaigns. Between 1998 and 2001, total spending on advertising increased by 75 percent, adjusting for inflation, to over $500 million a year. In just four years, the federal government spent over $1.6 billion on advertising to promote military service.[47]

The armed services also proved adept at responding to the changing tastes of its young audience. The Marines sponsored the X Games, an annual "extreme sports" competition. The U.S. Army contracted with a leading computer-game company to produce "America's Army," a "first-person shooter" computer game designed to allow young players to "stay alive, . . . advance in rank, . . . and eventually join the Special Forces" (fig. 5.3). Reviewers praised the game for its realism and sophisticated design, which allowed users to "cycle through your enemies and drop them with ease."[48]

The entertainment industry is an even more powerful engine for dissemination of martial virtues. War movies became a Hollywood staple in the quarter century after Pearl Harbor, when roughly one-fifth of all its films explored military themes.[49] By the late 1980s the industry had recoiled from the post-Vietnam malaise, producing blockbusters

FIG. 5.3. Screenshots from "America's Army," a computer game developed as a recruitment tool for the U.S. Army. The caption for one screenshot says, "This Soldier isn't here for the scenery." (http://www.americasarmy.com)

such as *Top Gun* and *The Hunt for Red October* that helped to rehabilitate the reputation of the armed services.[50] A decade later, the booming computer- and video-game business also exploited military motifs. "Shooter" and "fighting" games such as "Call of Duty," "Battlefield: Armored Fury," "SOCOM: U.S. Navy SEALs," and "Medal of Honor" were bought by millions of American households in the early 2000s.[51] There were growing commonalities between computer and video games played by consumers and programs used for training by the military itself.[52]

Transformations within the news industry have also helped to bolster support for the military. As CNN demonstrated during the Gulf War, cable news networks are capable of providing immediate and vivid coverage of U.S. military engagements. Furthermore, entertainment media proved more willing in the 1990s to exploit such news coverage as an inexpensive source of content. One consequence is broader public awareness of military conflict, particularly among less-educated or politically informed segments of the population.[53]

Throughout the 1990s, the American public saw repeated demonstrations of the nation's capacity to project force effortlessly—during the Gulf War itself, through cruise-missile attacks on three countries (Iraq, Afghanistan, and Sudan) in 1996–1998, and during the NATO bombing campaign in Kosovo in 1999. News and entertainment media were saturated with images of "'clean' techno-war, devoid of human suffering and death, conducted with surgical precision by wondrous mechanisms."[54] (General Charles Horner, head of U.S. air operations during the Gulf War, characterized it as "a technology war, although it is fought by men and women.")[55] Such engagements buoyed public support for the military and provided further evidence of its capacity to achieve victories with "remarkably low costs."[56] Political scientist Matthew Baum says that the changed media environment also intensified the tendency for public opinion to "rally-round-the-flag" during military engagements, precisely because of the newly heightened awareness of conflict among "the least politically sophisticated segments of the public."[57]

## Opportunism

The foreign policy articulated by the Bush administration in the wake of the 9/11 attacks had two main components. The first was an open embrace of the concept of preemptive war. "The war on terror will not be won on the defensive," President Bush told graduates at West Point in 2002, promising to take "preemptive action when necessary to defend our liberties."[58] The second component was a commitment to democratization as one of the main goals of U.S. foreign policy—as President Bush assured during his second inaugural address, the United States would "seek and support the growth of democratic movements and institutions in every nation and culture, with the ultimate goal of ending tyranny in the world."[59]

These two commitments were said to mark a radical turn in American foreign policy, away from a decades-long practice of restraint in the exercise of power and of realism in dealing with unsavory allies. "The events of September 11," said the Washington Post's Anne Applebaum, wrought "an extraordinary revolution" in U.S. foreign policy.[60]

"These developments represented . . . an epochal change," said James Mann, "the flowering of a new view of America's status and role in the world."[61]

The error in these assessments is the confusion of espoused policy with actual practice. In this respect, observers of foreign policy had much in common with civil libertarians who believed that the 9/11 attacks would lead to massive intrusions on the rights of citizens. Both groups treated their apprehensions about policy shifts as though they had actually been realized. However, the constraints that shaped existing policies were not so easily overcome.

After 9/11, the United States continued to cooperate with nations with blemished records on human rights, when it seemed prudent to do so. It carefully measured its pressure on strategically important states such as Russia and on major trading partners such as China.[62] U.S. intelligence services continued to collaborate with their Syrian counterparts even as the State Department condemned Syria as one of the junior partners of the Axis of Evil.[63] In other cases, the United States found that new security concerns actually compromised its capacity to promote democratization. The United States could not confront the military government of General Pervez Musharraf in Pakistan, or the House of Saud, because of its need for their support in the War on Terrorism.[64] Nor did it demand political reforms that would destabilize the government of Egyptian president Hosni Mubarak.[65] Troubled central Asian states were not pressured intensively because they were also being asked to host critical new defense and intelligence facilities.[66]

The Bush administration's commitment to a doctrine of preemption also seemed, in the words of *Washington Post* reporter Thomas Ricks, "an astonishing departure from decades of practice and two centuries of tradition."[67] This statement demands close consideration. As a matter of *practice*, the United States (like other great powers) has long been prepared to topple governments that threaten American interests, if circumstances permit it to do so. In the modern era, the United States participated in the 1953 coup against Iranian prime minister Mohammed Mosaddeq, organized the 1954 coup against Guatemalan president Jacobo Arbenz Guzmán, orchestrated a failed 1961 invasion of Cuba, supported the 1963 coup against South Vietnamese president Ngo Dinh Diem and the 1973 coup against Chilean president Salvador Allende, and armed the Nicaraguan opposition in the early 1980s.[68] The United States also took less-dramatic steps to shape other governments, by providing aid to anticommunist elements in Japan and Italy during the Cold War.[69]

Many of these activities were done covertly, without a pretense of legality. The novelty of the Bush Doctrine lay in its attempt to make the case *openly* for interventions to protect U.S. interests—to do overtly what had once been done covertly. This was, indeed, a significant shift in *espoused* policy. However, the United States had been edging toward such a policy for years. It invaded Grenada in 1983 and Panama in 1989, despite broad international condemnation of the attacks. (In both instances, UN Security Council resolutions condemning the invasions were vetoed by the United States.)[70] The United States explicitly invoked the right to self-defense to justify its 1986 attack on Libya, which supported the Abu Nidal group, after Abu Nidal's bombing of a West Berlin nightclub popular with U.S. servicemen. "We have heard it asserted that military action to retaliate or pre-empt terrorism is contrary to international law," said Secretary of State George Shultz, however,

> the [UN] Charter's restrictions on the use or threat of force in international relations include a specific exception for the right of self-defense. It is absurd to argue that international law prohibits us from capturing terrorists in international waters or airspace, from attacking them on the soil of other nations . . . or from using force against states that support, train and harbor terrorists or guerrillas. . . . A nation attacked by terrorists is permitted to use force to prevent or pre-empt future attacks, to seize terrorists or to rescue its citizens when no other means is available.[71]

The Clinton administration was sympathetic to Shultz's view. In 1996 President Clinton warned that the United States "cannot and will not refuse to do what we believe is right" in dealing with states that sponsor terrorism, even if allies do not agree.[72] The administration again invoked the right to self-defense to justify its 1998 cruise-missile attacks on Sudan and Afghanistan, following the bombing of U.S. embassies in Kenya and Tanzania. "This is not a one-shot deal," administration officials said at the time. "This is the war of the future."[73]

The attempt to loosen rules on military action may be troubling, but in practice U.S. policy was not unmoored. To a large degree, policy was driven (and checked) by bureaucratic and geopolitical realities. Thus, there were critical instances in which the Bush administration did not act against states that were alleged to pose "a grave and growing danger" to the United States.[74] When North Korea announced in 2005 that it had nuclear weapons, the Bush administration downplayed the statement ("We've heard this kind of rhetoric before") and encouraged North Korea to engage in multilateral talks.[75] Even after North Korea tested a nuclear device in 2006, President Bush insisted that diplomacy had not yet "run its course."[76] The United States took a similar approach to Iran as its leadership purged moderate elements within its government and accelerated its nuclear-weapons program.[77]

The decision to invade Iraq was taken precisely because it did *not* entail a dramatic change in the policy or operations of the U.S. government. The American interest in Iraq was longstanding. As President Bush himself conceded, this interest was partly rooted in the need to avoid disruptions in the supply of oil. ("We have a serious problem," Bush said in 2006. "America is addicted to oil, which is often imported from unstable parts of the world."[78] The United States accounts for 25 percent of world consumption of oil, and the Middle East has over 60 percent of the world's proven reserves.)[79] Iraq also threatened U.S. allies such as Israel. Its behavior throughout the 1990s suggested that it still had ambitions to acquire weapons of mass destruction.[80]

American policy after the cease-fire agreement of February 1991 was described antiseptically, and inaccurately, as "containment" of Iraq.[81] In reality, the two countries were engaged in a long, undeclared, and escalating war.[82] Only months after the 1991 ceasefire, U.S. troops entered northern Iraq to protect Kurds fleeing from persecution by the Hussein regime. While U.S. Marines feinted with the Iraqi troops, allied aircraft created a no-fly zone that barred Iraqi pilots from the topmost part of Iraqi territory. The intervention was "noble and ethically sound" but also led to an infringement of Iraqi sovereignty that was difficult to justify under international law.[83] In 1992, the allies added another no-fly zone to deter attacks on Shi'ite Muslims in southern Iraq, and they extended it in 1996. The Iraqi air force was constrained to a narrow band whose southern limit was only twenty miles from Baghdad.

Iraq continually tested the no-fly zones by building up missile sites, targeting allied aircraft with radar, firing antiaircraft weapons, and flying its own aircraft into the zones. An Iraqi MiG-25 was shot down in air combat in late 1992, and a short time later eighty allied planes attacked missile sites within Iraq.[84] In the next decade, allied pilots flew over three hundred thousand sorties in response to threats within the no-fly zones—many more sorties than were flown during the Gulf War itself.[85]

In 1994, Iraq began to assemble its armored forces on its southern border, raising the threat of a renewed attack on Kuwait. The United States responded vigorously, promising to land forty thousand troops in Kuwait within a week if Iraqi forces were not withdrawn.[86] The Iraqi government backed away from a confrontation. Nonetheless, the U.S. military began to rebuild its own capabilities. The number of U.S. military personnel deployed to the region rose from eight thousand in 1994 to thirty thousand in 2000.[87]

In the seven years after the 1991 cease-fire, the United States launched almost twice as many cruise missiles against Iraq as it had used during the Gulf War.[88] In 1993, the United States attacked a nuclear fabrication facility in Baghdad's suburbs with forty-five cruise missiles. Five months later, it fired twenty-three cruise missiles at the Iraqi intelligence headquarters in downtown Baghdad, in retaliation for an Iraqi plot to kill former president Bush. In 1996, forty-four cruise missiles were launched at military installations to punish an Iraqi raid into the Kurdish enclave in northern Iraq. In 1998, the United States undertook an even bigger assault, as a reply to Iraqi interference with UN weapon inspections. Over four hundred cruise missiles were launched in a four-day assault that also included 250 aerial sorties against targets across Iraq. Fourteen hundred elite Iraqi troops were killed in the attacks.[89]

By the late 1990s, the path for further escalation of conflict was cleared. The Clinton administration was adopting a tougher policy toward Iraq. The Iraqi government was intent on building "an arsenal of devastating destruction," President Clinton said during another buildup of allied forces in early 1998, "and some day, some way, I guarantee you, he'll use the arsenal."[90] Secretary of State Madeleine Albright affirmed that the United States now endorsed "regime change" in the country. Containment, said National Security Advisor Samuel Berger, "is not sustainable over the long run."[91]

The Clinton administration was also edging toward unilateralism.[92] By 1998, it had lost the support of two nations, Russia and France, which endorsed early measures against Iraq but opposed later cruise-missile attacks. The administration was not deterred by this or by complaints that it lacked authority from the United Nations to enforce no-fly zones and make retaliatory strikes against Iraq.[93] Defense Secretary William Perry said that the U.S. attack in 1996 was a response "to our national interest. We did not need assistance to carry out the mission."[94] "The Iraq problem," an independent study said in 1999, had mutated from "a multilateral conflict between Iraq and the United Nations to a bilateral one between Iraq and the United States."[95]

The military, meanwhile, was preparing for the possibility of escalation. As part of its standard practice, military staff within the U.S. Central Command (the lead for U.S. combat forces in the Middle East and Central Asia, known as CENTCOM) refined contingency plans for a full invasion of Iraq.[96] General Tommy Franks, head of CENTCOM from 2000 to 2003, was "deeply involved in this planning," according to his predecessor, Anthony Zinni. "He was more involved in it than just about anybody else. That was his life."[97] In the late 1990s, CENTCOM even dropped leaflets over Iraqi territory telling troops that they would be treated well if they refused to fight in a war with the United States.[98]

The American public broadly supported a more aggressive stance toward Iraq. Large majorities endorsed the major U.S. attacks in 1993, 1996, and 1998. Polls taken throughout the 1990s showed that even larger majorities favored taking "all military action necessary," including use of combat troops, to force Saddam Hussein from power. A February 1999 Gallup poll found that 74 percent of Americans favored "taking all-out military action against Iraq until the situation is resolved."[99]

In 1999–2000, conflict in the no-fly zones escalated. Iraq announced that it no longer recognized the no-fly zones and began acting more aggressively toward allied aircraft.[100] In response, the United States revised its rules of engagement so that pilots would have broader discretion to respond against threatened or actual attacks.[101] In the first eight months of 1999, the United States launched more than one thousand missiles against Iraqi targets. For the next sixteen months, Iraq was bombed on almost a daily basis.[102]

The Iraqi government was undeterred. On the eve of President Bush's inauguration, Iraqi forces fired more missiles at American and British pilots than they had in the whole of 2000.[103] The allies responded with an assault by two dozen aircraft on targets close to Baghdad, while Iraq retaliated with further missile attacks on allied aircraft. (The Bush White House called the allied strikes "routine."[104] Indeed, such conflict had become so habitual that Defense Secretary Rumsfeld was not consulted on the February 2001 assault.)[105] By the summer of 2001, Rumsfeld was considering another change to the rules of engagement in the no-fly zones, to add a more "muscular element" to U.S. policy.[106] CENTCOM, meanwhile, was "dusting off" its contingency plans for invasion of Iraq.[107]

A decade after the cease-fire, the groundwork for invasion of Iraq was well established. This is not to say that actions leading up to September 11 were taken with the expectation that they would lead to invasion. Nonetheless, the U.S. military was accustomed to conflict and understood its enemy. It had good intelligence about Iraq's conventional warfare capabilities and knew that those capabilities had been substantially degraded. An invasion would be "a cakewalk," said Republican defense adviser Ken Adelman in February 2002.[108] Moreover, it would be supported by the American public, which had witnessed ten years of military engagement in Iraq without U.S. casualties. In fall 2002, pollsters predicted that public approval of White House policies would surge once military action began—just as it had during the Gulf War and the 2001 invasion of Afghanistan.[109] Appointees within the Bush administration who lobbied for an invasion of Iraq were not advocating a radical shift in policy. They were pushing on an open door.

## FEMA on the Tigris

Narrowly considered, the invasion of Iraq *was* a cakewalk. Congress authorized the use of force against Iraq in October 2002. Within three months, 130,000 U.S. and British ground troops had been deployed to Kuwait. Allied forces crossed the Kuwait-Iraq border at dawn on March 20, 2003, and occupied the Iraqi capital on April 9. A decade of bombing had ruined Iraqi air defenses, retired Air Force chief of staff Merrill McPeak wrote in June 2003, so that "our aircraft were able to begin reducing opposing ground forces immediately. Army and Marine Corps formations, judged by 'experts' to be much too small for the job, captured Baghdad in just 22 days."[110] One hundred U.S.

soldiers died by hostile action, fewer than in the Gulf War. Public support for President Bush quickly spiked, as pollsters had anticipated (see fig. 1.1).

Three years later, Iraq had become a debacle, even when judged on the president's own terms. In 2002 Bush approved a war plan that said that his goal was to help Iraqis "build a society based on moderation, pluralism and democracy."[111] However, the number of civilians killed in Iraq rose year after year, largely because of growing sectarian violence.[112] Street violence had made daily life "unbearable."[113] Almost one million Iraqis had been forced to move from their homes.[114] Guerrilla warfare in Iraq was "shaping a new generation of terrorist leaders," according to a U.S. intelligence assessment.[115] The International Monetary Fund reported that the Iraqi economy was stagnating as violence undermined efforts to rebuild infrastructure and provide services.[116] Transparency International found that corruption had grown worse in every year of occupation.[117] Moreover, Iraq had become a major political liability—a main cause of the president's declining political fortunes.[118]

The federal government made these outcomes more likely because of its staggering incompetence in the postwar management of Iraq. Many people had warned the Bush administration that careful planning was essential. In January 2003 a bipartisan panel of retired military and civilian leaders cautioned,

> Given the sheer complexity of post-conflict reconstruction efforts, developing a clear strategic plan of action at the outset is critical to success. Such a plan should articulate the U.S. interests at stake, define U.S. objectives for the intervention, and lay out the strategy for achieving these policy objectives and a clear division of labor delineating who is responsible for what aspects of the plan's implementation. Perhaps even more important than the plan itself is the strategy development and planning process, which allows key players to build working relationships, hammer out differences, identify potential inconsistencies and gaps, synchronize their actions, and better understand their roles.

This was an appeal for rationality, foresight, and coherence in decision making. Unfortunately, the panel concluded, the federal government lacked mechanisms for proper planning and coordination of effort. The subject was an "orphan" within the federal bureaucracy.[119]

In the eighteen months between the September 11 attacks and the March 2003 invasion of Iraq, the U.S. government proved this point definitively. The U.S. military engaged in exhaustive planning of the invasion itself but neglected questions about the governance of Iraq after its occupation. This was not because of ignorance about the risk of a collapse in public order after the fall of Saddam Hussein. In fact, CENTCOM itself undertook a war game in 1999, Desert Crossing, that highlighted the danger that "fragmentation and chaos" would follow Hussein's fall.[120] However, the warnings of Desert Crossing were soon forgotten.[121] Although plans prepared by CENTCOM in August 2002 said that "the end state for this operation is regime change . . . [with] an acceptable provisional/permanent government in place,"[122] the plans did not say how this goal would be achieved or what American troops would be expected to do once they reached Baghdad.

There were two reasons for CENTCOM's neglect. First, occupation and reconstruction was not a core function for the military. There was no major component within the armed services whose main function was to assure that such tasks were done well. Military leaders, the products of organizations that were honed (as former CENTCOM chief Zinni said) to be "great at the tactical problems [of] killing and breaking," had little interest in the subject.[123] (Zinni's successor, General Tommy Franks, made clear that he had no patience for the subject derisively known as "nation-building.")[124] Second, this indifference could be rationalized because there were other components of government, such as the State Department, that historically had responsibility for the subject. The State Department, Franks told subordinates in August 2002, would have the lead once the Hussein regime was toppled.[125]

There were two difficulties with Franks's assumption. The first was an overestimation of the State Department's capacities. In October 2001, the State Department did begin an exercise that it called the Future of Iraq Project, intended to engage Iraqi exiles and specialists on postwar priorities. But the project was underfunded and undisciplined. The exercise did not produce an operational plan for management of postwar Iraq.[126] Several of its seventeen working groups still had not met a month after the occupation of Baghdad.[127] The second difficulty was the enmity between the Defense Department's civilian leadership and their counterparts at the State Department, a feeling that grew as the two organizations disagreed over the wisdom of invasion. The departments were "at war," a senior Pentagon official later said. "It was knee-jerk venom on both sides."[128]

In fall 2002 the Joint Chiefs of Staff, the top advisory body for the armed services, became concerned by the lack of a postwar plan and advanced its own proposal for a military command to govern Iraq. Rumsfeld modified the plan by insisting on a split of military and civilian functions, with planning for civilian administration to be undertaken within the Office of the Secretary of Defense, guided by Under Secretary for Policy Douglas Feith.[129] Feith was later criticized harshly for his incompetence in handling the brief.[130] The more serious difficulty, however, was one of *bureaucratic* rather than personal incompetence: the department was simply reaching beyond its abilities. As a Rand report later said, the Defense Department "lacked experience, expertise, funding authority, local knowledge, and established contacts with other potential civilian organizations."[131]

Consequently, it improvised. In January 2003, only eight weeks before invasion, President Bush approved a directive creating a new Office for Reconstruction and Humanitarian Assistance (ORHA) under Feith's supervision.[132] (It was, says Woodward, a "rush job.")[133] Jay Garner, a retired general who ran the relief effort for Kurds in northern Iraq after the Gulf War, was recruited as its head. However, Garner was handicapped by a late start, an uncertain budget, and continued interdepartmental strife. Most ORHA workers had not yet joined the office when the invasion began on March 20.[134] Attempts to recruit experts from the State Department and other federal agencies were blocked by Rumsfeld and Feith.[135] "We started very slowly," Garner conceded in a press conference on March 11. He told journalists that his team had scarcely finished its enumeration of the challenges likely to arise after the invasion.[136]

Garner finally arrived in Baghdad on April 21, almost two weeks after its occupation. In Washington, however, there was conflict over the Defense Department's postoccupation planning. The State Department, responding to pressure from allies concerned about the appearance of a military occupation, wanted another civilian to head the administration. The Defense Department also appeared to concede the need for a more prominent and politically influential chief. Even be-

fore the occupation of Baghdad, Rumsfeld's office had decided to replace Garner. ORHA would be absorbed into a new organization, the
Coalition Provisional Authority (CPA). Garner was told of the changes
three days after his arrival in Baghdad. News of the change quickly
leaked to the media, undercutting Garner's authority and sowing uncertainty about plans for reconstruction. The new CPA administrator,
Paul Bremer, arrived in Baghdad on May 14.[137]

In the words of the Special Inspector General for Iraq Reconstruction, the CPA became the "de facto government of Iraq."[138] And yet
there was confusion about its legal status. "Whether the CPA was
a federal agency was unclear," a congressional report said in 2005.
"Competing explanations for how it was established contribute to
the uncertainty. . . . Some executive branch documents supported the
notion that it was created by the President, possibly as a result of a
National Security Presidential Directive. This document, if it exists,
has not been made available."[139] This ambiguity had concrete implications for the accountability of the CPA. The Defense Department insisted that federal auditors did not have jurisdiction to investigate
CPA spending, because it was not a federal agency. Contractors were
warned that they might not have remedies in U.S. courts if the CPA
broke its commitments. Employees who suspected contractor fraud
were told that they could not pursue those suspicions under American law.[140]

The CPA, like ORHA, was an organization "invented on the
fly."[141] Lacking a plan for obtaining staff from other federal agencies,
it became one of those rare bureaucracies that never actually employed its quota of workers. In June 2004, the CPA conceded that it
did not have an accurate personnel count but "believed it had a total
of 1,196 workers" in Baghdad, about half the authorized number.[142]
The Defense Department improvised by recruiting hundreds of workers through its White House Liaison Office, which normally vets political appointees for the department. Many of these recruits possessed
what the inspector general delicately called "inconsistent skill sets."[143]
They were Republican loyalists with no military or government experience or familiarity with the Middle East.[144] A group of CPA workers
responsible for managing the Iraqi government's budget, all in their
twenties, were recruited because they had submitted resumes for un-
related jobs at the conservative Heritage Foundation.[145]

The occupation, a consultant's report said in 2003, gave American officials a "unique opportunity" for radical reconstruction of Iraqi society.[146] The inexperience and partisanship of many CPA workers encouraged them to seize the moment and pursue reforms that were unneeded or impracticable.[147] (Iraqi officials later disparaged the CPA's approach as "market fundamentalism.")[148] The CPA's ambitious plan for privatization of state-owned enterprises was ultimately shelved in response to complaints that the resulting unemployment would aggravate popular unrest.[149] Other plans were compromised by the turnover of CPA staff. A senior CPA adviser called many of the staff "90-day wonders, getting their tickets punched that said, 'I've been in Baghdad.'"[150]

Lacking its own capacity, the CPA depended on the cooperation of other actors in Iraq. However, it proved incapable of managing these relationships effectively. Dealings with the military were fraught with conflict; Bremer and General Ricardo Sanchez, commander of U.S. ground forces in Iraq, were scarcely speaking to each other.[151] A basic sign of the dysfunction was the CPA's decision to divide the country into administrative regions that did not match the regional commands used by the military.[152] The CPA's relationships with the chief development agency, USAID, and with the United Nations Mission to Iraq were similarly poor.[153]

The CPA also relied heavily on contractors, even to perform basic security functions. ("We are creating a private army on an unprecidented [sic] scale," a 2004 CPA memo said. "This will be the largest private security force ever assembled. It will be larger than Coalition Forces and will represent a force for good or harm depending on our insistance [sic] on the rule of law.")[154] However, an inspector general report concluded that the U.S. government was "not systemically well-poised" to provide the support needed to do this contracting properly.[155] "I didn't understand, and no one in my office understood, government procurement and contracting," a senior CPA official later admitted.[156]

Formally, Bremer was supposed to report to Defense Secretary Rumsfeld.[157] But Bremer soon asserted his independence from Rumsfeld, insisting that he reported directly to the White House.[158] "He doesn't work for me," Rumsfeld was reported to have said to National Security Advisor Condoleezza Rice in December 2003. "He works for you."[159] But the National Security Council (NSC) proved equally ineffectual in overseeing the CPA. The White House had said publicly that it did not intend to play a large role in guiding reconstruction, and the NSC's Executive Steering Group, set up in 2002 to coordinate war efforts, had been disbanded.[160] Rice was "profoundly frustrated" by the inability to obtain information from Bremer.[161]

Confusion about Bremer's place in the chain of command allowed him to make policy shifts that were opposed elsewhere in the government and that undercut efforts to stabilize Iraq. Two days after his arrival, Bremer announced a broad rule banning former Ba'ath Party members from jobs in the public sector.[162] A week later, Bremer disbanded the army, the security and intelligence services, and the defense ministry.[163] These were critical reversals of U.S. policy. Wide-scale debaathification stripped government ministries of thousands of their most experienced personnel, and dissolution of the Iraqi army denied the U.S. military a critical tool for maintaining order.[164] Both policies created a pool of aggrieved and unemployed Iraqis.[165] Only weeks earlier, Bush and Rumsfeld had been told that postwar planning was built on the assumption that debaathification would be restrained and that the Iraqi military would be kept intact. Neither military leaders nor the National Security Council were warned of Bremer's plans.[166] Bremer reversed the debaathification policy a year later, conceding that it had been "poorly implemented."[167]

American policy on the transfer of sovereignty to a new Iraqi government was equally erratic. Immediately after the occupation, Garner encouraged local elections and began organizing a national assembly that would establish a new provisional government for Iraq; outlines of the plan were made public in early May.[168] This was consistent with a plan summarized by National Security Advisor Rice in March.[169] But Bremer announced an abrupt reversal in U.S. policy two weeks later: there would be no quick transfer of powers to a provisional government.[170] Local elections were halted.[171] Bremer's CPA would retain authority, to be exercised with the help of a carefully selected twenty-five-person Governing Council.

Pressed for an explanation of how the United States would eventually give up authority, Bremer later published his plan in an unusual forum—the opinion page of the *Washington Post*.[172] Bremer's September 2003 column warned that immediate elections were "simply . . . not possible." The Governing Council would develop a plan for drafting and ratifying a new Iraqi constitution; this would be followed by elections and then by complete transfer of the CPA's powers. There was no timeline, but Bremer implied that the process would not end quickly. Influential Iraqis, and key allies such as France and Germany, were troubled by the prospect of an indefinite occupation.[173]

Rice and other senior Bush administration officials later claimed that they had been "blindsided" by Bremer's plan.[174] Bremer, said columnist David Brooks, "hadn't cleared the piece with his higher-ups in the Pentagon or the White House."[175] However, there is reason to doubt the surprise: Bremer's column was consistent with President Bush's statement on Iraqi governance the day before and also with the text of a resolution that the administration urged on the UN Security Council the following month.[176]

Clearly, however, there was unresolved disagreement within the administration about the wisdom of Bremer's approach. In late September, Rice established a new committee, the Iraq Stabilization Group, to oversee Bremer and referee on disagreements between the Defense and State Departments on Iraqi governance.[177] Even as the UN Security Council acceded to Bremer's September plan, the Bush administration rewrote its strategy on transfer of sovereignty.[178] Bremer was recalled to Washington for a round of impromptu consultations. On November 15, a new plan was announced. It was an exact reversal of the priorities laid out in September: first, a commitment to transfer sovereignty to a provisional government in seven months; next, elections for an interim government; and then finally, the drafting and ratification of a new constitution.[179]

Meanwhile, reform in Iraq was being undermined by the steady deterioration of public order. In January 2003 the bipartisan panel had warned that "security is the *sine qua non* of post-conflict reconstruction"; without it, any intervention was "doomed to fail."[180] However, the U.S. military had done little to stop the widespread looting that followed the collapse of the Iraqi government or to counter the subsequent wave of criminal violence. It failed to take steps such as securing the Iraqi borders that would have deterred the insurgency in later months.[181] The failure to act quickly and firmly had a profound effect on reconstruction efforts. Following a car-bomb attack on its Baghdad headquarters, the United Nations withdrew its personnel in late 2003. International relief organizations, contractors, and military forces supplied by smaller allies soon followed.[182] The CPA itself was driven into "a physical and psychological bunker" by escalating violence.[183]

The inability to maintain security was another consequence of the failure to plan adequately for occupation. In the weeks before invasion, the administration had refused to contemplate investing in a constabulary that would maintain order afterward.[184] But the collapse of security was also the consequence of Rumsfeld's determination to keep troop requirements for the invasion as low as possible. There was broad agreement among senior Army officers that several hundred thousand troops would be needed to occupy and secure the country. Franks's own initial estimate, provided to Rumsfeld in December 2001, was that 385,000 troops were required. Rumsfeld, convinced that the military was being unduly cautious, pressed for reductions. The invasion force eventually numbered 145,000 troops.[185] The count of troops in Iraq declined to 109,000 by February 2004. Although it was increased in response to mounting violence, the U.S. force never rose above 160,000 in the next two years.

## A Failure of Command

The Bush administration, like many of its predecessors, flattered itself by imagining that it had the freedom to articulate and realize a new grand strategy for American foreign policy. This, after all, is what we imagine that chief executives are supposed to do: they formulate ambitious goals and execute great plans. This is essential to our stereotyped view of executive decision making.

But the stereotype can be misleading. The rhetoric and behavior of chief executives is often shaped, perhaps unwittingly, by bureaucratic and political realities. In 2001 the U.S. government was dominated by the defense establishment, which was both trusted and increasingly capable of exercising force without imposing substantial costs on U.S. society. Its behavior after September 11 was opportunistic, shaped heavily by an understanding of what could be done easily and quickly. To a significant degree, action *preceded* deliberation: the major commitments that would dominate the Bush administration's agenda for the next five years were already being formed within days —indeed, hours—of the attacks.[186]

Strategy was driven by capacity and opportunity—that is, a sense of what could be done easily—but it was also undercut by incapacities, that is, by the inability of the federal government to execute certain tasks well. The Bush administration could invade Iraq; this routine was well practiced. But it could not sort out what to do once it had executed this routine. What is equally striking is the inability of the administration to recognize this limitation—to see what it could not do well—and tailor its behavior accordingly. An excuse might be that the administration operated on the assumption that events would turn in their favor; but there is no evidence that the administration recognized this *as an assumption* or asked itself what would be done if the assumption proved to be mistaken. Nor did the administration appear capable of responding coherently when confronted with mounting evidence that in fact it had made assumptions that were mistaken.

An awareness of capabilities and risks is one of the signposts of rationality in decision making, and it is largely absent in the history of the Bush administration's approach to the War on Terrorism. The administration followed the rituals of planning: accounts of its behavior in Iraq are replete with strategy statements, operational plans, priority lists, and "megabriefs." And Secretary Rumsfeld himself cautioned about the need to accommodate uncertainty. As he often said after the September 11 attacks, "There are things we know we don't know and that's really important to know, and not think you know them when you don't. But the tricky ones are the unknown unknowns, the things we don't know we don't know. They're the ones that can get you in a bucket of trouble."[187]

Unfortunately, much of this talk and paperwork was administrative flotsam. In reality, the Bush administration did not plan. It could articulate ambitious goals but could not marshal the administrative capacities of its agencies so that their work contributed directly to those goals. It could not induce agencies with overlapping responsibilities to collaborate. It could not anticipate curves in the road. The administration's problem, Henry Kissinger is reported to have said, was that it "did not have a system of national security policy decision making that ensured careful examination of the downsides of major decisions."[188] Or as the 2005 Rand analysis said regarding the administration's Iraq policy,

> Unity of command and broad participation are both important to the success of stabilization and reconstruction operations. . . . An active NSC interagency process [is] necessary to ensure that the State and Defense Departments are acting off the same sheet of paper and to

bring forward debate of alternative views and subsequent decision-making on important issues. Policy differences need to be expressed and adjudicated, if necessary by the President, as the planning process goes forward. . . . Some process for exposing senior officials to possibilities other than those being assumed in their planning also needs to be introduced.[189]

It is a damning comment on the quality of governance within the Bush administration that worn bromides such as these could be presented as major lessons from the invasion.

There was a temptation in some postwar commentaries to ascribe failings in decision making to the personal qualities of key players—such the president's incuriosity, Donald Rumsfeld's bullying, or Condoleezza Rice's inability to command the attention of her more experienced colleagues. (Senator Chuck Hagel told Bob Woodward that the administration's difficulty was that it "had no strategic thinker.")[190] However, the difficulties were more fundamental. After all, regime change in Iraq had been a publicly stated goal of the U.S. government since 1998, but in 2001 there was still no plan to assist Iraq when the regime did change.

There are also strong commonalities among the handling of Iraq, the development of policy on homeland security, and the response to Hurricane Katrina. In each case the administration wrestled with the challenge of setting clear goals and inducing agencies to collaborate in pursuing those goals. There are important similarities between FEMA and the CPA—two federal agencies (assuming, for the purpose of argument, that the CPA was a federal agency) with responsibilities that outstripped their capacities, whose success hinged materially on cooperation with others, and whose efforts were undone by the inability to achieve unified command.

This is, then, another story about structural limits on executive power. The Bush White House was proud of its decisiveness and its willingness to articulate a bold "grand strategy," but its policies were heavily shaped by existing capabilities and the inertial pressure of the status quo. When it adopted more-ambitious goals, it was thwarted by the inability to develop the administrative capabilities required for their accomplishment. A motif in Bob Woodward's account of the Iraq invasion, *State of Denial*, is the impatient White House official who, having heard the recounting of some difficult problem, tells his or her subordinate, "Just fix it."[191] This was the illusion of command. The reality was that the control cables had snapped.

The great irony is that this failure of command largely undercut the administration's effort to establish a new principle of preemptive self-defense. International law develops by example and by the evolution of international opinion about the wisdom of new practices. Few countries, or specialists in international law, accepted the wisdom of the preemption doctrine when it was articulated by the Bush administration in 2002. Success in Iraq might have persuaded diplomats and scholars that their initial reservations were misguided. Failure, on the other hand, simply reinforced doubts about the new doctrine. Who could defend preemption if, in practice, it actually *aggravated* security threats?

# 6

# The Collapse of Fortress Bush

> At some point, George W. Bush's administration became the literary
> equivalent of a television reality show.
>
> —Tim Rutten, "CIA, Under Tenet's Watch,"
> *Los Angeles Times*, April 30, 2007

APPREHENSIONS ABOUT THE concentration of power within the
executive branch during the Bush administration were encouraged by
the White House's own campaign to convey an impression of firmness
and determination. The immediate comparison was with the Clinton
White House, which was said to be marked by its managerial and
moral chaos. The Bush administration would be different. It would
avoid disorder and internecine warfare. Instead, it would build an organizational culture that valued discipline and loyalty.[1]

By December 2003 it was received wisdom that the Bush administration had succeeded in doing this. Michael Deaver, deputy chief of
staff to Ronald Reagan, said that the Bush administration ran "the
most disciplined White House in history." Ken Auletta called it Fortress Bush. The Bush administration, said Auletta, was "disciplined
like a private corporation," and turf wars among key advisers had
given way to "mind-meld."[2] This unrelenting emphasis on discipline
was said to percolate down to departments and agencies within the
executive branch. By appointing loyalists in key positions, the White
House had countered the "centrifugal forces" inherent in the Washington bureaucracy.[3] A presidential appointee called it the Cult of Bush.
"This group is all about loyalty," he told Elizabeth Drew, "and the definition of loyalty extends to policy-making, politics, and to the execu-
tion of policy."[4]

A new emphasis on secrecy was a critical part of this effort to assure order within the executive branch. Here, too, the Bush administration was said to have got what it wanted. It was generally accepted

that the Bush administration was, as Arthur Schlesinger Jr. said, "the most secretive administration since Nixon."[5] John Dean, President Nixon's legal counsel, went further, claiming that the administration's penchant for secrecy was "far worse than during Watergate."[6] Larry Klayman, chairman of Judicial Watch, a conservative watchdog organization, called the Bush administration the most secretive since Eisenhower.[7]

Once again, rhetoric ran ahead of realities. The discipline of the Bush administration was overstated. On the eve of the September 11 attacks—only eight months after Bush's inauguration—there were many signs that that the fortress walls were cracking. Polls showed that Bush had one of the lowest approval ratings in modern history for a president in his inaugural year. *Slate* magazine had pronounced a "Death Watch" for Defense Secretary Rumsfeld, and on September 10 *Time* magazine published a profile that described Secretary of State Powell as marginalized, frustrated, and contemplating resignation.[8] Conservative allies were turning on the administration for tactical errors and mismanagement of the economy. The administration, said the conservative journal the *Weekly Standard*, was "strategically crippled."[9] Only a few days before the attacks, prominent Republicans were invited to a private dinner at the White House for "an unvarnished critique of Mr. Bush's style and strategy." (The "urgent political task," Bush advisers told the *New York Times* after the meeting, was to "project the image [of Bush] as a commanding leader.")[10] These fissures likely would have widened if the September 11 attacks had not intervened.

Moreover, the administration proved incapable of sustaining discipline after the 9/11 attacks. For example, the White House quickly lost control over the biggest story of the first Bush term: the narrative of the 9/11 attacks themselves. In 2002, it opposed the establishment of a special commission to examine the "facts and circumstances" of the attack but was compelled to concede this battle. Its original choice for chair of the commission, Henry Kissinger, resigned as a consequence of the hostile reaction to his appointment. The commission, backed by a sympathetic public, pressured the White House and federal departments to provide, as the commissioners wrote in November 2003, "a degree of access to information unequalled in the history of the United States."[11]

From the point of view of Attorney General John Ashcroft, the 9/11 Commission appeared to be "veering dangerously out of control."[12] In the following months, the White House continued to lose struggles over its work. The administration relented on the question of access to the president's daily intelligence briefing, the Holy Grail of classified documents. The White House initially refused to allow the full commission to interview the president, but it again retreated under public pressure. It insisted that National Security Advisor Condoleezza Rice could not testify publicly before the commission without breaching executive privilege; nonetheless, Rice testified. Under questioning, Rice conceded that that the title of the August 6, 2001, intelligence briefing was "Bin Ladin Determined to Strike in U.S." The public reaction was so strong that the White House posted the briefing on the Internet ten days later.[13]

The commission became, in the words of its chairman, Thomas Kean, "the definitive arbiter of 9/11."[14] Its report was a publishing-industry phenomenon, selling over three hundred thousand copies in the three days after its release in July 2004. By 2006 it had become "the King James version of all September 11 accounts."[15] But the King James version was certainly not flattering to the White House. It showed that the Bush administration had dismissed the fight against al Qaeda as a priority during its first eight months in office and that top officials had responded sluggishly to threat reports in July and August 2001. "The system was blinking red," the commission said, but federal agencies "never mobilized in response to the threat. They did not have direction, and did not have a plan."[16]

By end of 2003 there was other evidence that the Bush administration's capacity to control the policy agenda was ephemeral. In March 2003, sources in the intelligence community who were frustrated by the White House's use of evidence about the Iraqi threat told journalists that one claim in the president's State of the Union Address— about Iraqi attempts to buy uranium ore in Africa—had been studied earlier and found baseless. The administration refused to concede its error, and in July the former ambassador who had investigated the allegations in Africa, Joseph Wilson, published a column in the *New York Times* that accused the White House of "twisting" intelligence on Iraq.[17] The White House attempted to defend itself by leaking, and later publishing, parts of an overall assessment of Iraqi capabilities prepared by the CIA in 2002, which seemed to bolster the president's January statement. However, this tactic backfired when the published document revealed other discrepancies between internal intelligence assessments and the administration's public statements on the danger posed by Iraq.[18]

More damage followed. Columnist Robert Novak reported that Wilson had been sent to Africa at the suggestion of his wife, Valerie Plame, "an agency operative."[19] Because Plame worked undercover, Novak's statement suggested that a federal official might have violated the Intelligence Identities Protection Act, which makes it a crime to disclose the identity of covert agents. By December 2003, a special prosecutor had been appointed to investigate. His two-year probe damaged the White House, revealing that Vice President Cheney had authorized the leaking of classified information to rebut Wilson's claims.[20] Cheney's chief of staff, I. Lewis Libby, resigned in 2005 after being indicted for obstructing the investigation. His resignation compromised Cheney's influence during the Bush administration's second term.[21]

Signs of decaying discipline were also evident in the field of domestic policy. *Esquire* magazine published a scathing review of tensions within the White House written by investigative journalist Ron Suskind. Suskind's main source was John J. DiIulio Jr., a professor of public policy at the University of Pennsylvania who was recruited in 2001 to run the White House's high-profile office for faith-based initiatives. DiIulio resigned after only seven months, denying rumors of tensions with other White House staff. However, DiIulio was more forthright with Suskind. The White House, he said, suffered from "a complete lack of a policy apparatus" and a "breathtaking . . . lack of even basic policy knowledge." The Bush administration's approach to homeland security—its decision to create an Office of Homeland Security and later to replace it with a new department—had not "received more than talking-points caliber deliberation," DiIulio complained.[22]

Suskind's *Esquire* article garnered substantial attention, but in December 2003 he was only weeks away from the release of an even bigger exposé. In fact, 2004 would prove to be the year in which claims about the Bush administration's effectiveness in maintaining discipline or secrecy collapsed entirely. It would become clear that the administration never achieved a "mind-meld" among key advisers; on the contrary, there was bitter dissent and an inability at the center to resolve disagreements amicably. Similarly the Bush administration did not establish control over the bureaucracy. Instead, Bush appointees waged a low-intensity war with the federal bureaucracy, and they lost many key battles in that war. All of this conflict become a matter of public record, as a consequence of leaks, special inquiries, tell-all books, and the routine operation of transparency laws.

The collapse of Fortress Bush was a moral tale about the difficulties of asserting control within contemporary U.S. government. In important respects it is a story driven by declining respect for the bureaucracy and the presidency and by the rise of market forces. Bush appointees made clear their deep distrust of the bureaucracy and handled it roughly; career bureaucrats, no longer bound by old concepts of strict fidelity, found ways to resist rough treatment. Political appointees who were dismayed by unfairness in policymaking at the center of government also felt free to vent that dismay. The news and entertainment industry, eager for sensation, allowed dissidents to express their discontent more forcefully than ever before and compensated them generously for doing so. The tell-all industry became a powerful engine of transparency.

## Distrusting the Servants

On the whole, the Bush administration evinced a deep antipathy toward the federal public service. Indeed, one of the ironies of the Bush administration is the extent of its estrangement from three bureaucracies that were essential to the achievement of its priorities: the Department of Defense, the Central Intelligence Agency, and the State Department. Moreover, the career public servants who worked in these bureaucracies were keenly aware of the antagonism.

The Republican Party is not usually regarded as hostile to the defense establishment. The technological revolution within the U.S. military began during the massive defense buildup under the Reagan presidency. And the Bush administration was widely perceived as one that would have a stronger rapport with the U.S. military's leadership than did the Clinton administration.[23] At the swearing-in of Defense

Secretary Rumsfeld in January 2001, the president adverted to the Clinton-era tensions, promising that his aim (and Rumsfeld's) would be to "strengthen the bond of trust" with the military.[24]

However, the Republican attitude toward the defense establishment was nuanced. The Republican leadership appreciated the military but disdained bureaucracy, and it believed that the Defense Department manifested the worst features of bureaucracy: inertia, hostility to fresh thinking, inefficiency, and self-aggrandizement. The military, it was thought, had wasted the opportunities presented by the end of the Cold War and technological change. It remained wedded to cumbersome and expensive weapons systems. And it had exploited President Clinton's inability to push the military leadership to pursue reforms.[25]

Rumsfeld expressed his reservations about the defense bureaucracy starkly. In a speech at the Pentagon the day before the September 11 attacks, Rumsfeld said,

> The topic today is an adversary that poses a threat, a serious threat, to the security of the United States of America. This adversary is one of the world's last bastions of central planning. . . . With brutal consistency, it stifles free thought and crushes new ideas. It disrupts the defense of the United States and places the lives of men and women in uniform at risk. . . . The adversary [is] Pentagon bureaucracy. Not the people, but the processes. . . . In this building, despite this era of scarce resources taxed by mounting threats, money disappears into duplicative duties and bloated bureaucracy—not because of greed, but gridlock. Innovation is stifled—not by ill intent but by institutional inertia.[26]

During his first eight months as defense secretary, Rumsfeld attempted to maintain a tight grip on Pentagon operations, constantly pushing military leaders to explain or reconsider existing practices. He became notorious for "snowflakes," memoranda that demanded an immediate answer to the secretary's queries. Rumsfeld's office challenged the role of the Joint Chiefs of Staff in providing military advice to the president, questioned existing force levels, and threatened cancellation of new weapons systems.[27]

Rumsfeld's drive to assert civilian control stirred broad resentment within the defense bureaucracy. By the summer of 2001 many military leaders were alienated by his confrontational style.[28] It had become difficult for officials to remember that the object of Rumsfeld's ire was "not the people, but the processes." The fundamental difficulty, Admiral Vernon Clark, chief of naval operations, reportedly told Rumsfeld, was that "you don't trust us."[29] The director of operations for the Joint Chiefs of Staff said that he also discovered that Rumsfeld's attitude "was one of fundamental mistrust."[30] Tommy Franks, chief of CENTCOM, confronted Rumsfeld in fall 2001 over his constant questioning of tactics in the Afghan campaign. "I'm either commander or I'm not, and you've got to trust me or you don't," Franks was reported to have told Rumsfeld.[31]

This habitual distrust of military judgment would have fatal consequences during planning for the invasion of Iraq, as Rumsfeld pushed Franks and CENTCOM planners to reduce their estimate of troop requirements. Rumsfeld said publicly that he had accepted military advice on the number of troops needed for invasion, but in actuality Rumsfeld pressed Franks to reduce his estimate of requirements. "There was always pressure from [the Office of the Secretary of Defense]," said a CENTCOM planner. "Could we do it smaller?"[32] Franks's earlier plans, which proposed higher troop deployments, were criticized for lack of creativity.[33]

There were widespread concerns within the military leadership about the drive to reduce troop requirements, evidenced in the public comments of their retired colleagues. In August 2002 General Frederick Kroesen, a former commander of U.S. forces in Europe, said that the Pentagon appeared to be embarking on a "campaign based on hope" that would end in disaster if its assumptions proved untenable.[34] In October 2002, former CENTCOM chief Anthony Zinni also "bristle[d] against ideas of small forces," warning that the United States would need to maintain order in Iraq during a lengthy period of transition to self-rule.[35] In January 2003, General Norman Schwarzkopf, commander of U.S. forces during the Gulf War, said that he was worried by the "cockiness" of the U.S. war plan. Schwarzkopf said his active-duty friends were preoccupied by "the Rumsfeld thing," the perception that the defense secretary had scant regard for their judgment.[36]

The chiefs of the armed services were largely sidelined in invasion planning.[37] Even so, Army Chief of Staff Eric Shinseki was candid when asked by the Senate Armed Services Committee to estimate how many troops would be required for an occupation of Iraq. Shinseki said that "several hundred thousand soldiers" were likely needed—far more than were provided for in the war plan. Under Secretary of Defense Paul Wolfowitz dismissed Shinseki's estimate as "outlandish" and "wildly off the mark." Neither Rumsfeld nor Wolfowitz attended Shinseki's retirement ceremony in June 2003. There is "an important distinction between command and effective leadership," Shinseki said at the ceremony. "Without leadership, command is a hollow experience—a vacuum often filled with mistrust and arrogance."[38]

The Bush administration managed the intelligence community—and in particular the lead organization in that community, the Central Intelligence Agency—in much the same way.[39] There were two major complaints against the CIA. The first was its ineffectiveness in collecting raw intelligence overseas. In 2004 the House Intelligence Committee called the agency's clandestine arm a "dysfunctional" and "stilted" bureaucracy, chary of dangerous intelligence-gathering projects. Compounding this problem was undue caution in interpreting data, leading to routine understatement of threats.[40] The CIA had "a culture of analytic risk aversion," the House Committee said, that led to intelligence reports "so caveated that they are of little use to consumers who are searching for some form of clarity."[41]

In the view of key members of the administration, the agency also had a long record of failure. (An anonymous official put the White House's attitude toward the agency more colorfully, saying that its "basic view of the world is that the CIA has blown it over and over again.")[42] Vice President Cheney remembered that the CIA had badly underestimated Iraq's nuclear weapons capabilities in 1990, an error discovered only when inspectors entered Iraq at the end of the Gulf War.[43] "The people working on the Persian Gulf at the CIA are pathetic," said Richard Perle, chairman of a board that advised Donald Rumsfeld on defense policy. "They have a record of over thirty years of being wrong."[44] In 1998, Rumsfeld himself chaired a congressionally mandated inquiry that concluded that the agency had underestimated ballistic-missile threats from Iraq, Iran, and North Korea.[45] (He told journalists at the time that the inquiry took "a somewhat different approach" to the available intelligence, weighing it "as senior decision-makers would.")[46] The CIA's failure to anticipate Indian nuclear weapons tests in 1998 also provoked widespread concern. Its analysts had dismissed the possibility of testing only three months earlier.[47]

The consequences of this distrust were threefold. The first was a complete inversion of the usual procedures for decision making. In the aftermath of 9/11, the Bush administration did not ask the CIA for "any strategic-level intelligence assessments on any aspect of Iraq" before deciding on invasion, according to the CIA officer responsible for such requests.[48] By the time the White House was seriously engaged with the CIA on its assessment of the Iraqi threat, its war planning was already well under way.[49] Senior decision makers could do this because of their certainty that existing assessments, which acknowledged dangers, were too cautious. Iraq "has aggressively pursued the development of additional weapons of mass destruction," Vice President Cheney told *Meet the Press* twelve weeks after the 9/11 attacks. Its links with al Qaeda were "pretty well confirmed."[50]

A second consequence was pressure on the intelligence community to "lean forward" in its Iraqi assessments. The Robb-Silberman Commission, appointed by the administration in 2004 to examine the intelligence community's performance before the invasion of Iraq, concluded that CIA analysts "operated in an environment shaped by intense policymaker interest in Iraq." They were aware of "the backdrop of impending war." Vice President Cheney was deeply engaged in the CIA's work, making an unprecedented number of visits to its headquarters to probe analysts about their conclusions. The commission found that analysts received no encouragement from top managers to challenge prevailing assumptions about the Iraqi threat. Certainly CIA director George Tenet, a Clinton appointee, would not do this. After President Bush expressed his displeasure about a briefing on Iraq in December 2003, Tenet promised that the agency could craft a "slam dunk case" against Iraq.[51] In his public statements, Tenet downplayed his analysts' reservations about the gravity or immediacy of the Iraqi threat.[52] "The overall climate," the Robb-Silberman Commission concluded, led to "an unwillingness even to consider the possibility that the conventional wisdom was wrong."[53]

A third consequence of distrust was the attempt to create new capacities for intelligence assessment—in other words, to find alternative ways of doing work that the intelligence community was believed to be incapable of doing properly. Under Secretary of Defense Feith created a small unit within his office to collect and scour raw intelligence about the link between Iraq and al Qaeda, a connection that was regarded skeptically by the CIA.[54] Feith's unit met with CIA analysts to argue for revision of the agency assessment—an unusual example, the Senate Intelligence Committee later found, of a "consumer organization" engaging in the actual production of intelligence findings.[55] Feith's unit also disparaged CIA analyses in White House briefings from which the agency was excluded.[56] (A "fundamental problem" with the CIA's work, Feith said in these private briefings, was its application of a "juridical" standard to available intelligence. This was essentially a restatement of Rumsfeld's complaint during the ballistic-missile inquiry four years earlier.)[57] Vice President Cheney later said that "alternative intelligence assessments" produced by Feith's unit were the "best source of information" about connections between Iraq and al Qaeda.[58]

Second-guessing of the CIA's judgment continued as the administration prepared to make its case against Iraq before the United Nations in February 2003. Unsatisfied with the brief provided by the CIA, the White House produced its own, more extensive dossier on the Iraqi threat, including material that had been "missed or overlooked" by the agency. This longer brief—"very compelling and very strong," in the eyes of Deputy Chief of Staff Karl Rove—was passed to Secretary of State Colin Powell, who would deliver the UN speech. Powell, in turn, spent "four very, very difficult days" reviewing the evidence amassed against Iraq, visiting the CIA's headquarters to examine raw intercepts of communications collected by the intelligence community.[59] This deep engagement of senior policymakers in the interpretation of intelligence was further evidence of their alienation from the bureaucracy: at a critical moment, they were using scarce hours to check the integrity of its work.

The State Department, too, was the object of distrust—perhaps even more intensely than either the Defense Department or the CIA. The indictment against the State Department was that it was insufficiently forceful in asserting U.S. interests and prone to distasteful foreign entanglements. Under Secretary of Defense Douglas Feith disparaged it as "the Department of Nice."[60] President Bush deplored its tendency to "striped pants formality."[61] (In October 2003, Iraq envoy Paul Bremer spoke with Bush about a planned replacement for Bremer in 2004. "What's needed is someone with significant political skills and preferably area expertise," Bremer said. "Perhaps you should look at someone from State." Bush grimaced.)[62] Vice President Cheney believed that there were too many people in the department who were hostile to the idea of serious change in the Middle East.[63] Even the deputy secretary of state, Richard Armitage, had "poked fun at [the department's] stereotypically effete culture" during his earlier service at the Pentagon.[64]

The consequence of these attitudes was a practice of subverting or ostracizing the State Department. In August 2002, Secretary Powell persuaded the president and other top advisers that the United States should attempt to build pressure on Iraq through the United Nations; ten days later, Vice President Cheney gave a high-profile speech that challenged the likely effectiveness of a UN initiative. Powell was "dumbfounded" by Cheney's speech.[65] A few months later, Cheney's office intervened to prevent State Department staff from participating in the Defense Department's planning for postwar Iraq.[66] This intervention fell on sympathetic ears: Defense Secretary Rumsfeld also expressed ambivalence about the involvement of "State Department types" in postwar planning.[67] Pentagon spokesman Lawrence DiRita was reported to have told General Jay Garner's postwar planning staff that the State Department could not be trusted with that responsibility because "they keep screwing things up."[68]

Only a week after the fall of Baghdad, the accumulated animosity toward the State Department was vented by Newt Gingrich, the former Speaker of the House of Representatives. The United States had achieved its "stunning victory" in Iraq, Gingrich said, only because responsibility for Iraq had finally shifted from the State Department to the Defense Department. The State Department was a "broken instrument." It had engaged in a "deliberate and systematic effort to undermine" the president's policies, allowing his goals to be diluted in "a murky and deceptive game" of diplomacy. Diplomats responsible for Middle Eastern affairs were alleged to be unsympathetic to administration priorities because of an organizational culture bent to "appeasing dictators and propping up corrupt regimes." World opinion had turned against the United States, Gingrich claimed, largely because of the failure of the State Department's global communications program.[69]

Practical men, John Maynard Keynes once said, are often the unwitting slaves of some defunct philosopher.[70] The same might be said of Bush administration appointees as they negotiated with the career bureaucracy. One of the remarkable features of the Bush administration's animosity toward the State Department, for example, was its consistency with half a century of Republican Party rhetoric. In the 1940s and 1950s, conservative Republicans also railed against the power of the "striped pants brigade" within the Department of State; indeed, Senator Joseph McCarthy routinely damned the diplomatic corps of the United States in such terms. Secretary of State Acheson, said McCarthy, was "a pompous diplomat in striped pants with a phony British accent." The department was said to be infiltrated by communists, homosexuals, and other un-American elements. The State Department responded with a campaign to "dispel the myths that [our] employees are pinks, snobs, and worse." Acheson himself hosted congressional smokers to cultivate, as the *Washington Times-Herald* said, a "'he-man' atmosphere."[71]

This was intelligible, if not defensible, as a kind of class warfare: an expression of populist midwestern antipathy to the northeastern Protestant elite that was perceived to dominate the federal bureaucracy in the first half of the twentieth century.[72] However, the hostile rhetoric persisted decades after the influence of the old-stock establishment (and striped pants themselves) had passed away. In 2005, conservatives endorsed the appointment of John Bolton as ambassador to the United Nations precisely because it would serve as a rebuff to "the striped-pants diplomat crowd, people who know what fork to use."[73] Colin Powell's deputy, Richard Armitage, could be accepted as a representative of the State Department because he was so clearly the antithesis of the archetype—"an outspoken, muscular, barrel-chested man who deplored fancy-pants, pin-striped diplomatic talk."[74]

In the 1960s, this populist disdain for the federal bureaucracy was generalized and given a patina of academic credibility. A group of conservative scholars argued that bureaucrats in the national government should be regarded in the same terms as entrepreneurs in the private sector: as self-interested actors, mainly interested in maximizing their salary and benefits, budgets, and authority. Unless forcefully checked, these scholars argued, bureaucrats would build administrative empires and resist uncomfortable changes in policy. "Budget-maximizing" bureaucrats were considered one of the main causes of overgrown federal government.[75]

These were presented as hypotheses about bureaucratic motivation, but for many conservative policymakers they were taken as fact. The federal bureaucracy, President Ronald Reagan's personnel chief said, is a "tough beast to tame."[76] During the Reagan administration, political appointees were encouraged to assert control firmly. A 1984 Heritage Foundation report told appointees to practice "jigsaw public management":

> Career staff will supply information, but they should never become involved in the formulation of agenda-related policy objectives. . . . Once controversial policy goals are formulated, they should not be released in total to the career staff. Thus the political executive and his political staff become "jigsaw puzzle" managers. Other staff see and work on the individual pieces, but never have enough of the pieces to be able to learn the entire picture.[77]

Seventeen years later, this suspicion of the career civil service persisted. The federal bureaucracy "jealously guards paychecks, pocketbooks, and power," a Heritage Foundation brief cautioned the incoming Bush administration in 2001. To break the hold of this "permanent government," the brief warned, it would be necessary to select political appointees who were prepared to assert their authority on the critical questions of policy and management.[78]

The Bush administration's approach to the management of the three agencies that were key to the Global War on Terrorism—Defense, State, and the CIA—was largely consistent with this advice. The White House and its appointees were determined to tame these three bureaucracies, and so made a practice of distrusting bureaucratic advice and substituting its own. Broadly speaking, this was evidence of a profound alienation between the governors and the agents on whom they relied to govern. The misfortune, in this case, is that in key respects the agents' advice was sound.

Moreover—and this was key to the Bush administration's eventual misfortunes—the agents were more willing to protest publicly about rough handling by their political masters. The Bush administration was partly undone by the collapse of the traditional ethos of fidelity within the federal bureaucracy, a code of conduct that at one time generally restrained public servants from speaking publicly (or leaking information) about misconduct within the executive branch.

## The Servants Talk Back

The extent to which understandings about loyalty and dissent have changed is illustrated by a thirty-year-old story that came back to life during the Bush presidency. In May 2005, *Vanity Fair* magazine revealed one of Washington's best-kept secrets: the identity of Deep Throat, the government official who had guided *Washington Post* reporters Bob Woodward and Carl Bernstein as they investigated the Watergate scandal. Mark Felt, associate director of the FBI during the scandal, became a source for Woodward and Bernstein out of frustration with White House interference in FBI investigations.[79]

A few weeks later, L. Patrick Gray III, who had been FBI director at the time, appeared on ABC's *This Week* to vent his anger at Felt, who had lied thirty years earlier when Gray asked whether he was the *Post*'s source. Gray had his own deep grievances about the Nixon White House. Nixon's advisers left him to "twist slowly in the wind" after he admitted in 1973 that he passed information about the Watergate investigation to the president's staff. "I was so hurt and so angry" about Nixon's conduct, Gray told *This Week*—but nonetheless he, like Felt, kept silent for decades.[80] Gray died of cancer two weeks after the interview.

For three decades, Felt and Gray said nothing about their role in one of the greatest political controversies in American history. This is a measure of restraint that is almost incomprehensible to a contemporary audience. Felt told friends that he was "concerned about bringing dishonor to our family." He believed that he had betrayed his obligations by leaking information and did not know whether he would be regarded "as a decent man or a turncoat."[81] J. Edgar Hoover, he may have remembered, kept a quotation from the long-dead writer Elbert Hubbard framed in FBI headquarters. "If you work for a man, in heaven's sake work for him," Hubbard wrote. "Speak well of him, stand by him, and stand by the institution he represents."[82] (Felt relented when his family, better attuned to postmillennial culture, persuaded him that there was no dishonor and that there was an opportunity to "make enough money to pay some bills.")[83] Gray was guided by the same stoic code. He kept voluminous files about the Nixon years and wrote a manuscript that defended his conduct, but he refused to publish it during his lifetime.[84] It was only Felt's treachery, and recognition of his own grave illness, that prompted Gray to speak.

In 2005, this vocabulary of strict obligation was clearly anachronistic. It had been qualified by a new understanding that government officials were entitled to protest publicly about improper conduct by superiors. Indeed, honor was sometimes found in disclosure, not secret keeping. Such officials were known as *whistleblowers*. This usage was familiar to most Americans in 2005, but that was not the case thirty years earlier. The *New York Times* first used the phrase in this sense in 1971, describing the attempt by Ralph Nader's Clearing House for Professional Responsibility to encourage leaks of confidential information from government employees. (Nader was "seeking tipsters," the *Times* said.)[85] Congress soon gave its imprimatur to the practice. The Civil Service Reform Act of 1978 provided new remedies to public servants who had been punished for disclosing official misconduct. These remedies were toughened by the Whistleblower Protection Act of 1989.[86]

It became quickly evident during the Bush administration that this change in ethical standards of lower-level bureaucrats constituted an important check on the power of senior officials. These public servants engaged in what Professor Rosemary O'Leary calls "guerilla government," a form of resistance to goals laid out by their political masters.[87]

Ironically, the FBI was once again at the heart of the story. Shortly after the 9/11 attacks, FBI director Robert Mueller denied that the bureau had warning signs of a hijacking plot within the United States. Within weeks, however, journalists learned of a July 2001 memorandum from the FBI's Phoenix office, raising questions about Arabs learning to fly big jets at Arizona flight schools.[88] A few months later, an FBI agent wrote to Senate investigators about the Minnesota office's unsuccessful attempt to obtain a warrant to search the property of Zacarias Moussaoui, the so-called twentieth hijacker, who had been regarded suspiciously by the flight school that he approached for instruction on how to fly a jumbo jet. The FBI, said agent Coleen Rowley, had "omitted, downplayed, glossed over and/or mischaracterized" the Moussaoui investigation "in an effort to avoid or minimize personal and/or institutional embarrassment on the part of the FBI and/or perhaps even for improper political reasons."[89] Far from bringing "dishonor to the family," as Felt had once feared, Rowley was publicly lauded for courage and patriotism.[90] Republican congressmen warned the FBI against retaliation, and *Time* magazine put Rowley on

FIG. 6.1. In May 2002, FBI employee Coleen Rowley publicly disclosed the unsuccessful efforts of the bureau's Minneapolis field office to obtain a warrant to search the computer of Zacarias Moussaoui, later known as the "twentieth hijacker." *Time* magazine selected Rowley as one of their Persons of the Year for 2002.

its cover as a Person of the Year (fig 6.1). The disclosure bolstered the case for establishing a special commission to investigate events leading to the 9/11 attacks.

Throughout the Bush presidency, top officials were dogged by public servants like Rowley. Officials in the FBI rebutted claims by Attorney General John Ashcroft that he had not been briefed on terrorist threats within the United States before the attacks.[91] The Justice

Department also fought claims of misconduct and sabotage within the FBI's translation unit made by a former employee, Sibel Edmonds. The Justice Department publicly denied the charges, but an internal report that bolstered some of the assertions was leaked to the *New York Times*.[92] In 2003, a recently retired employee of the Office of the Secretary of Defense, Lieutenant Colonel Karen Kwiatkowski, a self-described "conservative anarchist," became a prominent critic of the "subversion of constitutional limits on executive power" by the Bush administration in the months preceding the invasion of Iraq.[93] Within weeks of the occupation of Baghdad, many other officials within the Office of the Secretary of Defense were speaking to journalists anonymously about weaknesses in prewar planning.[94] The advent of war with Iraq also provoked several resignations by State Department officials. One, John Brady Kiesling, gained international attention for his complaint about the administration's "fervent pursuit of war with Iraq."[95] Another State Department official later told the Al Jazeera television network that the Bush administration's actions in Iraq had been tainted by "arrogance and stupidity."[96] These small acts of resistance had a powerful cumulative effect on public perceptions of the administration.

## The CIA versus Bush

This sporadic guerrilla warfare sometimes erupted into more-systematic conflict between the bureaucracy and the White House. Within the CIA, there was simmering frustration at the way in which the Bush administration had handled prewar intelligence about Iraq. Even in 2002, journalists were hearing rumors of dissent within the agency about the manipulation of intelligence. The Knight-Ridder newspapers reported in October 2002 that over a dozen officials had expressed concern about "very strong pressure . . . to cook the books."[97]

Animosities heightened after Ambassador Joseph Wilson's column in the *New York Times* on the president's misrepresentation of intelligence about Iraqi efforts to procure uranium ore in Niger. Vice President Cheney's chief of staff, I. Lewis Libby, saw the Niger stories as "selective leaking" by the CIA, designed to protect the agency if no weapons were found in Iraq.[98] CIA head George Tenet became enraged when the White House claimed erroneously that the agency had approved the president's statement.[99] A few days later, the White House acknowledged that the CIA had actually warned against using the Niger intelligence, but the damage was done. A group of retired CIA analysts published a letter criticizing the White House for behavior that it called "a deep insult to the integrity of the intelligence process."[100]

Tensions mounted as it became clear that weapons of mass destruction would not be found in Iraq. The head of the U.S. group charged with finding weapons of mass destruction conceded in January 2004 that "we were almost all wrong" on the Iraqi threat, and in April the Senate Intelligence Committee completed a report that concluded there was no evidence of an operational link between the Hussein regime and al Qaeda.[101] The White House, pressed on the misjudgments, insisted that it had relied on the advice of its intelligence services.[102] In February 2004 it attempted to shape the controversy by establishing an independent commission to examine the capabilities and performance of the intelligence community.

The restlessness within CIA was evidenced in June 2004 with the publication of *Imperial Hubris*.[103] The book was published anonymously, but the author was soon revealed to be Michael Scheuer, a senior CIA analyst who had led the agency's task force on Osama bin Laden. Scheuer's jeremiad condemned the "senior leaders" of the United States as "moral cowards" who ignored warnings about terrorist attacks and then responded with an ill-considered attack on Iraq. The invasion of Iraq was a "tremendous gift" to bin Laden, Scheuer said, because it would motivate radical Muslims to fight the United States and create a failed state in which terrorist organizations would thrive.[104]

Scheuer's book proved remarkably popular, remaining on the *New York Times* bestseller list for eight weeks in the summer of 2004.[105] CIA managers denied that Scheuer had been given permission to publish as a way of defending the agency against White House attacks and said that they were surprised by the book's success.[106] But Scheuer encouraged a more cynical interpretation. "As long as the book was being used to bash the President, they gave me carte blanche to talk to the media," Scheuer said. He claimed that the agency took a more restrictive position on his media appearances when he criticized the agency's leadership as well.[107] Scheuer ignored the restrictions and later resigned from the agency.

Conflict between the intelligence community and the White House escalated in the weeks preceding the 2004 election. In September 2004, details of a classified report on prospects for Iraq were leaked to the *New York Times*.[108] Noting the strong possibility of civil war, the report undercut White House claims of substantial progress in Iraq.[109] President Bush dismissed the analysis, saying that the CIA was "just guessing" about conditions in Iraq.[110] Bush subsequently conceded that his description of the CIA's work had been "unfortunate."[111] Later that day, a CIA official, Paul Pillar, gave a speech defending the analysis. Conservative columnist Robert Novak said that the exchange was evidence that the White House and CIA "are at war with each other."[112]

Leaks continued. The following week, two more classified intelligence summaries were provided to the *New York Times*. Prepared in January 2003, these reports had predicted that invasion would bolster Islamist radicals and trigger violent internal conflict.[113] Later, the Knight-Ridder newspaper chain received yet another CIA report, rebutting the administration's assertion of a link between the Hussein regime and al Qaeda.[114] A recently retired CIA official, James Pavitt, added to the controversy, telling journalists that "there was nothing in the [prewar] intelligence that was a casus belli" for war with Iraq. Pavitt conceded that the conflict between the White House and CIA had become "vicious and vindictive"—the worst in three decades, including the tumultuous 1970s.[115] Conservative commentators were outraged at what they regarded as CIA insubordination. It is "CIA v. Bush," David Brooks said in October 2004.[116]

Porter Goss, appointed by President Bush as director of the CIA in August 2004, attempted to squelch these leaks, reminding agency staff that they should "scrupulously honor our secrecy oath." His memo leaked to journalists the next day.[117] In the succeeding weeks, the media reported extensively on the conflict between Goss's aides and career public servants. Several top officials eventually resigned, bringing added scrutiny to the agency.[118]

Evidence of internal turmoil surfaced again in March 2005, after the public release of the report on intelligence capabilities that had been commissioned by President Bush a year earlier.[119] The report claimed that agency head George Tenet and his deputy, John McLaughlin, ignored warnings that a key source of intelligence on Iraqi biological weapons programs, code-named Curveball, had been judged to be unreliable. Tenet immediately attempted to shift blame, saying that it was "stunning and deeply disturbing" that he had not been warned about Curveball.[120] Other former CIA officials reacted strongly to Tenet's statement. "The fact is there was yelling and screaming about this guy," said James Pavitt.[121]

The CIA suffered other damaging leaks later in 2005. In November, the *Washington Post*, relying on sources in the intelligence community, described secret detention centers operated by the agency.[122] When Goss attempted to track down the source of the leak, these efforts were also publicly reported.[123] So, too, was a highly classified effort to improve the intelligence community's ability to track the development of nuclear weapons.[124] In February 2006, Goss publicly admonished the leakers, telling them that they were jeopardizing national security and the integrity of the agency.[125] However, former agency officials were deeply skeptical about the likely effectiveness of Goss's attempts to stop disclosures from the troubled agency.[126]

## Revolt by the Military

Disquiet also mounted within the military as the War on Terrorism progressed. One of the most damaging controversies of the Bush administration arose after the leak of a confidential CENTCOM report. Major General Antonio Taguba was directed to investigate allegations of mistreatment of detainees held by U.S. forces at Iraq's Abu Ghraib prison in January 2004. Taguba's report, completed in early March, found evidence of "sadistic, blatant, and wanton criminal abuses . . . intentionally perpetrated" by U.S. troops at Abu Ghraib.[127] The classified report quickly leaked to CBS News, which reported it (after twice deferring to Defense Department requests for delay) on April 28. Rumsfeld interpreted the leak as an act of subversion. He was "blindsided," he told Congress, when "someone took that secret report and gave it to the press."[128]

Rumsfeld had it largely right: the Abu Ghraib scandal exploded because military personnel refused to mind their place in the hierarchy. Gary Myers, lawyer for one of the seven soldiers charged with prisoner abuse, complained that they were scapegoats, who had orders to break prisoners before interrogation by military intelligence and the CIA. On April 30, investigative journalist Seymour Hersh detailed the soldiers' claims using letters written by Myers's client and transcripts of a military hearing on his case held earlier in the month. Much more damaging, however, were photographs of abuse—some collected during Taguba's investigation and leaked, and others provided directly to the media by soldiers who served at Abu Ghraib.[129]

In his report, Taguba recommended that Brigadier General Janis Karpinski, who led the brigade at the center of the controversy, should be reprimanded and relieved of command. When the Taguba report leaked, Karpinski declined to wait for the wheels of military justice to turn. In a series of high-profile television interviews in the following days, she also complained of scapegoating. "There is a shared responsibility in this," said Karpinski, pointing to her superior officer, Lieutenant General Ricardo Sanchez.[130] Karpinski was eventually relieved of command but wrote a book claiming that responsibility for the abuses went "to the summit of civilian leadership."[131]

Abu Ghraib revived debate over the Bush administration's policy on the interrogation of prisoners in its War on Terrorism and revealed internal disagreements as well. Two days after the CBS report on Abu Ghraib, the New York City Bar Association (NYCBA) published a report on the laws governing treatment of detainees.[132] The NYCBA was prompted to produce the report eight months earlier when the chairman of its human-rights committee was approached by a group of military lawyers concerned about the Bush administration's attempt to loosen restrictions on interrogation. "They were extremely upset," an NYCBA representative told journalists. "They said they were being shut out of the process."[133] Former military lawyers confirmed a struggle between civilian and military leaders. "If we had been listened to," said the recently retired head of the Navy's legal service, "these abuses would not have occurred."[134]

The military lawyers' visits to the NYCBA were triggered by an internal report that narrowed the definition of torture and asserted that the president's constitutional authority superceded statutory bans on torture. The memorandum had been classified by Secretary Rumsfeld, but in early June a copy was leaked to the media.[135] So too were earlier government memos that provided legal justifications for torture.[136] Military sources also confided to the *Los Angeles Times* that Rumsfeld's office had authorized interrogators to "take the gloves off" shortly after the September 11 attacks.[137] The string of leaks drove the administration to release hundreds of pages of classified documents on its interrogation policy.[138]

Nonetheless, evidence of tensions continued to surface. An independent panel appointed to investigate the treatment of military detainees conceded in fall 2004 that the military lawyers "were not utilized to their fullest potential" as the administration developed its interrogation policy; in March 2005 a second study acknowledged their reservations more frankly.[139] An inquiry by the Senate Armed Services Committee led to the release of internal documents in which the military lawyers protested that administration policies were "inconsistent with our most fundamental values."[140]

The careerists' concerns were not limited to interrogation. Many of them were also troubled by the administration's attempt to loosen rules for the trial of detainees charged with war crimes. In 2004, three officers serving as prosecutors for Guantánamo detainees protested about the unfairness of the trial rules and requested new assignments. (In an internal email, one officer complained that the administration was prosecuting "fairly low-level accused in a process that appears to be rigged.") The internal protests were leaked to U.S. and Australian media in 2005, compromising the government's case against Australian detainee David Hicks.[141] After the trial rules were struck down by the Supreme Court in 2006, the country's top military lawyers publicly opposed key parts of a new plan unveiled by the Bush administration. Marine Brigadier General James Walker told Congress that the plan contained elements that "no civilized country" should countenance.[142] The White House's attempt to convey the impression of a rapprochement with the group was immediately undercut when details of the internal wrangling leaked to the press.[143]

One prominent political appointee shared these concerns. Alberto Mora, the legal adviser to the secretary of the Navy, protested against the administration's interrogation policy in 2002–2003. He believed that he had persuaded the Defense Department's leadership to retreat from its proposed policy but learned following the Abu Ghraib leaks that his superior, Defense Department General Counsel William Haynes II, had simply cut Mora out of subsequent discussions. Mora resigned in January 2006. A few weeks later, the *New Yorker* described a leaked memorandum written by Mora that detailed his complaints.[144] By that time Haynes had been nominated for appointment to the U.S. Court of Appeals. Twenty retired flag officers publicly opposed the nomination, arguing that Haynes ignored "clear and unanimous concerns" by military lawyers about the corrosion of military values.[145] The nomination was later withdrawn by the administration.[146]

The Bush administration was also confronted with rising frustration within the military over the management of the Iraq invasion and the administration's treatment of military leadership.[147] In September 2003, General Anthony Zinni challenged Rumsfeld directly. At a conference of Marine and Navy officers near the Pentagon, Zinni recalled "the garbage and the lies" of leaders during the Vietnam War and asked, "Is it happening again?" Zinni's speech was "greeted warmly . . . with prolonged applause."[148] A few months later, Zinni went further. He appeared on CBS's *60 Minutes* to promote a new book coauthored by novelist Tom Clancy. The Iraq invasion, said Zinni, revealed "true dereliction, negligence and irresponsibility."[149] Zinni's book stayed on the *New York Times* bestseller list for five weeks in 2004.[150]

Zinni's voice was eventually joined by those of officers with immediate experience of the military action in Iraq. Major General Paul Eaton, a former commander of the U.S. Army's infantry school, had been responsible for training Iraqi security forces in 2003–2004. Within days of his retirement in January 2006, Eaton publicly criticized the administration's policy in Iraq. News reports said that his views were "broadly affirmed" by serving officers.[151] Weeks later, Eaton published a column in the *New York Times* that said that Rumsfeld "is not competent to lead our armed forces" and called for his resignation. Rumsfeld, Eaton said, had ignored and alienated seasoned officers. "Rumsfeld demands more than loyalty," Eaton wrote. "He wants fealty."[152]

As Eaton had shown, a demand for something "more than loyalty" would be strongly resisted. The following months were marked by an unusual series of protests by retired officers. Lieutenant General Gregory Newbold, director of operations for the Joint Chiefs of Staff until his retirement in late 2002, castigated the Bush administration for "successive policy failures" in Iraq. Writing "with the encouragement of some still in positions of military leadership," Newbold challenged colleagues to break their silence as well.[153]

Three other retired officers joined with Zinni, Eaton, and Newbold in April 2006 to make a public case for Rumsfeld's firing. "They only need military advice when it satisfies their agenda," said Major General John Riggs. "That's why I think he should resign."[154] Major General John Batiste, who commanded the 1st Infantry Division in

Iraq until 2005, told CNN that the Defense Department needed leadership "that respects the military as they expect the military to respect them."[155] Rumsfeld "oversteps his bounds," complained Major General Charles Swannack Jr., commander of the 82nd Airborne Division during its mission in Iraq. "He just controls our generals far too much."[156]

The media coined this the Revolt of the Generals. It was not the last expression of dissatisfaction with Rumsfeld's leadership. In 2006 alone, six major books documented missteps in Iraq, all relying on the cooperation of sources within the military.[157] (Zbigniew Brzezinski observes that the Iraq invasion is the first war in U.S. history to have produced such an "instant bibliography."[158] By contrast, only two books on Vietnam appeared on the *New York Times* bestseller list during that decade-long war.)[159] In one of these (Bob Woodward's *Plan of Attack*), NATO commander General Jim Jones is reported to have said that Rumsfeld had "systematically emasculated" the military's leadership. Jones publicly confirmed the report.[160] In October, a classified briefing showing the collapse of the U.S. strategy in Iraq was leaked from CENTCOM.[161] Rumsfeld is "losing control of the institution he ostensibly leads," the *Army Times* said in November 2006.[162] Rumsfeld resigned four days later. In 2001, he had spoken of a war on the Pentagon bureaucracy. A very public war is what Rumsfeld got—and lost.

## The Tell-All Industry

Wars between Bush appointees and key parts of the federal bureaucracy were eventually compounded by schisms at the very heart of the administration. The breakdown in internal discipline was remarkable and led to a spate of tell-all books, often published within months of the events they described, that provided an unprecedented view of the internal workings of the Bush White House. Precisely because the disclosures were driven by discontent, the view was rarely flattering.

Three considerations fueled this collapse in discipline. The ethic of fidelity had clearly frayed for top appointees, just as it had for bureaucrats. In the late 1950s, said former Eisenhower speechwriter Stephen Hess, "it was a rule of thumb that no one spoke" publicly about his or her service in government until the president had published his memoirs. "It was bad form" to do otherwise.[163] Clearly, this etiquette had eroded by 2004. Another consideration is the incentive offered by the publishing industry, which offers payments that dwarf government salaries. A final consideration is anger at mistreatment by the White House itself. Appointees who did not feel that their opinion had been given its due felt free to make their case in a public forum.

The year 2004 would be marked by a string of tell-all books. The first was *The Price of Loyalty*, written by Ron Suskind with the cooperation of Paul O'Neill, the former ALCOA executive who served as Bush's first treasury secretary until he was dismissed in December 2002. O'Neill provided Suskind with interviews and thousands of pages of documents accumulated during his tenure in the Cabinet. *The Price of Loyalty* topped the *New York Times* nonfiction bestseller list for five weeks after its publication in January 2004.[164] O'Neill, already wealthy, was not interested in royalties. However, he was deeply troubled—as John DiIulio Jr. had been before him—by the malfunctioning policy machinery within the Bush administration. There was no "honest broker" to assure that dissenting views received a fair hearing, O'Neill complained.

In April 2004, *The Price of Loyalty* was followed by Richard Clarke's *Against All Enemies*, which held first place on the nonfiction bestseller list for four weeks.[165] Clarke was a career public servant who had been the White House's counterterrorism coordinator at the time of the 9/11 attacks. After his resignation in February 2003, Clarke negotiated a book deal for which he was paid an advance in the "mid to high six figures"—in other words, a multiple of the $130,000 salary paid to civil servants of Clarke's rank.[166] Timed to coincide with his appearance before the 9/11 Commission, the book was a surprise hit, earning Clarke over a million dollars in royalties in its first weeks. Movie rights were purchased by Sony Pictures for "a sum in the low six figures."[167] Like O'Neill, Clarke debuted his book with an interview on CBS's *60 Minutes* and painted a similarly unflattering picture of policymaking in the Bush White House. Bush's advisers, Clarke said, "had no interest in complicated analysis" of policy problems, paid little attention to the terrorist threat before 9/11, and afterward became fixated with the threat posed by Iraq.

The White House's response to Clarke's allegations was frenzied and ultimately self-defeating. Condoleezza Rice appeared so often in television interviews to rebut Clarke that the White House proved incapable of maintaining its position that it would be a violation of confidentiality for her to appear as a witness before the 9/11 Commission.[168]

*Against All Enemies* was displaced by Bob Woodward's *Plan of Attack*, which dominated the *New York Times* nonfiction bestseller list in May 2004.[169] It was apparent that Secretary of State Colin Powell, equally frustrated by his inability to influence White House policies, was one of Woodward's main sources.[170] Woodward charted the deep estrangement between Powell, Defense Secretary Rumsfeld, and Vice President Cheney. Cheney had a "fever" over Iraq, Powell was alleged to have said, stoked by the "Gestapo office" run by Under Secretary of Defense Feith.[171] (In 2005, Powell's former chief of staff echoed these complaints, calling the White House's decision-making process "dysfunctional" and complaining that the State Department had been shunted aside by a "Cheney-Rumsfeld cabal.")[172]

More book deals followed. In late May, *Plan of Attack* was joined by Ambassador Joseph Wilson's *The Politics of Truth*, which retold the imbroglio over his mission to investigate allegations that Iraq had attempted to procure uranium ore in Niger. The *New York Times* later reported that Wilson's wife, CIA officer Valerie Plame, had negotiated a $2.5 million agreement for publication of her memoirs as well.[173] (Wilson and Plame subsequently sold the rights to their life stories to Warner Brother Pictures.)[174] In June 2004, CIA director George Tenet resigned and was offered a $4.5 million book contract.[175] This amount was astounding—likely more than Tenet had earned during the whole of his twenty years in government service.

And yet the amount offered Tenet was exceeded by the $5 million advance paid by HarperCollins to General Tommy Franks, who retired from government service in July 2003.[176] ("I am going to get my mains," Franks told one of his senior officers shortly before his retirement.[177] He told friends that he also earned $1 million in speaker's fees in his first months of retirement.)[178] Franks's memoirs reached the top of the nonfiction bestseller list in August 2004.[179] Although broadly supportive of the administration, Franks noted his early proposal for larger troop deployments in Iraq, criticized Rumsfeld for micromanaging, and called Feith "the dumbest fucking guy on the planet." (Feith, exasperated by the criticism of his performance, resigned from the Defense Department in 2005 and negotiated his own book deal with HarperCollins.)[180] Senior political appointees in the Defense and State Departments were censured for "disruptive and divisive" infighting, and the "narrow-minded four-stars" who led the armed services were castigated for "parochial bullshit."[181]

It is hardly surprising that Mark Felt's family, consumers of popular media, should have reached the conclusion that his restraint about Watergate was unnecessary and financially short-sighted. By the end of 2004 there was substantial evidence, all based on first-person accounts, of the dysfunctionality of the policy process within the Bush administration. Moreover, this string of disclosures continued in 2005 and 2006. Some of these disclosures were again contained in autobiographies written by former bureaucrats, such as *My Year in Iraq*, written by former envoy Paul Bremer with a main purpose of showing that the Pentagon and White House had been closely implicated in controversial decisions on postwar governance, or *Squandered Victory*, by former CPA adviser Larry Diamond, which documented the incompetence of the occupying power.[182] Colin Powell, no longer secretary of state, collaborated on a biography that again expressed his dismay with the irrationality of White House decision making.[183] Bob Woodward's *State of Denial*, released in September 2006, was a five-hundred-page catalogue of grievances at the highest levels of the Bush administration. The pretense of discipline and confidentiality had dissipated entirely.[184]

The spate of exposés was brought full circle with the release of *Tempting Faith*, a book written by David Kuo, who was appointed to work with John DiIulio Jr. as deputy director of the Office of Faith-Based Initiatives in 2001. Kuo resigned in December 2003. In 2005 he wrote an article about the torment that he imagined Mark Felt endured as he wrestled for three decades with his decision to leak information to Woodward and Bernstein.[185] As it happened, it was a subject close to home. Kuo was disturbed by manipulation of faith-based funds for partisan purposes and by private mocking of evangelical leaders by Bush advisers. Kuo moved more quickly than Felt. He negotiated a book deal and in October 2006 made the ritual appearance on *60 Minutes* to recount the White House's misdeeds.[186]

## The Fraying Secrecy System

The attempt to impose discipline within the Bush administration was an overwhelming failure, in two senses. With regard to concrete policy, the administration made ill-fated decisions that could have been avoided if top policymakers had given more weight to bureaucratic advice or had succeeded in inducing key bureaucracies to collaborate and develop the capacities needed to achieve the administration's goals. To the extent that the administration achieved control, it did so in the very narrow meaning of the term, in the sense of an assertion of the right to command. The administration did not achieve control in the broader sense of *mastery* of the public service—that is, the harnessing of bureaucratic power to its ends. This would have required time, negotiation, and a presumption of bureaucratic good faith. It might also have required a willingness to surrender the administration's ambition for substantial policy change. The price of comity might have been incrementalism.

Moreover (and this is the second sense in which the attempt to impose discipline failed), the Bush administration could not *sustain* control, even in the narrow meaning of the term. Quickly, and with increasing intensity, the administration encountered resistance from bureaucrats and political appointees who objected to such treatment. It is critical to note the terms in which protests against the Bush administration were couched: not only (or even primarily) as disagreements about the *substance* of policy but as complaints about the refusal to accord respect and allow a proper hearing to opposing views. Dissidents within the administration had coherent ideas about what fair treatment required—and they were prepared to resist unfairness. Appointees and bureaucrats alike knew that there were now alternatives to acquiescence.

The cumulative effect of these discrete acts of rebellion was a degree of transparency about the internal operations of the Bush presidency that was rarely acknowledged by its critics. To its deep frustration, the Bush administration was confronted by a "hemorrhaging of information," as Donald Rumsfeld rightly observed in 2004.[187] Indeed, one of the unrecognized casualties of the 9/11 crisis was the federal government's system of secret keeping. After five years of struggle, it became even more firmly established that the power to classify information as secret was grossly overused. ("Three-quarters of what I read that was classified shouldn't have been," said 9/11 Commission chairman Tom Kean in 2004.)[188] It was widely believed that decisions to classify or declassify information were driven by political rather than national-security considerations and that the highest officials in the country were prepared to leak classified material if it served their interests.[189] Campaigns against leakers were often regarded as a means of retribution against political opponents.

These were all symptoms of a collapse in the system's legitimacy —that is, the erosion of faith that rules governing secret information were reasonable, fairly applied, and worthy of respect. In the words of Republican Senator Trent Lott, frustrated by CIA stonewalling over the declassification of an Intelligence Committee report in 2004, there was something "seriously awry" with the secrecy system.[190] This collapse in legitimacy is not easily reversed, and it implies that future presidents will have an even more difficult task in controlling the outflow of sensitive information. If rules are not respected, they will not be obeyed.

# 7

# Beyond the Imperial Presidency

President Bush has broader goals than even fighting terrorism—he
has long intended to make reinvigorating the presidency a priority.
                                                    —John Yoo, September 2006[1]

Not only is President Bush's job approval down to a record-low level
for his administration, but public support for his handling of a variety of issues is washing out, along with perceptions of his leadership
qualities.                                          —Gallup analysis, May 2006[2]

CRITICAL COMMENT ON the George W. Bush administration has
been preoccupied, understandably, with the ways in which it has
sought to expand presidential authority. Supporters of the Bush administration's policies have characterized it as an attempt to "reinvigorate" the presidency.[3] Critics put it in less flattering language. Many
of them revived a term coined by Arthur Schlesinger Jr. over three
decades ago, at the zenith of the Nixon administration.[4] Bush, like
Nixon, is said to have established an "imperial presidency," distinguished by a dangerous concentration of executive authority over foreign and domestic affairs and by the erosion of traditional counterweights to that authority.
    Schlesinger himself encouraged the comparison, asserting in 2004
that the Bush administration had upended the constitutional balance
of powers and that the imperial presidency had, as a consequence,
been "born again."[5] Other scholars followed in Schlesinger's foot-
steps. In 2005, Professor Peter Irons invoked the same language as he
lamented the "vast expansion of federal power" and the erosion of
constraints on presidential control of the federal bureaucracy.[6] Professor Andrew Rudalevige argued that "a 'new' imperial presidency has
been cemented" after the 9/11 attacks.[7] The metaphor also permeated
popular discourse about the Bush administration—as a favorite rhe-

torical device of former Nixon aide John Dean and in scores of newspaper and magazine commentaries.[8] If other critics did not use the term, they often employed language that invoked the same underlying fear of untrammeled executive authority.

## Nine Critical Changes

This fear of expanding executive power is misguided, or at least it is too broadly stated to be helpful in understanding the central problem of contemporary American government. Critics of a resurgent "imperial presidency" underestimate the ways in which societal and institutional changes have undercut the power of the executive branch in the past three decades. In critical ways, contemporary presidents are weaker than in the era that spanned from Roosevelt to Nixon. We have discussed these constraints throughout this book, but it is useful to summarize nine of the most important changes here:

*1. Growing institutional complexity.* One important consideration is that critical components of the executive branch are now more complex than they were in the Nixon era. We may forget that critical components of the federal bureaucracy were, in 1968, still relatively young. (Like baby-boomers themselves, much of the national-security apparatus had just reached the age of majority in 1968; today, it approaches retirement age.) As institutions mature, they become more complex. Growth in size encourages formalization of rules about methods of work and leads to more elaborate and specialized bureaucratic structures. With time, organizational cultures (which include understandings about missions, techniques, and interorganizational antagonisms) become more elaborate and deeply entrenched. These considerations make it more difficult for presidents to accomplish significant changes in policy and in the organization of the executive branch. A similar trend toward complexity within the legislative branch and in state and local governments may also complicate federal efforts to change policy or rationalize bureaucratic structures.

*2. Post-Nixon controls.* Contemporary presidents are checked by a web of statutes, watchdog agencies, and nongovernmental constituencies that did not exist before Nixon's election in 1968. President Johnson did not need to deal with the Freedom of Information Act or a battery of other laws that require disclosure of government information or impose procedural requirements on federal agencies.[9] His departments were not supervised by a phalanx of inspectors general or a strengthened Government Accountability Office, and his Budget Bureau did not have its math checked by a Congressional Budget Office. Johnson-era bureaucrats also dealt with a smaller population of advocacy groups. (Many of today's most influential groups were not established even a quarter century ago.) We tend to exaggerate the breadth and effectiveness of the Bush administration's campaign against these formal and informal checks on executive power.

3. *Declining spending power.* The postmillennial president also has less freedom to wield influence through increased spending. As a percentage of GDP, total outlays under the Bush administration were not significantly different from those under the Nixon administration. However, a much larger share of that spending is now consumed by mandatory expenditures, such as Social Security. In 1968, mandatory spending consumed one-third of the federal budget. In 2001, the share was two-thirds. This share will rise as the number of older Americans dependent on federal entitlement programs grows.

4. *The neoliberal settlement.* Prevailing wisdom about the federal government's right to intervene in the market to achieve governmental objectives has changed radically over the past quarter century. Regulatory agencies that were lauded in 1970 as guardians of the public interest are now often criticized for abusing their regulatory powers. Attempts by government to intervene in market operations are regarded with suspicion, and expansion of trade is actively encouraged.

5. *Market complexity and market power.* Partly because of the neoliberal shift led by President Reagan, markets have grown in breadth and complexity over the past three decades. Greater breadth complicates governmental action because the federal government may not have jurisdiction over some market actors (such as those located overseas) or may confront conflicting claims for jurisdiction (for example, made by subnational or foreign governments). Greater complexity complicates action by making it difficult to anticipate the consequences of an intervention. Growing markets also enrich businesses, which use that wealth to lobby against governmental interventions.

6. *Declining public trust.* The public's trust in the federal government has collapsed over the past forty years. Nixon and his predecessors could rely on a supply of public goodwill that has now been depleted. Nixon himself helped to drain the reservoir, but the fault is

not entirely—or even principally—his.[10] The causes are more complicated. Low trust likely complicates presidential action in many ways,
for example, by encouraging antitax sentiment or priming the public
to mobilize against initiatives that appear to threaten their rights or
interests.

7. *Declining trust within elites.* There is anecdotal evidence that
trust *within* governing elites—that is, among political appointees, career bureaucrats, legislators and legislative staff, journalists, and heads
of nongovernmental organizations—has also declined. This might be
a natural consequence of the general decline of trust over the past
three decades: members of the country's governing elites may have
absorbed the antigovernment ethos that is deeply embedded in popular culture. It might also be caused by breakdown of old institutions
(such as the print or broadcast news media) and the influx of many
new players or by shifts in the character of party politics. Whatever
the cause, the decline in trust complicates the task of negotiating over
shifts in policy and, in particular, over shifts in authority from one
component of government to another.[11]

8. *The fraying ethos of fidelity.* A variation on the theme of declining
trust is the fraying of the ethos of fidelity within the federal bureaucracy. Dissent has been legitimized, by law and also by convention:
public servants have a right to express concern about wrongdoing and
misguided policy that was not recognized four decades ago. This, it
should be emphasized, is not inherently problematic: dissent can improve the accountability and performance of public institutions. At the
same time, however, it limits the capacity of the executive to control
the executive branch and also to control the policy agenda.

9. *Changes in information and communications technology.* The revolution in information and communications technology has undercut
presidential authority as well. Digitization has made it easier to leak
information, increased the volume of incriminating information (such
as email) that is available for leaking, and increased the impact of
leaks by allowing the instantaneous dissemination of leaked information. The communications revolution has also undercut the executive
branch's ability to say what the "facts on the ground" actually are in
remote locations (or even at home, as Hurricane Katrina showed).
Similarly, it has eroded the White House's ability to control the veloc-
ity and direction of policy debate. Increasingly, the president reacts to
the news, rather than making it.

## The Dysfunctional Presidency

Such difficulties have been evident to presidents and White House advisers for years. Advisers who encouraged President Bush to broaden presidential prerogatives were motivated by frustration over many of these constraints on executive authority and over the perceived inability to act decisively in the public interest because of them. We can disagree with the tactics used by the Bush White House to "reinvigorate" the presidency, but this does not imply that the diagnosis is entirely wrong. In an era that is typified by what I have earlier called entrenched liberalism, presidential leadership *is* a more challenging task.

The 9/11 attacks were regarded as an opportunity to revive presidential authority. More than five years after the attacks, it should be possible to assess whether this goal has been achieved. It is necessary, when doing this, to look beyond individual battles about presidential prerogative—the fight over presidential signing statements or over the breadth of executive privilege, for example—and consider instead the overall outcome of the struggle over executive power. When the smoke has drifted off the field, how much territory has the president actually gained? How much have the constraints on executive authority that I have enumerated actually changed?

The honest answer to both questions is: very little. The president's advocates may claim that he has reinvigorated the office, and critics may rail against the accretion of presidential power. Neither argument could be squared easily with the political realities. By the fifth anniversary of the 9/11 attacks, Bush's ship of state was listing badly. It had lost control of the policy agenda and lacked the capacity to frame debate on the most important issues. In many respects it had failed to impose its priorities on the federal bureaucracy or stanch the outflow of compromising information. The administration was on the cusp of a "thumping" (in the president's own words) in the 2006 midterm elections.[12]

Moreover, the Bush administration had failed to consolidate many of the expanded powers that it had claimed after 9/11. Consolidation could be achieved in two ways: through institutionalization and through legitimation. Expanded powers could be recognized in law (a form of institutionalization), or they could be broadly accepted as a reasonable expression of presidential authority (a form of legitimation). In some instances, new powers had been asserted but neither institutionalized nor legitimized. The NSA's Terrorist Surveillance Program, for example, was poorly understood and still highly controversial. There was also no clear and broadly accepted understanding about the collection and sharing of personal information by law-enforcement agencies or about the mining of government and commercial databases to identify potential security risks. There was no clear statutory basis for the preventive detention of individuals suspected of plotting imminent attacks. There was little agreement about the rules that should govern the practice of extraordinary rendition, or the detention, interrogation, and trial of citizens and aliens who appeared to be involved in terrorist plots. Policy over the control of sensitive information relating to national security was equally muddled.

Indeed, one of the startling truths about the 9/11 crisis is that the nation often failed to establish clear rules about the manner in which a long-term counterterrorism campaign would be waged.[13] In the immediate aftermath of an attack, improvisation is to be expected; but five years later we might reasonably expect that rules about new practices would be articulated and given a legislative sanction. The nation did not do this, because neither the president nor Congress wanted to engage directly with the question of what the new rules should be. The Bush administration preferred to act independently and often covertly. In the short term, this allowed the expansion of presidential power—but in the long term, expressions of power that are not institutionalized and legitimized are less likely to be enduring.

In fact, it could be argued that the administration's belligerence in asserting its prerogatives, and apparent indifference to the moral questions raised by its policies, actually undercut the capacity of future presidents to exercise similar powers. Its behavior undercut assumptions that the president would act in good faith. In this sense, the Bush strategy was myopic. It was, perhaps, not really intended to reinvigorate the presidency *as an institution* but, rather, to expand the powers of the current administration to meet the needs of the moment.

Even in the short term, however, the Bush administration encountered difficulties. For example, it proved unable to maintain significant public support. Of the five presidents reelected in the modern era, only Nixon had lower approval ratings in his second term, after the Watergate scandal began to unfold in April 1973. Bush's predicament —shared by anyone who hoped that his administration would reinvigorate presidential authority—was the broad public perception of his incompetence in managing important problems. Bush's image as an effective manager was "shattered" by 2006, in the view of the Gallup organization.[14] If the Bush presidency had been widely regarded as effective in managing key issues, prospects for a revived "imperial presidency" might have been better. But in the public's eyes, the imperial presidency failed the test of pragmatism: it simply did not work.

By 2006 the more common term to describe the Bush presidency —*dysfunctional*—captured this point precisely. The Department of Homeland Security was dysfunctional, said Republican Senator Susan Collins.[15] Relations between federal and state emergency-management agencies were "a dysfunctional mess" according to former FEMA head Michael Brown.[16] The team of national-security advisers was dysfunctional, according to Kenneth Adelman, a former member of Secretary Rumsfeld's Defense Policy Board.[17] Deputy Secretary of State Richard Armitage said the "foreign-policy-making system" was dysfunctional.[18] A "Republican former Cabinet secretary with decades of foreign-policy expertise" considered the "interagency process" to be "completely dysfunctional."[19] The CIA, said Senator John McCain, was a "dysfunctional organization."[20] The relationship between the intelligence community and Congress was dysfunctional, in the eyes of the 9/11 Commission.[21] The deteriorating situation in Iraq was aggravated by "the dysfunctional U.S. government," National Security Advisor Condoleezza Rice confided to a White House colleague.[22] These were Republicans; Democrats and nonpartisan observers used the term even more broadly.

Complaints about dysfunctionality had little to do with new claims of presidential power. They dealt, instead, with a sense that the executive branch had failed to work properly even within the generally recognized bounds of its authority. The word was imprecise, but it conveyed the point that something had gone badly wrong in the internal operations of government. The administration failed to perform basic tasks well. It had not formulated policies that were likely to advance the national interest, had not anticipated or responded properly to contingencies, and could not coordinate the bureaucratic limbs of government. It could not behave rationally. It could not achieve control, in the technical sense of inducing other actors, even within the executive branch, to collaborate in the achievement of its goals.[23]

Less-often acknowledged, but even more troubling, was a larger dysfunctionality in the Bush administration's response to 9/11. The

Bush administration flatly refused to challenge some of the most important constraints on executive authority in the post-Nixon era. For example, it did not challenge the broad public consensus in favor of lower taxes and did not seriously pursue reforms that would relieve the long-term budget pressures generated by federal entitlement programs, even though this meant that homeland-security programs would be underfunded. It actively promoted the increased consumption of imported goods, even though this exacerbated the threat posed by poorly supervised trade flows. It resisted a return to firm regulation of the private sector, even though the bulk of vulnerable facilities lay in private hands. In short, it attempted to craft a response to the 9/11 crisis that largely respected the neoliberal settlement crafted by Ronald Reagan and his successors in the waning years of the twentieth century.

The Bush administration could rationalize this policy because it seemed to have other ways of responding to terror threats. It could use the military to "take the fight to the enemy." This was a way of avoiding a response to the crisis that imposed significant costs on politically important constituencies at home. Military action served as a substitute for domestic policies that would entail difficult challenges to the neoliberal settlement or the civil-liberties regime. The military itself had also been restructured—through technological innovations and the abolition of conscription—to reduce the domestic impact of the use of force overseas. The War on Terrorism was not, therefore, a manifestation of resurgent presidential power. On the contrary, it was evidence of an administration attempting to respond decisively to crisis without perturbing, in any fundamental way, post-Nixon understandings about the place of government in Americans' everyday lives.

Even here, however, government policy was tainted by irrationality. The Bush administration did not establish its war aims and then determine what actions it should pursue. Rather, it was driven by opportunism and bureaucratic inertia, with justifications largely crafted *ex post*. As Thomas Ricks has observed, there was effectively no war plan for Iraq, no explanation of how actions on the ground (such as invasion and occupation) would eventually lead to broader strategic goals (such as regional transformation).[24] When actions failed to yield the expected results, the administration proved incapable of learning and adapting to new realities. The consequence, as the Iraq Study Group observed in December 2006, was that U.S. national security was actually undermined by U.S. policy. Al Qaeda had been given a new base of operations and a major propaganda victory.[25] Global perceptions of U.S. power had been badly shaken, and its moral leadership undermined.

## The Problem of Authority

It is difficult to avoid speculating about counterfactuals. Suppose that the 2000 election has produced a Democratic, rather than a Republican, president. Would the broad path of policy after the 9/11 attacks have been dramatically different? The answer is not so clear. The failure of Democratic leaders to provide a coherent alternative to the Bush administration's counterterrorism program, and the quiescence of many senior Democrats as the Bush administration made critical decisions in its War on Terrorism, should tell us that they were equally sensitive to the institutional and societal constraints on federal action.

Indeed, there was broad agreement among Democrats and Republicans about the boundaries of federal policy. For example, the Clinton administration had been strongly committed to the neoliberal settlement. It was President Clinton, after all, who promised the American people that "the era of big government is over," that the federal bureaucracy would shrink, and that the federal government would remain committed to a program of fiscal balance, regulatory restraint, and free trade.[26]

The Clinton administration also understood the other constraints that typified the American polity at the turn of the millennium. Its own attempt to reform surveillance rules had been undermined because of civil-liberties concerns, and a series of initiatives to reorganize the federal bureaucracy was undone by resistance from Congress, nongovernmental stakeholders, and federal employees. It is not hard to imagine that a post-9/11 Democratic administration would have felt the temptation to exploit transient "windows of opportunity" (as the Bush administration did with the Patriot Act) or to proceed covertly on sensitive matters of surveillance. As we have seen, the Clinton administration had also begun to experiment with military interventions that were justified in terms similar to those used by the Bush administration in 2002—and which were sometimes interpreted as attempts to divert attention from less-tractable domestic problems.

The Democratic-controlled Congress also trod warily after November 2006 while managing the conflict between national security and the rights of aliens. Democratic leaders in Congress condemned the U.S. detention facility in Guantánamo Bay but had not passed legislation to close the facility by June 2007. Although many leaders also condemned the denial of habeas corpus rights for prisoners at Guantánamo, Congress had not passed legislation that would restore those rights. Despite evidence that the CIA continued to keep secret detainees, Congress failed to bar the practice. The Democratic majority on the Senate Select Committee on Intelligence split on a legislative proposal that would restrict the CIA to interrogation techniques already approved for use by the military, even with an exception in cases of "national exigency."[27] Editorialists bemoaned Democrats' preoccupation with "tactical political calculations."[28] "Some Democrats," said a human rights activist, "are still worried these issues aren't political winners for them."[29]

Personnel may change, but the broad constraints on federal action do not shift so readily. It is not difficult to imagine, therefore, that a future president, confronted with instantaneous and intense pressure to *do something* in response to a domestic attack, would respond with policies that are broadly comparable to those pursued by the Bush administration after 9/11. This is an alarming prospect, and it is not hypothetical. In 2006, *Foreign Policy* surveyed national-security specialists for their appraisal of the terrorist threat. More than 80 percent said an attack on the scale of 9/11 was likely or certain to happen within the United States before 2011. The probability of smaller-scale attacks was judged to be much higher.[30]

We could envisage a set of policies that might reduce the possibility of comparable attacks or minimize the prospect of an equally pathological response to future attacks. We could reform tax and entitlement policies so that homeland-security programs can be properly funded. We could regulate privately held infrastructure more forcefully. We could rationalize the federal bureaucracy and congressional oversight. We could strengthen mechanisms for interagency coordination. We could take steps to revive the senior ranks of the career civil service and check the influence of political appointees in areas of critical importance. We could develop explicit rules about the boundaries of surveillance and data mining, about preventive detention, and about the trial and imprisonment of terrorists.

Most of these reforms are, of course, highly impracticable, not only because they involve adjustment of deeply entrenched arrangements but also because they seem to collide directly with the liberal credo. Such reforms entail an expansion of federal responsibilities and, in particular, an expansion of the authority of the executive branch. Critics would assail some of these reforms as dangerous accretions of executive power, and some would invoke the image of the imperial presidency while making that case.

Scholars who deploy the image of the imperial presidency may argue that their concern is not with executive power per se but with unregulated executive power—that is, authority that is unconstrained by laws or procedures designed to ensure that it is exercised properly. This is a critical distinction, but it is also one that is missed by many of those who echo the refrain of the imperial presidency. In truth, the rhetoric of the imperial presidency gains currency by playing on the centuries-old fear of central government, and it in turn reinforces the perception that the main problem in contemporary American governance is "big government" and a too-powerful executive branch. (A 2006 Gallup poll found that a large majority of Americans, Republicans and Democrats alike, believed that "big government" posed the biggest threat to the country in the future.)[31] The very language of the imperial presidency conveys this point. The root of "imperial" is the Latin verb *imperare*, "to command." If the imperial presidency is problematic, it is presumably because of this excess in its capacity to command.

In critical respects the predicament of contemporary governance is precisely the opposite of this formulation. In the postmillennial liberal state, the president often lacks the power to command. He has not been given authority to act. He cannot command nonstate actors, and he cannot exercise authority intelligently within the executive branch. This weakness encourages (but does not justify) a variety of perverse responses to crisis: the displacement of attention to military action, covert policies, and open disdain of law. The central challenge, therefore, is not simply to *restrain* presidential authority but to decide what powers the president must have and in what way that authority should be regulated.

In a sense, the question of whether the president should have extensive powers in moments of crisis is moot. As I have noted, new information and communications technologies generate intense pressure on the chief executive to respond authoritatively to crises. We might even say that new technologies *create* crises more quickly. We saw this phenomenon at work after 9/11 and also after Hurricane Katrina. No president facing such pressure will decline to respond decisively. The real question is what shape that response will take. The lull between attacks is the time in which we should agree on the terms that will govern the nation's response to future crises.

# Notes

### Notes to the Preface

1. There is an extensive literature that establishes this point. See, for example, James Ettema and Theodore Glasser, "Narrative Form and Moral Force," *Journal of Communication* 38, no. 3 (1998): 8–27.

### Notes to Chapter I

1. Joe Conason, *It Can Happen Here: Authoritarian Peril in the Age of Bush* (New York: Thomas Dunne Books, 2007), 9.

2. This was the proportion of respondents who said that they trusted government most or all of the time. Dana Milbank and Richard Morin, "Public Is Unyielding in War against Terror," *Washington Post*, September 29, 2001, A1.

3. James A. Stimson, *Tides of Consent: How Public Opinion Shapes American Politics* (New York: Cambridge University Press, 2004), 4–5.

4. The war in Iraq provoked broad concern, but by 2006 most Americans saw no connection between the war in Iraq and the broader antiterror effort. Carl Hulse and Marjorie Connelly, "51% in Poll See No Link between Iraq and Terror Fight," *New York Times*, August 22, 2006.

5. Hubert Vedrine, foreign minister from 1997 to 2002, quoted in Phillip Stephens, "Distant Friends," *Financial Times*, September 5, 2002.

6. Josef Joffe, *Überpower: The Imperial Temptation of America* (New York: Norton, 2006).

7. Bo Larsson, "Sweden, Germany Boost European Social Democracy," *Dawn*, Internet edition, September 27, 2002, http://www.dawn.com/2002/09/27/int14 .htm (accessed July 10, 2006).

8. "It's Time for Bush to Listen to Us," *Northern Echo*, November 17, 2003.

9. Philippe Sands, *Lawless World: America and the Making and Breaking of Global Rules from FDR's Atlantic Charter to George W. Bush's Illegal War* (New York: Viking, 2005), xii.

10. Timothy Garton Ash, "Us and the Hyperpower," *Manchester Guardian Weekly*, April 17, 2002, 11.

11. Michiko Kakutani, "Rise of the Vulcans: Review," *International Herald Tribune*, March 10, 2004, 9.

12. Niall Ferguson, "Empire of the Gun," *Daily Mail*, June 21, 2003, 18.

13. "Bush and Blair Need Each Other, Says Russian Commentary on London Summit," *BBC Monitoring International Reports,* November 18, 2003.

14. Francis Fukuyama, *America at the Crossroads: Democracy, Power, and the Neoconservative Legacy* (New Haven, CT: Yale University Press, 2006), 189.

15. Andrew Bacevich, "Why Read Clausewitz When Shock and Awe Can Make a Clean Sweep of Things?" *London Review of Books,* June 8, 2006, 3–6.

16. Dan Froomkin, "Executive Power Outage," *Washington Post,* June 6, 2006.

17. Arthur M. Schlesinger Jr., *War and the American Presidency* (New York: Norton, 2004). See also Andrew Rudalevige, *The New Imperial Presidency: Renewing Presidential Power after Watergate* (Ann Arbor: University of Michigan Press, 2005).

18. Constitution Project, "Statement of the Coalition to Defend Checks and Balances," February 27, 2006, available online at http://www.constitutionproject .org/article.cfm?messageID=197 (accessed July 10, 2006).

19. Glenn Greenwald, *How Would a Patriot Act? Defending American Values from a President Run Amok* (San Francisco: Working Assets Publishing, 2006).

20. David Cole, "In Case of Emergency," *New York Review of Books,* July 13, 2006, 42.

21. Stuart Taylor Jr., "The Man Who Would Be King," *Atlantic,* April 2006, 25–26.

22. "It is starting to look like an elected dictatorship." Stein Ringen, "Going Soft," *Times Literary Supplement,* November 3, 2006, 5–6.

23. Bob Herbert, "The Nixon Syndrome," *New York Times,* January 9, 2006, 21.

24. Richard Schmitt, "Senate Blocks the Renewal of the Patriot Act," *Los Angeles Times,* December 17, 2005.

25. Elizabeth Drew, "Power Grab," *New York Review of Books,* June 22, 2006, 15.

26. Paul Krugman, "The Treason Card," *New York Times,* July 7, 2006, A17. Joe Conason later argued that "the name for . . . the threat embedded within the Bush administration . . . is authoritarianism." Conason, *It Can Happen Here,* 11.

27. "The Real Agenda," *New York Times,* July 16, 2006, 11 (emphasis added).

28. Peter Baker and Jim VandeHei, "Clash Is Latest Chapter in Bush Effort to Widen Executive Power," *Washington Post,* December 21, 2005, A1. See also the March 13, 2002, statement by President Bush: Executive Office of the President, "President Bush Holds Press Conference" (Washington, DC: Office of the Press Secretary, March 13, 2003).

29. John Yoo, *The Powers of War and Peace: The Constitution and Foreign Affairs after 9/11* (Chicago: University of Chicago Press, 2005); Jane Mayer, "The Hidden Power," *New Yorker,* July 3, 2006, 44–55.

30. In the first five years of the Bush administration, the number of civilians employed by the federal government averaged about 1.85 million. In the half century before 2005, it averaged 2.01 million. In the same five years, nondefense discretionary spending averaged about 3.7 percent of GDP; in the period from 1962 to 2005, the average was 3.9 percent.

31. Executive Office of the President, "Vice President's Remarks to the Traveling Press" (Washington, DC: Office of the Vice President, December 20, 2005).

32. In popular discourse in the United States, "liberal" is often taken to mean socialist or social-democratic, particularly on matters of economic policy. I am not using the term in this sense. Rather, I refer to the older understanding of liberalism, which emphasizes a commitment to political liberties, limited government, and a free-market economy. Deepak Lal discusses the shift in meaning of the term in *Reviving the Invisible Hand: The Case for Classical Liberalism in the Twenty-First Century* (Princeton, NJ: Princeton University Press, 2006), 237.

33. Local government is not recognized within the federal Constitution but was, at the time, so deeply entrenched in Anglo-American political practice that it might reasonably be said to have quasi-constitutional status.

34. *The Federalist No. 51*.

35. Walter Dean Burnham, *Critical Elections and the Mainsprings of American Politics* (New York: Norton, 1970), 176.

36. Francis Fukuyama, "The End of History?" *National Interest* 16 (summer 1989): 3–16.

37. Irving Kristol, *Neoconservatism: The Autobiography of an Idea* (Chicago: Elephant Paperbacks, 1999), 211.

38. Most major OECD countries, Peter Hall and David Soskice argue, can be characterized as *coordinated market economies,* because they rely more heavily on nonmarket mechanisms to solve critical problems of coordination between economic actors—such as the negotiation of relationships between firms and workers or between firms and investors or between suppliers and clients. The Anglo-American countries, by contrast, are *liberal market economies,* because they eschew these mechanisms and rely more heavily on competitive markets to resolve problems of coordination. Peter A. Hall and David W. Soskice, *Varieties of Capitalism: The Institutional Foundations of Comparative Advantage* (Oxford: Oxford University Press, 2001), 1–68. A sharp distinction between the Anglo-American and continental European economies is also drawn by Edmund Phelps in "Dynamic Capitalism," *Wall Street Journal,* October 10, 2006, A14. A good description of the major variants of European capitalism is also provided in Will Hutton, *A Declaration of Interdependence* (New York: Norton, 2003), 240–253; and Barry J. Eichengreen, *The European Economy since 1945: Coordinated Capitalism and Beyond* (Princeton, NJ: Princeton University Press, 2006).

39. The same equation is made in Gøsta Esping-Andersen, *The Three Worlds of Welfare Capitalism* (Cambridge, UK: Polity, 1990).

40. This is not to say that fundamental rights are unprotected in these other countries: governments may be constrained by rights implied by other parts of their written constitutions, by convention or tradition, or by international agreements.

41. Arend Lijphart, *Patterns of Democracy: Government Forms and Performance in Thirty-Six Countries* (New Haven, CT: Yale University Press, 1999).

42. Indeed, the liberal ethos is so deeply engrained in American culture that it is regarded as a natural stance rather than a consciously chosen ideological position. Louis Hartz, *The Liberal Tradition in America,* 2nd ed. (San Diego: Harcourt Brace Jovanovich, 1991), 3–32.

43. The Dutch scholar Geert Hofstede finds that Americans are more individualist in their orientation than the citizens of the other fifty countries included in his research. Geert H. Hofstede, *Culture's Consequences: Comparing Values, Behaviors, Institutions, and Organizations across Nations,* 2nd ed. (Thousand Oaks, CA: Sage, 2001).

44. Samuel P. Huntington, *American Politics: The Promise of Disharmony* (Cambridge, MA: Belknap, 1981), 33.

45. These attacks on Roosevelt are now attributed to his "court-packing" scheme, but other proposals stirred opposition as well, such as plans to expand the White House staff, incorporate independent regulatory agencies into executive departments, and weaken the Comptroller General.

46. Paul Pierson, *Politics in Time: History, Institutions, and Social Analysis* (Princeton, NJ: Princeton University Press, 2004), 17–53.

47. For a discussion of many of these laws, see David H. Rosenbloom, *Building a Legislative-Centered Public Administration: Congress and the Administrative State, 1946–1999* (Tuscaloosa: University of Alabama Press, 2000).

48. A useful overview on this subject is provided by Daniel Yergin and Joseph Stanislaw, *The Commanding Heights* (New York: Simon and Schuster, 1998).

49. James Reston, "Uniquack on the Nixon Budget," *New York Times,* January 31, 1971, E13. For a discussion of Nixon's pragmatism in economic management, see Robert M. Collins, *More: The Politics of Economic Growth in Postwar America* (New York: Oxford University Press, 2000), 98–131.

50. Herbert Stein, *Presidential Economics: The Making of Economic Policy from Roosevelt to Clinton,* 3rd rev. ed. (Washington, DC: American Enterprise Institute, 1994), 190. On the Nixon-era trend toward increased regulation, see also Marc Allen Eisner, *Regulatory Politics in Transition,* 2nd ed. (Baltimore, MD: Johns Hopkins University Press, 2006), chap. 6; Marc Allen Eisner, *Governing the Environment: The Transformation of Environmental Protection* (Boulder, CO: Lynne Rienner, 2007), chap. 4.

51. The statement was made in Reagan's first inaugural address, in January 1981 (emphasis added).

52. David Harvey, *A Brief History of Neoliberalism* (New York: Oxford University Press, 2005).

53. On the shift in regulatory philosophies, see Eisner, *Regulatory Politics in Transition,* chap. 8; Eisner, *Governing the Environment,* chaps. 5–7.

54. Anthony Giddens discusses this shift in the United States and a comparable shift in the United Kingdom in *The Third Way and Its Critics* (Cambridge, UK: Polity, 2000), chap. 1. Streeck and Thelen argue that "the dominant trend" in the United States and other advanced political economies is "liberalization: the steady expansion of market relations in areas that under the postwar settlement of democratic capitalism were reserved to collective political decisionmaking." Wolfgang Streeck and Kathleen Thelen, eds., *Beyond Continuity: Institutional Change in Advanced Political Economies* (New York: Oxford University Press, 2005), 30.

55. Stockholm International Peace Research Institute, *SIPRI Yearbook 2005*

(Stockholm, Sweden: Stockholm International Peace Research Institute, 2005), table 8A.

56. L. Zecchini, "Le gigantisme militaire de Bush," *Le Monde,* February 6, 2002.

57. Christopher Wilkinson, "Perestroika: The Role of the Defense Sector," *NATO Review* 38, no. 1 (1990): 20–25.

58. The operating budget is the amount spent by the federal bureaucracy directly on its own personnel and operations. It does not include payments to individuals, such as Social Security; grants to state and local governments; and interest on the federal debt. The data is taken from table 17.5 of the Budget of the United States, FY 2007.

59. Paul Light, *The True Size of Government* (Washington, DC: Brookings Institution Press, 1999), table 2-2.

60. National Statistics, *Public Sector Employment Trends 2005* (Washington, DC: Office for National Statistics, October 2005).

61. Philip Harling and Peter Mandler, "From 'Fiscal-Military' State to Laissez-Faire State, 1760–1850," *Journal of British Studies* 32, no. 1 (1993): 44–70, tables 1 and 2.

62. Reserve forces are organized within state National Guards, but these may be called into service by the president without the consent of state governments.

63. A Gallup poll conducted June 8–10, 2001, asked respondents "how much confidence you, yourself have" in the military; 32 percent said "a great deal," and 34 percent said "quite a lot." Gallup Poll On Demand, www.gallup.com.

64. World Values Survey, http://www.worldvaluessurvey.org.

65. The term *neomilitarism* was first used by Edwin Lieuwen in 1964, while describing the reappearance of military governments in Latin America in the preceding two years. Edwin Lieuwen, *Generals vs. Presidents: Neomilitarism in Latin America* (New York: Praeger, 1964). However, Lieuwen did not invest the term with special meaning: he did not suggest that there was any qualitative difference in the character of old and new military governments. Perhaps for this reason, the term was not widely adopted in succeeding years. I am using the term in a quite distinct sense.

66. Lester M. Salamon and Odus V. Elliott, *The Tools of Government: A Guide to the New Governance* (New York: Oxford University Press, 2002).

67. Graham T. Allison and Philip Zelikow, *Essence of Decision: Explaining the Cuban Missile Crisis,* 2nd ed. (New York: Longman, 1999).

68. It is not always easy to militarize policy problems. Powerful constituencies must be persuaded that the problem really is one that falls within the sphere of military operations, and agencies within the defense establishment may themselves resist new tasks that they regard as inconsistent with their mission. Morton Halperin, "Why Bureaucrats Play Games," *Foreign Policy* 2 (1971): 70–90.

69. This phrase is used in the Department of Defense's *Quadrennial Defense Review Report* (Washington, DC: Department of Defense, February 6, 2006).

70. Dana Priest, *The Mission: Waging War and Keeping Peace with America's Mil-

*itary* (New York: Norton, 2003); Idl Oyman, "The Causes of Militarization of U.S. Foreign Policy: A Story of Inadequate Civilian Capabilities and a Reluctant Pentagon" (M.A. thesis, Johns Hopkins University, April 2005).

71. Alister Cooke, *American Home Front, 1941–1942* (New York: Grove/Atlantic, 2006).

72. Pew Research Center for the People and the Press, survey conducted by Princeton Survey Research Associates International, August 9–13, 2006, available online at http://www.pollingreport.com/terror2.htm (accessed November 15, 2006).

73. Jonathan Raban, "September 11: The View from the West," *New York Review of Books* 52, no. 14 (2005): 4.

74. Executive Office of the President, "Press Gaggle with Scott McClellan" (Washington, DC: Office of the Press Secretary, October 1, 2004).

75. Bob Woodward, "CIA Told to Do 'Whatever Necessary' to Kill Bin Laden," *Washington Post*, October 21, 2001, A1.

76. Lawrence Kaplan, "American Idle," *New Republic*, September 12, 2005, 19.

77. For accounts of the meeting, see Patrick Smith, "Looking over Powell's Shoulder with Unease," *Irish Times*, September 29, 2001, 12; and James Mann, *Rise of the Vulcans* (New York: Viking, 2004), 298–299.

78. Michael Tomasky, "The Democrats," *New York Review of Books* 14, no. 4 (2007): 16.

79. Lawyers Committee, *Assessing the New Normal: Liberty and Security for the Post–September 11 United States* (Washington, DC: Lawyers Committee for Human Rights, September 2003).

80. Ron Paul, "Homeland Security Is the Largest Federal Expansion in 50 Years," Texas Straight Talk, website of U.S. Rep. Ron Paul, November 25, 2002, http://house.gov/paul/tst/tst2002/tst112502.htm (accessed May 20, 2006).

81. Chalmers A. Johnson, *The Sorrows of Empire: Militarism, Secrecy, and the End of the Republic* (New York: Metropolitan Books, 2004), 287.

82. John W. Kingdon, *Agendas, Alternatives, and Public Policies*, 2nd ed. (New York: Longman, 2003), 166–168.

83. Charles Krauthammer, "The Obsolescence of Deterrence," *Weekly Standard*, December 9, 2002, 22–25.

84. State of the Union Address, January 29, 2002. The Axis of Evil later expanded to include Libya, Syria, and Cuba. John Bolton, "Remarks to the Heritage Foundation: 'Beyond the Axis of Evil: Additional Threats from Weapons of Mass Destruction'" (Washington, DC: Office of the Undersecretary of State for Arms Control and International Security, May 6, 2002).

85. Executive Office of the President, "Press Briefing by Scott McClellan" (Washington, DC: Executive Office of the President, June 16, 2005), available online at http://www.whitehouse.gov/news/releases/2005/06/20050616-5.html (accessed June 20, 2006).

86. Stephen Flynn, *America the Vulnerable* (New York: Harper Perennial, 2005), 11, 38.

87. David Sanger, "In Full Flight Regalia, the President Enjoys a 'Top Gun' Moment," *New York Times,* May 2, 2003, A1.

88. Ken Auletta, "Fortress Bush," *New Yorker,* January 19, 2004, 53.

### Notes to Chapter 2

1. R. Jeffrey Smith, "Many Rights in U.S. Legal System Absent in New Bill," *Washington Post,* September 29, 2006, A13.

2. There was "a pervasive sense," says Michael Flamm, "that American society was coming apart at the seams" during the law-and-order crisis. Michael Flamm, *Law and Order: Street Crime, Civil Unrest, and the Crisis of Liberalism in the 1960s* (New York: Columbia University Press, 2005), 1, 143. For a recent survey of the response to the law-and-order crisis, see Philip Jenkins, *Decade of Nightmares: The End of the Sixties and the Making of Eighties America* (New York: Oxford University Press, 2006).

3. Alan Brinkley, "A Familiar Story: Lessons from Past Assaults on Freedoms," in *The War on Our Freedoms,* ed. Richard C. Leone, 23–46 (New York: Public Affairs, 2003).

4. Geoffrey R. Stone, "Civil Liberties in Wartime," *Journal of Supreme Court History* 28, no. 3 (2003): 245. Stone made the same argument in an October 2003 amicus brief to the Supreme Court: Geoffrey R. Stone, David A. Strauss, and Stephen J. Schulhofer, *Brief of Amicus Curiae Fred Korematsu in Support of Petitioners in Odah, et al. v. United States, et al.* (Chicago: University of Chicago, October 2003).

5. Haynes Johnson, *The Age of Anxiety* (Orlando, FL: Harcourt Books, 2005), 466–493.

6. Stephen Magagnini, "Internment Memories Spur Fears," *Sacramento Bee,* March 19, 2003, A1.

7. Patricia Yollin, "A Secret History," *San Francisco Chronicle,* October 21, 2001, 8.

8. Steve Weinberg, "Becoming the Enemy: A Case for Balancing Freedom, Security," *Seattle Times,* November 2, 2003, K9.

9. Matthew Rothschild, "The New McCarthyism," *The Progressive,* January 2002, 18.

10. David Cole, "Taking Liberties: The War on Our Rights," *Nation,* January 12, 2004; Richard C. Leone and Greg Anrig, *The War on Our Freedoms: Civil Liberties in an Age of Terrorism* (New York: BBS PublicAffairs, 2003).

11. Public Interest Pictures, press materials for *Unconstitutional: The War on Our Civil Liberties* (2004), available online at http://www.publicinterestpictures.org/unconstitutional (accessed December 12, 2005).

12. Gara LaMarche, "Uncivil Liberties," *Democracy Journal* 3 (2007): 88.

13. Bill Carter and Felicity Barringer, "In Patriotic Time, Dissent Is Muted," *New York Times,* September 28, 2001.

14. "Just so you know," Maines told a British audience, "we're ashamed the president of the United States is from Texas." Johnson, *Age of Anxiety,* 489–490.

15. Timothy Gray, " 'Fahrenheit' Fever Pitch," *Variety,* May 17, 2004, 1.

16. Maher said that cruise-missile reprisal attacks were cowardly, whereas the 9/11 hijackings were not. For Fleischer's response, see Executive Office of the President, "Press Briefing by Ari Fleischer" (Washington, DC: Office of the Press Secretary, September 28, 2001), available online at http://www.whitehouse.gov/news/releases/2001/09/20010928-8.html (accessed December 14, 2005). For two reactions to Fleischer's statement, see "Democracy and Dissent," *St. Louis Post-Dispatch,* September 30, 2001; Timothy Noah, "Retract This, Please, Part 3," *Slate,* September 27, 2001, http://www.slate.com/id/1008366/.

17. Department of Justice, *Testimony of Attorney General John Ashcroft before the Senate Committee on the Judiciary* (Washington, DC: Department of Justice, December 6, 2001), available online at http://www.usdoj.gov/ag/testimony/2001/1206 transcriptsenatejudiciarycommittee.htm (accessed December 15, 2005).

18. Transcript, *NewsHour with Jim Lehrer,* PBS, November 11, 2004, available online at http://www.pbs.org/newshour/bb/law/july-dec04/ashcroft_11-11.html (accessed December 14, 2005).

19. Nick Salvatore, *Eugene V. Debs: Citizen and Socialist* (Urbana: University of Illinois Press, 1982).

20. Geoffrey R. Stone, *Perilous Times: Free Speech in Wartime from the Sedition Act of 1798 to the War on Terrorism* (New York: Norton, 2004), 172–173; Stone, "Civil Liberties in Wartime," 227n. 73.

21. Lawrence Preuss, "Denaturalization on the Ground of Disloyalty," *American Political Science Review* 36, no. 4 (1942): 701–702. Disloyal utterances were said to reveal a "mental reservation" that was held when the oath of allegiance was made, thereby vitiating the oath. For a recent study of sedition trials of German Americans during the First World War, see Clemens P. Work, *Darkest before Dawn: Sedition and Free Speech in the American West* (Albuquerque: University of New Mexico Press, 2006).

22. Criminal-syndicalism laws, such as the California Criminal Syndicalism Act of 1919, prohibited membership in organizations that advocated the use of unlawful means to effect a change in industrial ownership or control or any political change.

23. Robert K. Murray, *Red Scare: A Study in National Hysteria, 1919–1920* (Minneapolis: University of Minnesota Press, 1955), 181–184.

24. Berger was eventually defeated after a second special election in 1920. After his conviction was reversed, Berger regained his seat in 1923.

25. Murray, *Red Scare,* 226–237.

26. The attorney general identified seventy-eight subversive organizations by 1948. The count later went much higher. Richard M. Fried, *Nightmare in Red: The McCarthy Era in Perspective* (New York: Oxford University Press, 1990), 71.

27. Ibid., 182.

28. The only American charged with treason during the 9/11 crisis was Adam Gadahn, who served as a spokesman for al Qaeda and made several videotapes for the group urging violence against the United States. Gadahn, who was believed to

be hiding in Pakistan, was charged in October 2006. He was the first U.S. citizen to be charged with treason in over fifty years. Eric Lichtblau, "American in Qaeda Tapes Accused of Treason," *New York Times*, October 12, 2006. However, the related charge of seditious conspiracy was used successfully in the prosecution of individuals responsible for the World Trade Center bombing in 1993 and was also brought against John Walker Lindh and other alleged al Qaeda affiliates after 2001. In all of these cases, however, the alleged wrongdoing went beyond speech acts.

29. Fleischer called Maher's comment "unfortunate" but affirmed his right to say it. Executive Office of the President, "Press Briefing by Ari Fleischer" (Washington, DC: Office of the Press Secretary, September 28, 2001), available online at http://www.whitehouse.gov/news/releases/2001/09/20010928-8.html.

30. Vladimir Skaletsky, "Phantoms of Lost Liberty," *Maine Campus*, December 10, 2001.

31. Thomas Shevory describes the Clear Channel radio corporation's attempt to limit the playing of "inappropriate songs" after 9/11. Shevory notes that this was "a distinctively post-modern form of censorship . . . in the sense that it was imposed, not by the authority of the modern state, but by large, multi-national corporate interests." But Shevory also observes that "reaction against the Clear Channel policy demonstrated the power and vitality of popular culture, and an eventual recognition that its suppression would not be a simple undertaking." Thomas Shevory, "From Censorship to Irony: Rhetorical Responses," *Poroi: An Interdisciplinary Journal of Rhetorical Analysis and Invention* 2, no. 1 (2003), http://inpress.lib .uiowa.edu/poroi/papers/shevory030816_outline.html.

32. Matthew Ross, "Moore for the Money," *Variety*, November 7, 2004.

33. *Pierce et al. v. United States*, 252 U.S. 239 (1920); *Schaefer v. United States*, 251 U.S. 266 (1920); *Gilbert v. Minnesota*, 254 U.S. 325 (1920); *Milwaukee Social Democratic Publishing Company v. Burleson*, 255 U.S. 407 (1921); *Gitlow v. New York*, 268 U.S. 652 (1925); *Burns v. United States*, 274 U.S. 328 (1927); and *Whitney v. California*, 274 U.S. 357 (1927).

34. *Baumgartner v. United States*, 322 U.S. 665 (1944). See also *Schneiderman v. United States*, 320 U.S. 125 (1943).

35. An excellent summary of key decisions is provided in Albert Fried, *McCarthyism: The Great American Red Scare* (New York: Oxford University Press, 1997), 194–215. As to missteps: In 1948 the federal government successfully prosecuted the leadership of the Communist Party of the USA (CPUSA) for advocating the overthrow of the government. The conviction was upheld on appeal by Justice Billings Learned Hand, famous for his defense of the First Amendment, and later by the Supreme Court, which said that the improbability of an actual revolution was irrelevant to the case. *Dennis v. United States*, 341 U.S. 494 (1951). The Justice Department then began a prosecution of lower-level CPUSA officials.

36. Greg Robinson, *By Order of the President: FDR and the Internment of Japanese Americans* (Cambridge, MA: Harvard University Press, 2001), 4.

37. *Hirabayashi v. United States*, 320 U.S. 81 (1943); and *Korematsu v. United States* 323 U.S. 214 (1944).

38. Also known as Title II of the Internal Security Act of 1950.

39. Daniel J. B. Mitchell, "Warren's Wedge: An Historical Perspective on Wedge Issues in California Politics," in *California Policy Options 1999*, ed. Daniel J. B. Mitchell and Patricia Nomura, 99–111 (Los Angeles: UCLA School of Public Policy and Social Research, 1999), 109–110.

40. Hirabayashi and Korematsu also had their convictions vacated in the mid-1980s.

41. A third U.S. citizen, John Walker Lindh, was captured (like Hamdi) in Afghanistan. However, the U.S. government brought charges against Lindh within ten weeks of his capture. Lindh pled guilty to two of these charges in a plea bargain in July 2002.

42. Peter Canellos, "Japanese Internees See Modern Parallels," *Boston Globe*, November 2, 2003.

43. *Hamdi v. Rumsfeld*, 542 U.S. 507 (2004).

44. *Rumsfeld v. Padilla*, 542 U.S. 426 (2004).

45. In 2007, Benjamin Wittes observed that the Padilla case "stands for the proposition that, more than five years into the war on terror, America has no coherent legal strategy for thinking about those of its own who fight for the other side." Benjamin Wittes, *José Padilla: Would-Be Terrorist or White House Victim?* (Washington, DC: Brookings Institution, March 6, 2007).

46. A comparison of U.S. and UK antiterrorism legislation is provided by Clare Feikert, *Anti-Terrorism Authority under the Laws of the United Kingdom and the United States*, RL33726 (Washington, DC: Congressional Research Service, September 7, 2006).

47. For proposals, see Thomas F. Powers, "When to Hold 'Em," *LegalAffairs*, September-October 2004, available online at http://www.legalaffairs.org/issues/September-October-2004/argument_powers_sepoct04.msp; and Bruce A. Ackerman, *Before the Next Attack: Preserving Civil Liberties in an Age of Terrorism* (New Haven, CT: Yale University Press, 2006). For a criticism of the Ackerman plan, see David Cole, "In Case of Emergency," *New York Review of Books*, July 13, 2006.

48. Attorney General John Ashcroft later acknowledged that measures pursued by the Justice Department functioned in place of a formal preventive detention policy. John D. Ashcroft, *Never Again: Securing America and Restoring Justice* (New York: Center Street, 2006), 176. To a lesser degree, the federal government also used its material-witness powers to craft an ad hoc detention policy. Of the seventy individuals held as material witnesses after the 9/11 attacks, fifty-three were noncitizens. Human Rights Watch, *Witness to Abuse: Human Rights Abuses under the Material Witness Law since September 11* (New York: Human Rights Watch, June 2005), 16. Section 412 of the Patriot Act also gave the attorney general the authority to detain aliens if he had reasonable grounds to believe that they were engaged in activities that endangered national security. The provision required the attorney general to commence deportation proceedings, or bring criminal charges, within seven days. However, this provision was not used, largely because the fed-

eral government found it more convenient to use powers already available under immigration law.

49. Donald Johnson, *The Challenge to American Freedoms: World War I and the Rise of the American Civil Liberties Union* (Lexington: University Press of Kentucky, 1963); Judy Kutulas, *The American Civil Liberties Union and the Making of Modern Liberalism, 1930–1960* (Chapel Hill: University of North Carolina Press, 2006).

50. Kutulas, *The American Civil Liberties Union*, 98, 103–107, 224–225.

51. Jim Drinkard, "ACLU Membership Surges in Post-9/11 World," *USA Today*, December 11, 2002.

52. The ACLU's finances are difficult to gauge because of its federal structure and the division of the organization into educational and lobbying functions for tax reasons. Contributions to the American Civil Liberties Union Foundation, the educational arm of the national organization, increased from $37 million in 2000 to $48 million in 2005, according to IRS Form 990 data collected by GuideStar.org. Contributions to forty-three state foundations increased from $18 million in 2000 to $36 million in 2005. Complete data for other states' foundations, and for contributions to national and state lobbying organizations, could not be obtained.

53. Anick Jesdanun, "Defending Liberties in a High-Tech World," Associated Press, May 7, 2006.

54. The data is based on responses to the question, "How much of the time do you think you can trust the government in Washington to do what is right?" This question has been posed in surveys since 1958 by the American National Election Studies, undertaken by the Center for Political Studies at the University of Michigan.

55. For reviews of the debate over the determinants of trust in government, see Luke Keele, *Social Capital, Government Performance, and the Dynamics of Trust in Government* (Oxford, UK: Nuffield College, October 23, 2004); John R. Hibbing and Elizabeth Theiss-Morse, eds., *What Is It about Government That Americans Dislike?* (New York: Cambridge University Press, 2001); Russell J. Dalton, *Democratic Challenges, Democratic Choices: The Erosion of Political Support in Advanced Industrial Democracies* (New York: Oxford University Press, 2004); Stimson, *Tides of Consent: How Public Opinion Shapes American Politics*. In a comparative study of OECD countries, Pharr, Putnam, and Dalton suggest that the downtrend in trust has been "longest and clearest" in the United States. Susan Pharr, Robert Putnam, and Russell Dalton, "A Quarter-Century of Declining Confidence," *Journal of Democracy* 11, no. 2 (2000): 9.

56. Michael Freeman, *Freedom or Security: The Consequences for Democracies Using Emergency Powers to Fight Terror* (Westport, CT: Praeger, 2003), 1.

57. "Proposed Anti-Terrorism Measures Overstep Reason," *Houston Chronicle*, December 20, 1995, 34.

58. Gallup poll conducted August 11–14, 1995.

59. Louis J. Freeh, *My FBI* (New York: St. Martin's, 2005), 284.

60. "Americans Distrust Government, but Want It to Do More," National

Public Radio, July 28, 2000, available online at http://www.npr.org/programs/
specials/poll/govt/summary.html (accessed May 30, 2006).

61. Emphasis added. The survey was conducted by Gallup May 18–20, 2001.

62. "Too much power": Gallup poll conducted September 5–8, 2002. "Immediate threat": Gallup polls conducted September 8–10, 2003 (30 percent perceive
immediate threat); September 13–15, 2004 (35 percent); and September 12–15, 2005
(37 percent). The Gallup organization changed the wording of this latter question
after 2001, omitting the reference to the "large and powerful" federal government;
this may have contributed to the decline in proportion of respondents answering
affirmatively.

63. Public Agenda, "Confidence in U.S. Foreign Policy Index," June 2005.

64. Ashcroft, *Never Again*, 154.

65. Public Law 107-56 (2001). The official title is the USA PATRIOT Act, an
acronym for Uniting and Strengthening America by Providing Appropriate Tools
Required to Intercept and Obstruct Terrorism.

66. Leahy statement: *This Week*, ABC News, November 18, 2001. American Library Association, "Resolution on the USA Patriot Act," January 29, 2003, available
online at http://www.ala.org/ala/washoff/WOissues/civilliberties/theusapatriot
act/alaresolution.htm (accessed December 19, 2005).

67. Patty Reinert, "Experts Fear Net Ensnarls Liberties," *Houston Chronicle*,
October 7, 2001, A1.

68. Elaine Scarry, "Resolving to Resist," *Boston Review* 29, no. 1 (2004): 8–13.

69. Flamm, *Law and Order*, 118; Kathryn S. Olmsted, *Challenging the Secret Government* (Chapel Hill: University of North Carolina Press, 1996), 94–95; Stone, *Perilous Times*, 442, 451, 462.

70. Stone, *Perilous Times*, 495, David Cunningham, *There's Something Happening Here: The New Left, the Klan, and FBI Counterintelligence* (Berkeley: University of
California Press, 2004), 33.

71. Select Senate Committee to Study Government Operations, *Final Report
with Respect to Intelligence Activities* (Washington, DC: U.S. Senate, 1976) (hereafter
cited as "Church Committee report"), book 3, *Intelligence Activities and the Rights
of Americans*, 789, available online at http://www.aarclibrary.org/publib/church/
reports/contents.htm.

72. Details about COINTELPRO became known following the disclosure of
documents stolen from an FBI field office in 1971. The *New York Times* and *Washington Post* published exposés in 1974–75 that resulted in the Church Committee's investigation, as well as parallel inquiries established by President Ford and the
House of Representatives.

73. COINTELPRO was halted in 1971; the CIA's mail-opening program, in
1973; Operation CHAOS, in 1974. Army intelligence reduced its activities in 1971.
See Church Committee, book III.

74. Executive Order 11905, February 18, 1976, sec. 5.

75. The 2002 amendments included changes allowing the FBI to attend public

meetings, surf the Internet, and extract information from commercial databases without the need to show that a crime may have been committed.

76. Elizabeth Bazan, *The Foreign Intelligence Surveillance Act: An Overview of the Statutory Framework and Recent Judicial Decisions*, RL30465 (Washington, DC: Congressional Research Service, September 22, 2004).

77. James Kuhnhenn, "Anti-Terror Act Passes Senate," *Milwaukee Journal Sentinel*, October 26, 2001, 1A.

78. Several state associations used similar language; see, for example, New York Library Association, "Letter to Senator Charles Schumer, May 21, 2003," available online at http://www.nyla.org/index.php?page_id=662, (accessed December 19, 2005).

79. Michael Doyle, "No Haven from Politics for Librarians Leader," *Sacramento Bee*, July 21, 2005.

80. HR 1157, 108th Cong., 1st sess., 2003.

81. Ellen Goodman, "Snooping on Readers," *Boston Globe*, July 24, 2003.

82. Edward Kennedy, "On Wiretapping, Bush Isn't Listening to the Constitution," *Boston Globe*, December 22, 2005.

83. Jonathan Saltzman, "Student's Tall Tale Revealed," *Boston Globe*, December 24, 2005.

84. Eric Lichtblau, "At FBI, Frustration over Limits on an Antiterror Law," *New York Times*, December 11, 2005. The documents were released under the Freedom of Information Act.

85. Department of Justice, *Review of the Federal Bureau of Investigation's Use of Section 215 Orders for Business Records* (Washington, DC: Office of the Inspector General, March 2007), xv.

86. Department of Justice, "News Release: Attorney General Alberto R. Gonzales Calls on Congress to Renew Vital Provisions of the USA Patriot Act," April 5, 2005, available online at http://www.usdoj.gov/opa/pr/2005/April/05_ag_161.htm (accessed December 19, 2005). An investigation by the department's inspector general subsequently calculated that twenty-one "pure" section 215 applications were made to the Foreign Intelligence Surveillance Court between 2002 and 2005; none of these pertained to library records. Some other section 215 applications were made to acquire telephone-subscriber information, because of defects in the language of the FBI's pen-register/trap-and-trace authority that were corrected during the reauthorization of the Patriot Act. Department of Justice, *Review of the Federal Bureau of Investigation's Use of Section 215 Orders for Business Records*, v–xi.

87. An overview of National Security Letters and other forms of administrative subpoenas is provided by Charles Doyle, *Administrative Subpoenas and National Security Letters in Criminal and Foreign Intelligence Investigations* (Washington, DC: Congressional Research Service, April 2005).

88. Barton Gellman, "The FBI's Secret Scrutiny: In Hunt for Terrorists, Bureau Examines Records of Ordinary Americans," *Washington Post*, November 6, 2005, A1.

89. Department of Justice, *Review of the Federal Bureau of Investigation's Use of*

*National Security Letters* (Washington, DC: Office of the Inspector General, March 2007), xx.

90. In a report given to Congress in May 2006, Assistant Attorney General William Moschella gave a partial enumeration of letters issued in 2005; he said that the 9,254 letters counted in his report related to investigations of 3,501 individuals. William Moschella, "Letter to the Hon. J. Dennis Hastert Regarding Application of the Foreign Intelligence Surveillance Act," Department of Justice, Office of Legislative Affairs, April 28, 2006. On the proportion of National Security Letter requests that related to investigation of non-U.S. persons, see Department of Justice, *Review of the Federal Bureau of Investigation's Use of National Security Letters*, xxi.

91. Gellman, "The FBI's Secret Scrutiny." An audit by the Justice Department's inspector general found serious procedural problems with the use of National Security Letters but did not provide evidence of concrete harm to citizens. Department of Justice, *Review of the Federal Bureau of Investigation's Use of National Security Letters*. A subsequent FBI internal audit undertaken following the inspector general's study also found a large number of procedural violations that warranted tighter controls, most arising because communications companies provided more information than had been sought by the FBI. However, the audit found no evidence that FBI agents knowingly or willingly violated the law. John Solomon, "FBI Finds It Frequently Overstepped in Collecting Data," *Washington Post,* June 14, 2007, A1.

92. The decision of the U.S. District Court for the Southern District of New York in *John Doe v. Ashcroft* was given in September 2004; the decision of the U.S. District Court for the District of Connecticut in *John Doe v. Gonzales* was given in September 2005. In the Connecticut case, the "gag provisions" were found to violate the First Amendment. In the New York case, the Court also found that the terms governing the National Security Letter itself violated the Fourth Amendment. In May 2006, the U.S. Court of Appeals for the Second Circuit found that the arguments in both cases were affected by changes to the Patriot Act made earlier in the year, which allowed for judicial review of letters and loosened the gag rule. It dismissed the Connecticut case and returned the New York case for reconsideration by the lower court.

93. Robert O'Harrow, *No Place to Hide* (New York: Free Press, 2005), 24–27.

94. David Sarasohn, "DC Dangers: How a Rumor Becomes a Law," *Oregonian,* May 9, 2003, C11.

95. Brian Yeh and Charles Doyle, *USA Patriot Improvement and Reauthorization Act of 2005: A Legal Analysis* (Washington, DC: Congressional Research Service, March 24, 2006).

96. Department of Justice, *Review of the Federal Bureau of Investigation's Use of National Security Letters,* 124.

97. Associated Press, "ACLU Withdraws Lawsuit Challenging Patriot Act," *Washington Post,* October 29, 2006, A10.

98. There were, however, legislative limitations on warrantless interception, and courts also introduced rules that barred the introduction of evidence gained

through warrantless interception. A short history of judicial and legislative attitudes toward the interception of telegraphic and telephonic communication is provided in *Berger v. New York,* 388 U.S. 41 (1967). The two U.S. Supreme Court decisions that affirmed that warrantless interception did not raise Fourth Amendment issues, so long as premises were not entered, were *Olmstead v. United States,* 277 U.S. 438 (1928) and *Goldman v. United States,* 316 U.S. 129 (1942).

99. The quotation comes from *Lopez v. United States,* 373 U.S. 427 (1963); the reversing decision was *Katz v. United States,* 389 U.S. 347 (1967).

100. Lawrence Meir Friedman, *American Law in the 20th Century* (New Haven, CT: Yale University Press, 2002), 326–328.

101. Gallup poll, July 1–2, 1986.

102. See, generally, Charles J. Sykes, *The End of Privacy* (New York: St. Martin's, 1999); Reginald Whitaker, *The End of Privacy: How Total Surveillance Is Becoming a Reality* (New York: New Press, 1999); Simson Garfinkel, *Database Nation: The Death of Privacy in the 21st Century* (Cambridge, MA: O'Reilly, 2000); Christian Parenti, *The Soft Cage: Surveillance in America from Slavery to the War on Terror* (New York: Basic Books, 2003); O'Harrow, *No Place to Hide*; Colin J. Bennett and Charles D. Raab, *The Governance of Privacy: Policy Instruments in Global Perspective,* 2nd and updated ed. (Cambridge, MA: MIT Press, 2006).

103. "The United States is now the only advanced industrial state that has not passed, or is not in the process of passing, a data protection law covering private sector activities." Bennett and Raab, *The Governance of Privacy,* 131.

104. Federal Communications Commission, *Trends in Telephone Service* (Washington, DC: Federal Communications Commission, 2005); Peter Lyman and Hal Varian, *How Much Information? 2003* (Berkeley: University of California at Berkeley, October 27, 2003), table 8.6.

105. "Ashcroft vs. Americans," *Boston Globe,* July 17, 2002. TIPS is an acronym for the Terrorist Information and Prevention System. The prohibition was contained in section 880 of the Homeland Security Act.

106. John Markoff, "Pentagon Plans a Computer System That Would Peek at Personal Data of Americans," *New York Times,* November 9, 2002.

107. "Big Brother 2003," *USA Today,* June 23, 2003. The ban was contained in the 2004 defense appropriations bill. Congress permitted the continuance of elements of the TIA program that dealt with non-U.S. persons. See also Shane Harris, "TIA Lives On," *National Journal* 38, no. 8 (2006): 66–67.

108. Mark Clayton, "U.S. Plans Massive Data Sweep," *Christian Science Monitor,* February 9, 2006, 1; Ellen Nakashima and Alec Klein, "New Profiling Program Raises Privacy Concerns," *Washington Post,* February 28, 2007, D3. See also Conference Report 109-699, 109th Cong., 2d sess., September 28, 2006, on Homeland Security appropriations bill for fiscal year 2007.

109. O'Harrow, *No Place to Hide,* 119–124. Privacy concerns are also canvassed in Department of Homeland Security, *Report Concerning the Multistate Anti-Terrorism Information Exchange (MATRIX) Pilot Project* (Washington, DC: DHS Privacy Office, December 2006).

110. General Accounting Office, *Aviation Security: Long-Standing Problems Impair Airport Screeners' Performance*, GAO/RCED-00-75 (Washington, DC: General Accounting Office, 2000), 41.

111. Ken Kaye, "ACLU Questions Airport Pat Downs," *Seattle Times*, November 25, 2004, A11.

112. Department of Homeland Security, *Review of the Transportation Security Administration's Use of Pat-Downs in Screening Procedures*, OIG-06-10 (Washington, DC: Office of Inspector General, November 2005).

113. Timothy Sparapani, *Testimony before the Senate Committee on Commerce, Science, and Transportation Regarding the Transportation Security Administration's Physical Screening of Airline Passengers* (Washington, DC: American Civil Liberties Union, April 4, 2006); Paul Giblin and Eric Lipton, "New Airport X-Rays Scan Bodies, Not Just Bags," *New York Times*, February 24, 2007.

114. "Airport Security," *Washington Post*, August 20, 2006, B6. For a description of El Al's methods, see Rafi Ron, *Remarks to the Aviation Subcommittee, House Committee on Transportation and Infrastructure* (Washington, DC: U.S. House of Representatives, February 27, 2002).

115. An ACLU analyst told *USA Today*, "If you're going to allow police to make searches, question people and even make arrests based on criteria rather than actual evidence of criminality, you're going to have racial profiling." Thomas Frank, "Airport Security Uses Talk as Tactic," *USA Today*, December 28, 2005.

116. Eric Lipton, "Faces, Too, Are Screened at U.S. Airports," *New York Times*, August 17, 2006, A1.

117. "Airport Screening," *Detroit Free Press*, December 30, 2005.

118. National Commission on Terrorist Attacks upon the United States, *Final Report* (New York: Barnes and Noble Books, 2004), 83–84.

119. Paul Shukovsky, "Suit over Terrorism 'No-Fly' List Rejected," *Seattle Post-Intelligencer*, January 12, 2005, B2.

120. The Department of Homeland Security finally established a clear process for dealing with targeting errors, the Travel Redress Inquiry Program, in February 2007.

121. See, for example, General Accounting Office, *Aviation Security: Computer-Assisted Passenger Prescreening System Faces Significant Implementation Challenges*, GAO-04-385 (Washington, DC: General Accounting Office, February 2004).

122. Sara Kehaulani Goo and Robert O'Harrow, "TSA Readies Revised Aviation Screening," *Washington Post*, August 26, 2004, A12.

123. See, for example, Department of Homeland Security, *Report on the Transportation Security Administration's Security Flight Program* (Washington, DC: DHS Privacy Office, December 2006).

124. Kip Hawley, *Testimony before the U.S. Senate Committee on Commerce, Science, and Technology* (Washington, DC: Transportation Security Administration, February 9, 2006).

125. Section 514 of the Homeland Security Department FY2007 Appropriations bill, Public Law 109-295.

126. Leslie Harris, *Statement before the Senate Committee on the Judiciary* (Washington, DC: Center for Democracy and Technology, January 2007), 8–9.

127. Electronic Privacy Information Center, *Comments of Thirty Organizations on the Automated Targeting System* (Washington, DC: Electronic Privacy Information Center, December 4, 2006).

128. Sheldon Alberts, "Critics of U.S. Watchlist 'Just Paranoid,'" *Ottawa Citizen,* December 20, 2006, A5. Homeland Security Secretary Michael Chertoff also expressed his frustration with criticisms of the ATS. Shane Harris, "No Secret . . . Maybe," *National Journal* 38, no. 49 (2006): 54–55.

129. Harris, *Statement before the Senate Committee on the Judiciary.*

130. James Risen and Eric Lichtblau, "Bush Lets U.S. Spy on Callers without Courts," *New York Times,* December 16, 2005.

131. President Bush first used the title in a speech on January 23, 2006. Executive Office of the President, "President Discusses Global War on Terror at Kansas State University" (Washington, DC: Office of the Press Secretary, January 23, 2006).

132. Gen. Keith B. Alexander, "Response to Questions following 'FISA for the 21st Century' Hearing" (Fort George Meade, MD: National Security Agency, December 19, 2006).

133. The legal issues raised by the NSA program are canvassed in a letter to Congress written by several distinguished legal scholars in January 2006: Geoffrey R. Stone, "Why the NSA Surveillance Program Is Unlawful," *Huffington Post,* January 9, 2006, http://www.huffingtonpost.com/geoffrey-r-stone/why-the-nsa-surveillance-_b_13522.html (accessed January 10, 2006). On the failure to consult with Congress, see Alfred Cumming, *Statutory Procedures under Which Congress Is to Be Informed of U.S. Intelligence Activities* (Washington, DC: Congressional Research Service, January 18, 2006).

134. "Spying on Ordinary Americans," *New York Times,* January 18, 2006; Bob Herbert, "The Nixon Syndrome," *New York Times,* January 9, 2006, 21.

135. Richard Schmitt, "Senate Blocks the Renewal of the Patriot Act," *Los Angeles Times, December 17, 2005.*

136. James Bamford, "The Agency That Could Be Big Brother," *New York Times,* December 25, 2005.

137. Chris Cilizza, "Gore Says Bush Broke the Law with Spying," *Washington Post,* January 17, 2006.

138. Gary Hart, "Intelligence Abuse Déjà Vu," *Los Angeles Times,* December 21, 2005. In December 2005, President Bush conceded that the war in Iraq had likely caused about thirty thousand civilian deaths. In addition, the U.S. military had lost over two thousand soldiers in Afghanistan and Iraq by the end of 2005. Three thousand lives lost in the 9/11 attacks might also be added to the count.

139. In a FOX News/Opinion Dynamics poll conducted May 16–18, 2006, 30 percent of respondents believed that the government was listening to their phone calls, and 14 percent were unsure. In a CNN poll conducted May 16–17, 2006, 26 percent of respondents thought it somewhat or very likely that they were being

wiretapped; another 31 percent thought it possible or were unsure. http://www
.pollingreport.com/terror2.htm (accessed December 20, 2006).

140. Risen and Lichtblau, "Bush Lets U.S. Spy on Callers without Courts." A
later *Washington Post* account put the number of Americans whose communications had been monitored at about five thousand. Barton Gellman, Dafna Linzer,
and Carol Leonnig, "Surveillance Net Yields Few Suspects," *Washington Post*, February 5, 2006, A1.

141. Gellman, Linzer, and Leonnig, "Surveillance Net Yields Few Suspects."

142. Scott Shane and Eric Lichtblau, "Cheney Pushed U.S. to Widen Eavesdropping," *New York Times*, May 14, 2006.

143. Carol Leonnig, "Secret Court's Judges Were Warned about NSA Spy
Data," *Washington Post*, February 9, 2006, A1; Dan Eggen and Charles Lane, "On
Hill, Anger and Calls for Hearings Greet News of Stateside Surveillance," *Washington Post*, December 17, 2005, A1; Eric Lichtblau and James Risen, "Justice Deputy
Resisted Parts of Spy Program," *New York Times*, January 1, 2006; Eric Lichtblau,
"Bush Defends Spy Program and Denies Misleading Public," *New York Times*, January 2, 2006. In May 2007, former Deputy Attorney General James Comey testified
before the Senate Judiciary Committee about the Justice Department's refusal,
three years earlier, to condone the continuation of the program without modifications. Comey revealed that he and other officials in the Justice Department threatened to resign unless adjustments were made to the program. David Johnston,
"Bush Intervened in Dispute over N.S.A. Eavesdropping," *New York Times*, May 16,
2007.

144. Executive Office of the President, "Press Briefing by Attorney General
Alberto Gonzales and General Michael Hayden, December 19, 2005" (Washington, DC: Executive Office of the President, 2005), available online at http://www
.whitehouse.gov/news/releases/2005/12/20051219-1.html (accessed January 31,
2006); Department of Justice, *Legal Authorities Supporting the Activities of the National Security Agency Described by the President* (Washington, DC: Department of
Justice, January 19, 2006), 5.

145. In Orwell's novel *Nineteen Eighty-Four,* citizens constantly confront
posters that warn, "BIG BROTHER IS WATCHING YOU," with an image of Big Brother
"so contrived that the eyes follow you about when you move." They are monitored by highly visible "telescreens," installed so that citizens understood that they
"might be watched at any given moment." George Orwell, *Nineteen Eighty-Four*
(London: Secker and Warburg, 1949).

146. American Civil Liberties Union, *ACLU et al. v. NSA et al., Memorandum
in Support of Plaintiff's Motion for Partial Summary Judgment* (New York: American
Civil Liberties Union, March 9, 2006). In another case, the prosecution of Iyman
Faris, a federal judge dismissed claims that the government had relied improperly
on evidence collected through the TSP. However, the same charge was still being
pursued in 2007 with regard to the prosecution of an Oregon charity, the al-Haramain Islamic Foundation.

147. The activities of the FBI and other intelligence agencies were eventually

described in the Church Committee report; see in particular book 2 (*Intelligence Activities and the Rights of Americans*) and book 3 (*Supplementary Detailed Staff Reports on Intelligence Activities and the Rights of Americans*).

148. Executive Office of the President, "Press Conference of the President" (Washington, DC: Office of the Press Secretary, December 19, 2005).

149. "What the *New York Times* has done is nothing less than to compromise the centerpiece of our defensive efforts in the war on terrorism." Gabriel Schoenfeld, "Has the *New York Times* Violated the Espionage Act?" *Commentary,* March 2006, 23–32.

150. The "Al Qaeda Training Manual" was discovered during a police raid of an al Qaeda member's home in Manchester, England, and subsequently introduced as evidence during the trial of suspects in the 1998 U.S. embassy bombings in Tanzania and Kenya. It was posted on the Justice Department website in December 2001.

151. Executive Office of the President, "Press Briefing by Attorney General Alberto Gonzales and General Michael Hayden, December 19, 2005" (Washington, DC: Office of the Press Secretary, 2005).

152. David Savage, "Words, Deeds on Spying Differed," *Los Angeles Times,* January 26, 2006.

153. Attorney General Alberto Gonzales announced that the TSP would be terminated and replaced with a new program approved by the Foreign Intelligence Surveillance Court, in a January 17, 2007, letter to Senator Patrick Leahy, chairman of the Senate Judiciary Committee.

154. Eric Lichtblau and David Johnston, "Court to Oversee U.S. Wiretapping in Terror Cases," *New York Times,* January 18, 2007. Of course, the prospect of closer oversight by the newly elected Democratic Congress likely played a critical role in this decision as well. In April 2007, the Bush administration unveiled a proposal to "modernize" federal surveillance law. However, Democrats in Congress refused to consider reforms until the administration provided more details on the Terrorist Surveillance Program.

155. Jean-Marie Colombani, "We Are All Americans," *Le Monde,* September 12, 2001.

156. Seven French nationals were held at Guantánamo. Four were transferred to the control of French authorities in July 2004, and the remaining three were transferred in March 2005.

157. David Cole estimates that over five thousand foreign nationals were detained by federal authorities; none was found to have a connection to al Qaeda. David Cole, *Enemy Aliens: Double Standards and Constitutional Freedoms in the War on Terrorism* (New York: New Press, 2003), 25–26.

158. Office of the Inspector General, *The September 11 Detainees: A Review of the Treatment of Aliens Held on Immigration Charges in Connection with the Investigation of the 9/11 Attacks* (Washington, DC: Department of Justice, June 2003).

159. Richard Serrano, "9/11 Prisoner Abuse Suit Could Be Landmark," *Los Angeles Times,* November 20, 2006.

160. Martha Mendoza, "One Man Still Locked Up from 9/11 Sweeps," *Washington Post*, October 14, 2006.

161. *Turkmen v. Ashcroft*, U.S. District Court for the Eastern District of New York, judgment issued June 14, 2006, 77–79.

162. The December 28, 2001, memo is reproduced in Karen J. Greenberg and Joshua L. Dratel, *The Torture Papers: The Road to Abu Ghraib* (New York: Cambridge University Press, 2005), 29–37.

163. Lord Phillips, speaking in the case of *Abbasi and Anor v. Secretary of State for Foreign and Commonwealth Affairs*, Court of Appeal, November 6, 2002.

164. Department of Defense, "Secretary Rumsfeld Media Availability En Route to Guantanamo Bay, Cuba" (Washington, DC: Department of Defense, January 27, 2002), available online at http://www.dod.gov/transcripts/2002/t01282002 _t0127enr.html (accessed January 23, 2006). The administration reasoned that al Qaeda, as a nonstate actor, was not party to the Geneva Conventions and therefore not protected by them. It concluded that the Afghan state, which was a party to the Geneva Conventions, had ceased to exist, so that the Taliban militia was also a nonstate actor. The internal documents justifying the decision are reproduced in Greenberg and Dratel, *The Torture Papers*, 38–133. A helpful summary of the legal issues is provided by David Sloss, "Commentary on Rasul v. Bush," *American Journal of International Law* 98, no. 4 (2004): 788–798.

165. Executive Office of the President, *Military Order on Detention, Treatment and Trial of Certain Non-Citizens in the War against Terrorism* (Washington, DC: Office of the Press Secretary, November 13, 2001), available online at http://www .whitehouse.gov/news/releases/2001/11/20011113-27.html (accessed September 14, 2006).

166. Human Rights First, *Trials under Military Order: A Guide to the Final Rules for Military Commissions* (New York: Human Rights First, June 2004).

167. Vice President Dick Cheney, quoted in "Rumsfeld: Afghan Detainees at Gitmo Bay Will Not Be Granted POW Status," *FoxNews.com*, January 28, 2002, http://www.foxnews.com/story/0,2933,44084,00.html (accessed February 10, 2006).

168. Gallup poll conducted in January 2002; 71 percent regarded the treatment as acceptable, and 24 percent did not know enough to express an opinion.

169. *Rasul v. Bush*, 542 U.S. 466 (2004).

170. Michael Faul, "Guantanamo Detainees Say Arabs, Muslims Sold for U.S. Bounties," Associated Press, May 31, 2005.

171. Mark Denbeaux and Joshua Denbeaux, *Report on Guantanamo Detainees: A Profile of 517 Detainees through Analysis of Department of Defense Data* (South Orange, NJ: Seton Hall University School of Law, February 2006).

172. Tribunals concluded that thirty-eight individuals were not enemy combatants, out of a total of 558 reviews. American Forces Press Service, "38 Guantanamo Detainees to Be Freed after Tribunals" (Washington, DC: U.S. Department of Defense, March 30, 2005).

173. Title XIV of the National Defense Authorization Act for Fiscal Year 2006, Public Law 109-63.

174. *Congressional Record,* December 21, 2005, p. S14256.

175. Josh White, "Detainees Face Limited Access to Courts," *Washington Post,* December 24, 2005.

176. *Ex parte Milligan,* 71 U.S. 2 (1866).

177. Tim Golden, "The Battle for Guantánamo," *New York Times,* September 17, 2006.

178. Faul, "Guantanamo Detainees Say Arabs, Muslims Sold for U.S. Bounties."

179. Neil Lewis and David Johnston, "New FBI Files Describe Abuse of Iraq Inmates," *New York Times,* December 21, 2004. The documents were released under the U.S. Freedom of Information Act. An internal investigation by the U.S. Army later documented "degrading and abusive treatment" of at least one detainee. U.S. Army, *Army Regulation 15-6: Final Report of Investigation into FBI Allegations of Detainee Abuse at Guantanamo Bay Detention Facility* (Washington, DC: U.S. Army, June 9, 2005).

180. "Guantanamo Suicide Tries Called 'Coordinated Effort,'" *CNN.com,* January 24, 2005, http://www.cnn.com/2005/US/01/24/suicidal.gitmo (accessed January 23, 2006).

181. In a Gallup poll conducted June 16–19, 2005, 52 percent of respondents said that they approved of the treatment given to detainees; 36 percent disapproved, and 11 percent did not know. Fifty-seven percent said that the United States should continue to operate the facility. An ABC News/Washington Post poll conducted June 22–25, 2006, found that 57 percent of respondents supported "the federal government holding suspected terrorists without trial at the U.S. military prison in Guantanamo Bay."

182. ABC News/Washington Post poll, June 22–25, 2006, available online at http://www.pollingreport.com/terror2.htm (accessed February 15, 2007).

183. Golden, "The Battle for Guantánamo." "And so it goes," says Joseph Margulies, counsel for one of the Guantánamo detainees, reflecting on the Detainee Treatment Act. "Camp Delta continues in 2006 much as it began in 2002." Joseph Margulies, *Guantánamo and the Abuse of Presidential Power* (New York: Simon and Schuster, 2006), 251.

184. Human Rights Watch, *Enduring Freedom: Abuses by U.S. Forces in Afghanistan* (New York: Human Rights Watch, March 2004).

185. Douglas Jehl, "Army Details Scale of Abuse of Prisoners in an Afghan Jail," *New York Times,* March 12, 2005.

186. The list of abuses is taken from the March 2004 Taguba report; see Greenberg and Dratel, *The Torture Papers,* 417.

187. Josh White, "Documents Tell of Brutal Improvisation by GIs," *Washington Post,* August 3, 2005. In 2006, Human Rights First counted thirty-four suspected or confirmed homicides of detainees, including eight to twelve deaths resulting from torture. Human Rights First, *Command's Responsibility: Detainee Deaths in U.S. Custody in Iraq and Afghanistan* (Washington, DC: Human Rights First, 2006).

188. The *Los Angeles Times* reported that Defense Secretary Rumsfeld's office

told military interrogators to "take the gloves off" in late 2001. Richard Serrano, "Prison Interrogator's Gloves Came Off before Abu Ghraib," *Los Angeles Times,* June 9, 2004. A few months later a chief counterterrorism official publicly affirmed the administration's view that the "the gloves came off" after 9/11. Congressional Joint Inquiry, *Findings and Conclusions of the Congressional Joint Inquiry into September 11* (Washington, DC: Government Printing Office, December 2002), 232. Three years later, a U.S. Army intelligence officer charged with the murder of an Iraqi detainee testified that he had been pressured in 2003 by commanders who told him in an email that there were no rules for interrogation and that they "tired of taking casualties and the gloves were coming off." Jon Sarche, "Accused Interrogator Describes Tense Situation," Associated Press, January 20, 2006. See also Thomas Ricks, *Fiasco: The American Military Adventure in Iraq* (New York: Penguin, 2006), 197. Convicted of negligent homicide, the officer received a reprimand, a six-thousand-dollar fine, and two months of house arrest.

189. The January 25, 2002, memorandum is reproduced in Greenberg and Dratel, *The Torture Papers,* 118.

190. The August 1, 2002, memorandum from Assistant Attorney General Jay S. Bybee to Attorney General Gonzales is reproduced in ibid., 172. The position was affirmed by an interdepartmental working group in 2003. Ibid., 241, 286.

191. Human Rights First, *Behind the Wire* (New York: Human Rights First, March 2005), 24.

192. The national survey of 1,006 respondents was undertaken between April 29 and May 1, 2005. Data obtained from the Gallup organization.

193. Alasdair Roberts, *Blacked Out: Government Secrecy in the Information Age* (New York: Cambridge University Press, 2006), chap. 10.

194. *In Re Iraq and Afghanistan Detainees Litigation,* U.S. District Court for the District of Columbia, judgment issued March 27, 2007.

195. An overview of the publicly available evidence on the CIA's practices is provided by Jennifer Elsea and Julie Kim, *Undisclosed U.S. Detention Sites Overseas: Background and Legal Issues,* RL33643 (Washington, DC: Congressional Research Service, September 12, 2006).

196. Brian Ross and Richard Esposito, "CIA's Harsh Interrogation Techniques Described," *ABCNews.com,* November 18, 2005, http://abcnews.go.com/WNT/Investigation/story?id=1322866 (accessed January 27, 2006).

197. Douglas Jehl, "Report Warned CIA on Tactics in Interrogation," *New York Times,* November 9, 2005.

198. Ross and Esposito, "CIA's Harsh Interrogation Techniques Described."

199. Stephen Grey, *Ghost Plane: The True Story of the CIA Torture Program* (New York: St. Martin's, 2006), 137–139.

200. Dana Priest, "Wrongful Imprisonment: Anatomy of a CIA Mistake," *Washington Post,* December 4, 2005.

201. Jane Mayer, "Outsourcing Torture," *New Yorker,* February 14, 2005, 106.

202. Arar Commission, *Report of the Events Relating to Maher Arar: Analysis and*

*Recommendations* (Ottawa, Canada: Commission of Inquiry into the Actions of Canadian Officials in Relation to Maher Arar, September 18, 2006), 59.

203. According to Lexis-Nexis, no more than thirty major U.S. newspapers published editorials about the CIA detention sites in the two weeks following the *Washington Post*'s November 2005 exposé. Over one hundred newspapers wrote editorials in the two weeks following the December 2005 exposé on NSA surveillance.

204. ABC News/Washington Post poll, December 15, 2005, available online at http://www.pollingreport.com/terror2.htm (accessed February 15, 2007).

205. Regarding the House of Representatives, see William Mann, "House Committee Squashes Torture Queries," Associated Press, February 8, 2006. Republican senators also blocked attempts to adopt legislation that would require reports from the CIA on its detention facilities. The reporting requirements were added to the Intelligence Authorization Act for Fiscal Year 2006; as a consequence, the Senate's Republican leadership blocked the entire bill. Tim Starks, "Intelligence Bill Endangered for Second Year as Frist Delays Senate Debate," *CQ.com,* September 1, 2006, http://www.cq.com/public/20060905-05intel.html (accessed September 19, 2006). A Republican senator also blocked the 2007 intelligence authorization bill because it contained the same provision. Walter Pincus, "Who Stalled the Intelligence Bill?" *Washington Post,* March 8, 2007, A21.

206. Attempts by two victims of rendition, Maher Arar and Khaled al-Masri, to seek civil remedies in the United States were undercut when the federal government asserted its state-secrets privilege.

207. *Sandra K. Omar et al. v. Francis J. Harvey et al.,* U.S. District Court for the District of Columbia, Memorandum Opinion of February 6, 2006. The Court of Appeals for the District of Columbia affirmed this decision in February 2007.

208. Known as the McCain Amendment, this provision was contained in the defense appropriations bill for fiscal year 2006. The legal issues raised by the amendment are discussed in Michael Garcia, *Interrogation of Detainees: Overview of the McCain Amendment* (Washington, DC: Congressional Research Service, 2006), 4.

209. This statement was made by Senator McCain during the 2005 debate over his amendment to the defense appropriations bill. Senator John McCain, "Statement of Senator John McCain: Amendment on Army Field Manual" (Washington, DC: Office of Senator John McCain, July 25, 2005), available online at http://mccain.senate.gov/index.cfm?fuseaction=NewsCenter.ViewPressRelease&Content_id=1595 (accessed September 19, 2006). However, the same logic was articulated during the 2006 debate by senators McCain, John Warner, and Lindsey Graham, as well as former secretary of state (and former chairman of the Joint Chiefs of Staff) Colin Powell. Said Senator Graham, "I don't want the tools [defense and intelligence agencies] are given to become clubs to be used against our people." Carl Hulse, Kate Zernike, and Sheryl Gay Stolberg, "How 3 GOP Veterans Stalled Bush Detainee Bill," *New York Times,* September 17, 2006.

210. Executive Office of the President, "President's Statement on Signing of HR 2863" (Washington, DC: Office of the Press Secretary, December 30, 2005).

211. *Hamdan v. Rumsfeld*, 548 U.S. (2006).

212. Executive Office of the President, "President Discusses Creation of Military Commissions to Try Suspected Terrorists" (Washington, DC: Office of the Press Secretary, September 6, 2006). However, the practice of secret CIA detentions continued after September 2006. At least one prisoner, Abd al-Hadi al-Iraqi, was secretly held by the CIA after his capture in fall 2006. He was turned over to the military for detention at Guantánamo Bay in April 2007.

213. The administration's proposals were contained in S. 3861, the Bringing Terrorists to Justice Act of 2006, introduced in September 2006 by Senator Bill Frist.

214. Military Commissions Act, Public Law 109-366.

215. Jeffrey R. Smith and Charles Babington, "White House, Senators Near Pact on Interrogation Rules," *Washington Post*, September 22, 2006, A1. In February 2007, a federal appeals court upheld the constitutionality of the Military Commissions Act's restrictions on the writ of habeas corpus, although another appeal to the Supreme Court was expected.

216. Part IV of the Anti-Terrorism, Crime, and Security Act 2001.

217. *A (FC) and others (FC) v. Secretary of State for the Home Department*, House of Lords, December 16, 2004.

## Notes to Chapter 3

1. Douglas Brinkley, *The Great Deluge* (New York: William Morrow, 2006), 530.

2. David Henderson, "Why Spending Has Got to Give," *Policy Review* 136 (2006): 6.

3. Karlyn Bowman, *Public Opinion on Taxes* (Washington, DC: American Enterprise Institute, April 12, 2006), 4–5.

4. In figure 3.1, the tax burden is the average for the preceding five years. A few years are omitted because of lack of survey data. Budget of the United States, Fiscal Year 2007, Historical Tables, table 1.2; Bowman, Public Opinion on Taxes.

5. Bowman, *Public Opinion on Taxes*, 12–13.

6. Bureau of Labor Statistics, Consumer Expenditure Survey. In a New York Times/CBS poll taken in September 2006, 66 percent of respondents said that their household income was "just enough to pay bills and obligations" or not enough to do so; 44 percent were "very concerned" about their ability to meet major obligations.

7. The proportion of disposable income that is committed to financing household debt has increased steadily over the past quarter century, to almost one-fifth of disposable income. See data on the Financial Obligations Ratio, an estimate of the ratio of debt payments to disposable personal income, provided quarterly by the Federal Reserve Board: http://www.federalreserve.gov/releases/housedebt/default.htm. This trend is not unique to the United States.

8. This program had three major components. In June 2001, Bush signed into law a sweeping package of reforms to be phased in over several years: Economic Growth and Tax Relief Reconciliation Act of 2001, Public Law 107-16 (June 7, 2001).

Most of these reductions were scheduled to expire in 2011. A second law, adopted in May 2003, accelerated some changes in the 2001 law and introduced new reductions in taxes on investment income: Jobs and Growth Tax Relief Reconciliation Act of 2003, Public Law 108-27 (May 28, 2003). Further changes were made in a law adopted in October 2004: Working Families Tax Relief Act, Public Law 108-311 (October 4, 2004). The Bush administration claimed that tax reductions would spur growth, thus actually boosting revenue in the long run; but a "dynamic analysis" commissioned by the administration showed this claim to be unsustainable. Jason Furman, *A Short Guide to Dynamic Scoring* (Washington, DC: Center on Budget and Policy Priorities, July 27, 2006).

9. Gallup poll, October 5–7, 2001.

10. Gallup poll, November 8–10, 2002.

11. Gallup poll, January 28, 2003.

12. Bowman, *Public Opinion on Taxes*, 51.

13. Ibid., 34.

14. David M. Walker, *Managing in the New Millennium: Testimony before the Senate Committee on Governmental Affairs*, GAO/T-GGD-00-121 (Washington: General Accounting Office, March 29, 2000).

15. Congressional Budget Office, *The Long-Term Budget Outlook* (Washington, DC: Congressional Budget Office, December 2005).

16. Theda Skocpol, *Social Policy in the United States* (Princeton, NJ: Princeton University Press, 1995), 278–281.

17. Alasdair Roberts, "In the Eye of the Storm? Societal Aging and the Future of Public Service Reform," *Public Administration Review* 63, no. 6 (2003): 720–733.

18. Congressional Budget Office, *The Long-Term Budget Outlook.*

19. In 2007 Professor Martin Feldstein, former chief economic adviser to President Ronald Reagan, suggested that a reasonable target for defense expenditure was 6 percent of GDP. Feldstein suggested that this increase could be accomplished partly by avoiding any real increase in nondefense discretionary spending. Martin Feldstein, "The Underfunded Pentagon," *Foreign Affairs* 86, no. 2 (2007): 134–140.

20. Projections that showed continued surpluses often made heroic assumptions about the federal government's ability to restrain expenditure.

21. Henderson, "Why Spending Has Got to Give," 13.

22. Nondefense, nonentitlement spending grew from 3.1 percent of GDP in 2000 to 3.5 percent of GDP in 2005, according to the Congressional Budget Office's estimate.

23. Congressional Budget Office, *An Analysis of the President's Budgetary Proposals for Fiscal Year 2007* (Washington, DC: Congressional Budget Office, March 2006), 15–22. Statistics on the percentage growth of homeland-security programs since 2001 may not convey this reality sufficiently. It may be that in certain areas spending has grown "hugely" (as David Benjamin and Steven Simon argue) in percentage terms, but in some areas pre-9/11 expenditure was negligible. Daniel Benjamin and Steven Simon, *The Next Attack: The Failure of the War on Terror and Blueprint for Getting It Right* (New York: Times Books, 2005), 249.

24. Clark Kent Ervin, *Open Target: Where America Is Vulnerable to Attack* (New York: Palgrave Macmillan, 2006), 225–227.

25. General Accounting Office, *Aviation Security: Long-Standing Problems Impair Airport Screeners' Performance*, GAO/RCED-00-75 (Washington, DC: General Accounting Office, 2000), 41. See also Michael Moss and Leslie Eaton, "Security Firms Ever Mindful to Cut Costs," *New York Times*, November 15, 2001, B1.

26. "Now the Hard Part: Make Air-Security Plan Work," *USA Today*, November 19, 2001, 14A; Aviation and Transportation Security Act, Public Law 107-71, signed by President Bush on November 19, 2001.

27. The original cap of forty-five thousand screeners was contained in the Homeland Security Appropriations for FY 2004, Public Law 108-90, October 2003. It was repeated in subsequent appropriation bills.

28. Ervin, *Open Target*, 115.

29. The appropriation bill for fiscal year 2006 provided funding for only forty-three thousand screeners.

30. General Accounting Office, *Aviation Security: Challenges Exist in Stabilizing and Enhancing Passenger and Baggage Screening Operations*, GAO-04-440T (Washington, DC: General Accounting Office, February 12, 2004); Government Accountability Office, *Aviation Security: Enhancements Made in Passenger and Checked Baggage Screening*, GAO-06-371T (Washington, DC: Government Accountability Office, April 4, 2006). Turnover rates for government and private industry are collected by the federal Bureau of Labor Statistics and are summarized by Nobscot Corporation on its website, http://www.nobscot.com/survey/index.cfm.

31. Department of Homeland Security, *Follow-Up Audit of Passenger and Baggage Screening Procedures at Domestic Airports*, OIG-05-16 (Washington, DC: Office of the Inspector General, Department of Homeland Security, March 2005).

32. Government Accountability Office, *Aviation Security: Enhancements Made*, 23, 27. In December 2005, members of the 9/11 Commission criticized Congress for failing to provide funding that would allow faster adoption of improved screening technologies. 9/11 Public Discourse Project, *Final Report on 9/11 Commission Recommendations* (Washington, DC: 9/11 Public Discourse Project, December 2005).

33. General Accounting Office, *Aviation Security: Challenges Exist*, 3, 32, 36.

34. Spencer Hsu, "DHS Terror Research Agency Struggling," *Washington Post*, August 20, 2006, A8.

35. Two key programs—the National Bioterrorism Hospital Preparedness Program and the Centers for Disease Control's Cooperative Agreement on Public Health Preparedness and Emergency Response—were frozen or reduced during President Bush's second term. For references to the need for "tough choices" among "competing priorities," see Mike Leavitt, *Releasing the HHS Proposed Budget for FY 2006* (Washington, DC: Department of Health and Human Services, February 7, 2005). Centers for Disease Control and Prevention, *CDC FY 2006 and FY 2007 Budget Fact Sheet* (Atlanta: Centers for Disease Control and Prevention, March 31, 2006).

36. David Rosner and Gerald E. Markowitz, *Are We Ready? Public Health since 9/11* (Berkeley: University of California Press, 2006), 160.

37. Government Accountability Office, *Passenger Rail Security: Enhanced Federal Leadership Needed to Prioritize and Guide Security Efforts*, GAO-05-851 (Washington, DC: Government Accountability Office, September 2005).

38. The estimate was made by the Coast Guard in 2002. See the *Federal Register*, December 30, 2002, p. 79745. In 2002 the GAO reported that demand for grants substantially exceeded supply. General Accounting Office, *Port Security: Nation Faces Formidable Challenges in Making New Initiatives Successful*, GAO-02-993T (Washington, DC: General Accounting Office, August 5, 2002), 14–15. On grant spending up to 2005, see Government Accountability Office, *Risk Management: Further Refinements Needed to Assess Risks and Prioritize Protective Measures at Ports and Other Critical Infrastructure*, GAO-06-91 (Washington, DC: Government Accountability Office, December 2005), 3, 51.

39. Andrea Stone, "Readiness Problems Plague Coast Guard," *USA Today*, May 16, 2000, 19A.

40. Thomas H. Collins, *Statement on Deepwater Implementation before the Subcommittee on Coast Guard and Maritime Transportation* (Washington, DC: United States Coast Guard, April 20, 2005); James Jay Carafano and Laura Keith, *Learning Katrina's Lessons: Coast Guard Modernization Is a Must*, Backgrounder 1950 (Washington, DC: Heritage Foundation, July 7, 2006); Anne Laurent, "The Curse of Can-Do," *Government Executive* 32, no. 3 (2000): 41–47.

41. A 1997 GAO report suggested that the Coast Guard would be compelled to consider eliminating services or introducing user fees for some services. General Accounting Office, *Coast Guard: Challenges for Addressing Budget Constraints*, GAO/RCED-97-110 (Washington, DC: General Accounting Office, May 1997).

42. Laurent, "The Curse of Can-Do"; Ronald O'Rourke, *Coast Guard Deepwater Program: Background, Oversight Issues, and Options for Congress* (Washington, DC: Congressional Research Service, December 18, 2005), 2; Stephen Caldwell, *Coast Guard: Status of Efforts to Improve Deepwater Program Management*, GAO-07-575T (Washington, DC: Government Accountability Office, March 8, 2007), 10.

43. U.S. Department of Transportation, *Coast Guard Deepwater Acquisition Project Designated as Government Reinvention Laboratory* (Washington, DC: U.S. Department of Transportation, Office of Public Affairs, June 24, 1999). For details of the flexibility allowed to contractors by the Clinton administration, see Office of the Inspector General, *Acquisition of the National Security Cutter*, OIG-07-23 (Washington, DC: Department of Homeland Security, January 2007), appendix C.

44. See, for example, Eric Pianin, "GOP Targets 61 Programs for Cuts," *Washington Post*, February 2, 2000, A19.

45. Government Accountability Office, *Coast Guard: Observations on Agency Priorities in Fiscal Year 2006 Budget Request*, GAO-05-364T (Washington, DC: Government Accountability Office, March 17, 2005), 16.

46. General Accounting Office, *Coast Guard: Deepwater Program Acquisition Schedule Update Needed*, GAO-04-695 (Washington, DC: General Accounting Office, June 2004).

47. Caldwell, *Coast Guard*, 3; Office of the Inspector General, *Maritime Patrol*

*Boat Modernization Project,* OIG-07-27 (Washington, DC: Department of Homeland Security, February 2007); Office of the Inspector General, *Acquisition of the National Security Cutter.*

48. In February 2007, the Homeland Security Department's inspector general observed that the Coast Guard had adopted a "high-risk" procurement model and that staffing shortfalls in the department reduced the capacity to manage such risks. Richard Skinner, *Statement before the House Committee on Oversight and Government Reform* (Washington, DC: Department of Homeland Security, Office of the Inspector General, February 8, 2007). Eric Lipton, "Coast Guard to Manage Fleet Modernization," *New York Times,* April 18, 2007.

49. Collins, *Statement on Deepwater Implementation.* The Coast Guard's measure of defense readiness declined in each year between 2003 and 2006. U.S. Coast Guard, *2008 Budget in Brief and Performance Report* (Washington, DC: U.S. Coast Guard, February 2007), 27. The fleet, said homeland-security specialist Stephen Flynn, a former Coast Guard officer, operates "at the level, in many instances, of a Third World Navy." Mimi Hall, "Coast Guard Plagued by Breakdowns," *USA Today,* July 5, 2005.

50. General Accounting Office, *INS' Southwest Border Strategy,* GAO-01-842 (Washington, DC: General Accounting Office, August 2001).

51. Department of Justice, *Follow-Up Report on the Border Patrol's Efforts to Improve Northern Border Security,* I-2002-004 (Washington, DC: Department of Justice, Office of the Inspector General, February 2002), 1.

52. National Commission on Terrorist Attacks upon the United States, *Final Report* (New York: Barnes and Noble Books, 2004), 81.

53. Budget data is provided in Blas Nuñez-Neto, *Border Security: The Role of the U.S. Border Patrol,* RL32562 (Washington, DC: Congressional Research Service, May 10, 2005), 6. The deflator is provided in table 10.1 of the Historical Tables for the Fiscal Year 2007 Budget.

54. Congress's target was set in the Intelligence Reform and Terrorism Prevention Act of 2004, Public Law 108-458, section 5202.

55. Department of Homeland Security, "Transcript of Press Conference with Acting Secretary of Homeland Security Admiral James Loy on the FY 2006 Budget" (Washington, DC: Department of Homeland Security, February 7, 2005). Congress eventually funded fifteen hundred new positions for fiscal year 2006, still short of its own target.

56. George W. Bush, "President Bush Addresses the Nation on Immigration Reform" (Washington, DC: Executive Office of the President, May 15, 2006). On the fifth anniversary of the 9/11 attacks, the Border Patrol had 11,032 agents on the southwest border and 919 on the northern border. Government Accountability Office, *Homeland Security: Information on Training New Border Patrol Agents,* GAO-07-540R (Washington, DC: Government Accountability Office, March 30, 2007), 6. This was an increase of 1,971 agents on the southwest border since September 2001 and an increase of 649 on the northern border. Transactional Records Access Clearinghouse, *Border Patrol Expands but Growth Rate after 9/11 Much Less than Before* (Syra-

cuse, NY: Transactional Records Access Clearinghouse, 2005), available online at http://trac.syr.edu/immigration/reports/143/.

57. Thomas H. Kean, Lee Hamilton, and Benjamin Rhodes, *Without Precedent: The Inside Story of the 9/11 Commission* (New York: Knopf, 2006), 334–335, 339.

58. Anthony Wier, William Hoehn, and Matthew Bunn, *Threat Reduction Funding in the Bush Administration: Claims and Counterclaims in the First Presidential Debate* (Cambridge, MA: Harvard University, October 6, 2004).

59. Matthew Bunn and Anthony Wier, *Securing the Bomb 2006* (Cambridge, MA: Kennedy School of Government, July 2006), 105.

60. U.S. Commission on National Security/21st Century, *Road Map for National Security: Imperative for Change* (Washington, DC: U.S. Commission on National Security/21st Century, February 15, 2001), vii–viii, 10. The 9/11 Commission reached similar conclusions about the costs of bureaucratic fragmentation. National Commission on Terrorist Attacks, *Final Report.*

61. Homeland Security Act, Public Law 107-296, signed by President Bush on November 25, 2002.

62. Twenty agencies were taken from six federal departments. FEMA, which had been independent of any department, was also included in the merger. Another agency had been a component of the General Services Administration, also an independent entity.

63. George W. Bush, "Address to a Joint Session of Congress and the American People" (Washington, DC: Executive Office of the President, September 20, 2001).

64. Harold Relyea, *Homeland Security: Department Organization and Management—Implementation Phase,* RL31751 (Washington, DC: Congressional Research Service, January 3, 2005), 1–2. Ridge's predicament was complicated by the lack of legal or constitutional authority; he could trade only on his status as a presidential adviser.

65. Alison Mitchell, "Official Urges Combining Several Agencies to Create One That Protects Borders," *New York Times,* January 11, 2002, 8; John J. Miller, "The Impossible Position of Tom Ridge," *National Review,* June 17, 2002, 34–37.

66. Richard A. Clarke, *Against All Enemies: Inside America's War on Terror* (New York: Free Press, 2004), 24.

67. Michael Chertoff, "Remarks at the George Washington University Homeland Security Policy Institute" (Washington, DC: Department of Homeland Security, March 16, 2005).

68. James Jay Carafano and David Heyman, *DHS 2.0: Rethinking the Department of Homeland Security* (Washington, DC: Heritage Foundation, December 2004), 7. The study was undertaken by the Heritage Foundation and the Center for Strategic and International Studies.

69. John Mintz, "Infighting Blamed for Reducing Effectiveness," *Washington Post,* February 2, 2005, A1.

70. Jason Peckenpaugh, "ICE Releasing Illegal Aliens on Nationwide Basis," *Government Executive,* July 2, 2004; Justin Rood, "Homeland Security Agency Be-

gins Hiring after Lengthy Hiatus," *Government Executive,* August 3, 2005; Justin Rood, Chris Strohm, and Katherine McIntire Peters, "Wasted Year," *Government Executive,* March 1, 2006, 38–52.

71. Department of Homeland Security, *Review of the Status of Department of Homeland Security Efforts to Address Its Major Management Challenges,* OIG-04-21 (Washington, DC: Office of the Inspector General, March 2004); Department of Homeland Security, *Major Management Challenges Facing the Department of Homeland Security,* OIG-06-14 (Washington, DC: Office of the Inspector General, December 2005).

72. Relyea, *Homeland Security,* 10.

73. Thomas E. Mann and Norman J. Ornstein, *The Broken Branch: How Congress Is Failing America* (New York: Oxford University Press, 2006), 131–134.

74. In 1996, the Federal Aviation Administration was exempted from civil-service rules. Although it was not obliged to do so, the Clinton administration continued to comply with statutory requirements on union representation and collective bargaining. For a broader discussion of Clinton-era attempts at reform, and its relationship with federal unions, see Richard K. Johnson, "National Performance Review and Reinvention: Should It 'Reinvent' Our Federal Labor-Management Relations?" *Federal Depository Library Electronic Collection* 40, no. 2 (1996); Donald P. Moynihan, "Homeland Security and the U.S. Public Management Policy Agenda," *Governance* 18, no. 2 (2005): 171–196. On Bush policies, see George Nesterczuk, Donald Devine, and Robert Moffit, *Taking Charge of Federal Personnel* (Washington, DC: Heritage Foundation, January 10, 2001), available online at http://www.heritage .org/Research/GovernmentReform/BG1404.cfm (accessed September 23, 2006); George Nesterczuk, *A Successful Start for the Department of Homeland Security Requires Management Flexibility* (Washington, DC: Heritage Foundation, July 19, 2002), available online at http://www.heritage.org/Research/HomelandDefense/BG1572 .cfm (accessed September 24, 2006). In fact, the Bush administration made proposals to overhaul civil-service legislation *before* 9/11, but these proposals encountered stiff resistance. Jonathan Bruel, "Three Bush Administration Management Reform Initiatives," *Public Administration Review* 67, no. 1 (2007): 23–24.

75. Diane E. Watson, "News Release: Congresswoman Watson Opposes Flawed Homeland Security Act" (Washington, DC: Office of Congresswoman Diane Watson, November 14, 2002). Congresswoman Watson made this comment about HR 5710, the final version of the homeland-security bill.

76. *National Treasury Employees Union et al. v. Michael Chertoff et al.,* U.S. District Court for the District of Columbia, Civil Action No. 2005-0201, judgment issued August 12, 2005.

77. *National Treasury Employees Union et al. v. Michael Chertoff,* U.S. Court of Appeals for the District of Columbia, No. 05-5436, judgment issued June 27, 2006. The court agreed that collective-bargaining rights had not been protected but said that the complaint on appeals procedures was premature.

78. Brittany Ballenstedt, "DHS Scales Back Pay for Performance Ambitions," *Government Executive,* February 28, 2007.

79. Partnership for Public Service, *Best Places to Work 2005* (Washington, DC: Partnership for Public Service, 2005), available online at http://www.ourpublic service.org/research/research_show.htm?doc_id=297293 (accessed August 8, 2006).

80. Results of the Office of Personnel Management's 2006 Federal Human Capital Survey were released in January 2007. Of thirty-six agencies included in the survey, DHS ranked last in job satisfaction, leadership, and results-oriented culture and thirty-third in talent management.

81. Ervin, *Open Target*, 19. There was little evidence, a Century Foundation study concluded in 2004, that the creation of DHS had given Ridge "more clout in pulling disparate functions together." Donald Kettl, ed., *The Department of Homeland Security's First Year: A Report Card* (New York: Century Foundation, 2004), 7.

82. On the inexperience of senior DHS personnel, see Mintz, "Infighting Blamed for Reducing Effectiveness."

83. Wilson P. Dizard, "Who's at Home for DHS," *GCN.com*, April 18, 2005, http://www.gcn.com/print/24_8/35527-1.html (accessed July 31, 2006).

84. Eric Lipton, "Former Antiterror Officials Find Industry Pays Better," *New York Times*, June 18, 2006; Eric Lipton, "Homeland Security Inc.," *New York Times*, June 19, 2006.

85. Homeland Security Advisory Council, *Report of the Culture Task Force* (Washington, DC: Homeland Security Advisory Council, January 2007).

86. Norman Ornstein and Thomas Mann, *Perspectives on House Reform of Homeland Security* (Washington, DC: American Enterprise Institute, May 19, 2003); Mark Preston and Susan Crabtree, "Turf Battles Erupt over New Department," *Roll Call*, June 10, 2002.

87. Lee Hamilton, *Testimony before the Select Committee on Homeland Security* (Washington, DC: Wilson International Center for Scholars, September 9, 2003), 5.

88. National Commission on Terrorist Attacks, *Final Report*, 419–421.

89. Mann and Ornstein, *The Broken Branch*, 150–151. Three years after the passage of the Homeland Security Act, Congress's committee system looked "much as it did before 9/11." John Fortier, "Security Mishmash," *The Hill*, October 26, 2005. For a more optimistic view of the reforms, see Chris Strohm, "Further Streamlining of Homeland Security Oversight Unlikely," *GovExec.com*, September 11, 2006, http://www.govexec.com/story_page.cfm?articleid=34985&dcn=todaysnews (accessed September 15, 2006).

90. Richard A. Posner, *Remaking Domestic Intelligence*, Hoover Institution Press Publication 541 (Stanford, CA: Hoover Institution Press, 2005), 50.

91. The history of intelligence reform is canvassed by Amy B. Zegart, *Flawed by Design: The Evolution of the CIA, JCS, and NSC* (Stanford, CA: Stanford University Press, 1999).

92. See Commission on Intelligence Capabilities of the United States Regarding Weapons of Mass Destruction, *Report to the President* (Washington, DC: Commission on Intelligence Capabilities, March 31, 2005), 288–295; Helen Fessenden, "The Limits of Intelligence Reform," *Foreign Affairs* 84, no. 6 (2005): 106–120; Karen DeYoung, "A Fight against Terrorism—and Disorganization," *Washington Post*,

August 9, 2006, A1; Scott Shane, "Year into Revamped Spying, Troubles and Some Progress," *New York Times,* February 28, 2006, 12; Bill Gertz, "Intelligence Intransigence," *Washington Times,* February 6, 2006; Amy B. Zegart, "American Intelligence: Still Stupid," *Los Angeles Times,* September 17, 2006; Mark Lowenthal, *Intelligence: From Secrets to Policy,* 3rd ed. (Washington, DC: CQ Press, 2006), 276–279. "Our government," said a 2006 Markle Foundation study of antiterror information-sharing, "seems to have lost its sense of the broader mission." Markle Foundation Task Force, *Mobilizing Information to Prevent Terrorism* (New York: Markle Foundation, July 2006), 1.

93. Guy Dinmore, "U.S. Spy Chief Quits Post to Join Rice," *Financial Times,* January 5, 2007, 7.

94. "In terms of their effects on administrative costs, size of staff, productivity, or spending, most major reorganization efforts have been described by outsiders, and frequently by participants, as substantial failures." James G. March, Johan P. Olson, and John P. Olsen, "Organizing Political Life: What Administrative Reorganization Tells Us about Government," *American Political Science Review* 77, no. 2 (1983): 288. See also General Accounting Office, *Implementation: The Missing Link in Planning Reorganizations,* GGD-81-57 (Washington, DC: General Accounting Office, March 20, 1981); James P. Pfiffner, *The Strategic Presidency: Hitting the Ground Running,* 2nd ed. (Lawrence: University Press of Kansas, 1996), 91.

95. Canada created a new Department of Public Safety and Emergency Preparedness.

96. In the United Kingdom, decisions over the design of the "machinery of government" have been described as a form of executive self-regulation. Iain Maclean, *Machinery of Government Reform: Principles and Practice* (Oxford, UK: ESRC Whitehall Programme, 1997), available online at http://www.nuff.ox.ac.uk/politics/whitehall/Machinery.html (accessed September 4, 2006). A Westminster view of the aims of reorganization is provided in a recent World Bank summary: Neil Parison and Nick Manning, *Machinery of Government* (Washington, DC: World Bank, 2000), available online at http://web.worldbank.org/WBSITE/EXTERNAL/TOPICS/EXTPUBLICSECTORANDGOVERNANCE/EXTADMINISTRATIVEANDCIVILSERVICEREFORM/0,,contentMDK:20132487~menuPK:1919141~pagePK:210058~piPK:210062~theSitePK:286367,00.html (accessed September 4, 2006).

97. Donald Kettl, *System under Stress: Homeland Security and American Politics* (Washington, DC: CQ Press, 2004), 122. Herbert Emmerich observed that the drive for autonomy was "an apparently innate characteristic" of bureaus. Herbert Emmerich, *Federal Organization and Administrative Management* (Tuscaloosa: University of Alabama Press, 1971), 17.

98. Michael Nelson, "A Short, Ironic History of American National Bureaucracy," *Journal of Politics* 44, no. 3 (1982): 755.

99. Edward Page, *Political Authority and Bureaucratic Power: A Comparative Analysis* (Knoxville: University of Tennessee Press, 1985), 63–64; Daniel P. Carpenter, *The Forging of Bureaucratic Autonomy: Reputations, Networks, and Policy Innovation in Executive Agencies, 1862–1928* (Princeton, NJ: Princeton University Press, 2001),

18–20. By contrast, the military has been encouraged to develop such a cadre: under the Defense Reorganization Act of 1986, field officers cannot be promoted to the grade of flag officer until they have undertaken a joint duty assignment.

100. Kelly Chang, David Lewis, and Nolan McCarty, "The Tenure of Political Appointees" (paper presented at the meeting of the Midwest Political Science Association, University of Wisconsin, Madison, April 2001), 30.

101. Richard Cheney, "Vice President Cheney's Remarks in Sheboygan Falls, Wisconsin" (Washington, DC: Executive Office of the President, September 11, 2004).

102. George W. Bush, "Message to the Congress of the United States" (Washington, DC: Executive Office of the President, June 18, 2002).

103. Lauren Edelman, "Legal Environments and Organizational Governance," *American Journal of Sociology* 95, no. 6 (1990): 1401–1440; Frank Dobbin and Frank Sutton, "The Strength of a Weak State: The Rights Revolution and the Rise of Human Resources Management Divisions," *American Journal of Sociology* 104, no. 2 (1998): 441–476.

104. On unionization trends, see Richard Freeman, "Unionism Comes to the Public Sector," *Journal of Economic Literature* 24, no. 1 (1986): 45–46; Melvin Reder, "The Rise and Fall of Unions: The Public Sector and the Private," *Journal of Economic Perspectives* 2, no. 2 (1988): 103–104; Chester Newland, "Public Personnel Administration: Legalistic Reforms vs. Effectiveness, Efficiency and Economy," *Public Administration Review* 36, no. 5 (1976): 534–537. On the policy influence of unions, see Moynihan, "Homeland Security and the U.S. Public Management Policy Agenda," 174.

105. Fortier, "Security Mishmash," 303.

106. Frank Baumgartner, Bryan Jones, and Michael MacLeod, "The Evolution of Legislative Jurisdictions," *Journal of Politics* 62, no. 2 (2000): 336.

107. On the number of committees and staffing, see Steven Haeberle, "The Institutionalization of the Subcommittee in the United States House of Representatives," *Journal of Politics* 40, no. 4 (1978): 1059; Rosenbloom, *Building a Legislative-Centered Public Administration*, 78; Donald Wolfensberger, *A Reality Check on the Republican House Reform Revolution at the Decade Mark* (Washington, DC: Woodrow Wilson International Center for Scholars, January 24, 2005), 9. On expenditure and activity, and the phenomenon of institutionalization within the committee system, see Nelson Polsby, "The Institutionalization of the U.S. House of Representatives," *American Political Science Review* 62, no. 1 (1968): 144–168; Thomas Cavanagh, "The Dispersion of Authority in the House of Representatives," *Political Science Quarterly* 97, no. 4 (1983): 623–637. On resistance to reform, see Mann and Ornstein, *The Broken Branch*, 149–150.

108. Brian Riedl, *$20,000 per Household: The Highest Level of Federal Spending since World War II*, Backgrounder #1710 (Washington, DC: Heritage Foundation, December 3, 2003).

109. The ratio does not include civilian workers in the federal defense establishment or employees of the U.S. Postal Service. Data is provided in statistical

abstract of the U.S. Census Bureau, http://www.census.gov/prod/www/abs/statab.html.

110. John D. Donahue, *Disunited States* (New York: Basic Books, 1997), 10. Donahue excludes federal transfer payments in his calculation. See also Thomas Gais and James Fossett, "Federalism and the Executive Branch," in *The Executive Branch*, ed. Joel Aberbach and Mark Peterson, 486–524 (New York: Oxford University Press, 2006), 502–503.

111. For a pessimistic view of the federal government's capacity to influence state and local policy, see John J. DiIulio and Donald F. Kettl, *Fine Print: The Contract with America, Devolution, and the Administrative Realities of American Federalism* (Washington, DC: Brookings Institution Press, 1995), 18.

112. For a summary of writing on the backlash against federal controls, see Ann Bowman and George Krause, "Measuring Policy Centralization in U.S. Intergovernmental Relations," *American Politics Research* 31, no. 3 (2003): 304. On the decline of legitimacy of the federal government relative to state and local governments, see Donahue, *Disunited States*, 12. On the rising strength of intergovernmental lobbies, see Gais and Fossett, "Federalism and the Executive Branch," 502–504, 514. For a discussion of the federal-state relations at the moment of the 9/11 attacks, see Peter Eisenger, "Imperfect Federalism: The Intergovernmental Partnership for Homeland Security," *Public Administration Review* 66, no. 4 (2006): 537–538.

113. For example, see General Accounting Office, *Federal Assistance: Grant System Continues to Be Highly Fragmented*, GAO-03-718T (Washington, DC: General Accounting Office, April 29, 2003), 8–9.

114. The language was that of the National Conference of State Legislatures.

115. Dennis Bailey, *The Open Society Paradox* (Washington, DC: Brassey's, 2004), 60.

116. Office of Homeland Security, *National Strategy for Homeland Security* (Washington, DC: Executive Office of the President, July 16, 2002), 49.

117. National Commission on Terrorist Attacks, *Final Report*, 390.

118. Executive Office of the President, *Statement of Administration Policy on HR 10* (Washington, DC: Executive Office of the President, October 7, 2004), 2.

119. Intelligence Reform and Terrorism Prevention Act of 2004, sections 7211 and 7212.

120. Kathy Kiely, "House Passes Bill That Would Tighten Driver's License Rules," *USA Today*, February 11, 2005, 8A.

121. See, for example, the McKinsey studies of the response of the New York Fire and Police Departments: McKinsey & Company, *Improving NYPD Emergency Preparedness and Response* (New York: McKinsey & Company, August 19, 2002); McKinsey & Company, *Increasing FDNY's Preparedness* (New York: McKinsey & Company, August 19, 2002).

122. Council on Foreign Relations, *Emergency Responders: Drastically Underfunded, Dangerously Unprepared* (Washington, DC: Council on Foreign Relations, June 2003), 8. See also Brian A. Jackson, *Protecting Emergency Responders: Lessons*

*Learned from Terrorist Attacks* (Santa Monica, CA: Rand, 2002); Tom LaTourrette, *Protecting Emergency Responders* (Santa Monica, CA: Rand, Science and Technology Policy Institute, 2003).

123. Department of Homeland Security, *Nationwide Plan Review Phase 2 Report* (Washington, DC: Department of Homeland Security, June 16, 2006), xii.

124. Government Accountability Office, *DHS' Efforts to Enhance First Responders' All-Hazards Capabilities Continue to Evolve*, GAO-05-652 (Washington, DC: Government Accountability Office, July 2005), fig. 7. The three largest grant programs, accounting for three-quarters of spending in 2005, were the State Homeland Security Grant Program, the Urban Area Security Initiative, and the Law Enforcement Terrorism Prevention Program.

125. Department of Homeland Security, *The State of Indiana's Management of State Homeland Security Grants Awarded during Fiscal Year 2002 and 2003*, OIG-06-19 (Washington, DC: Office of Inspector General, December 2005), 1.

126. House Select Committee on Homeland Security, *An Analysis of First Responder Grant Funding* (Washington, DC: House Select Committee on Homeland Security, April 2004); Government Accountability Office, *DHS' Efforts to Enhance First Responders' All-Hazards Capabilities Continue to Evolve*; Michael B. D'Arcy and Brookings Institution, *Protecting the Homeland, 2006/2007* (Washington, DC: Brookings Institution Press, 2006), 120.

127. House Select Committee on Homeland Security, *An Analysis of First Responder Grant Funding*, 7. DHS released its interim "National Preparedness Goal" in 2005: Department of Homeland Security, *Interim National Preparedness Goal* (Washington, DC: Department of Homeland Security, March 31, 2005).

128. Veronique de Rugy, *What Does Homeland Security Spending Buy?* Working Paper 107 (Washington, DC: American Enterprise Institute, April 2005), 17.

129. House Select Committee on Homeland Security, *An Analysis of First Responder Grant Funding*, 4–5.

130. National Commission on Terrorist Attacks, *Final Report*, 396.

131. Senator Patrick Leahy, "News Release: Bush Budget Would Shortchange Smaller States" (Washington, DC: Office of Senator Patrick Leahy, February 2, 2004).

132. *Congressional Record*, July 12, 2005.

133. House Select Committee on Homeland Security, *An Analysis of First Responder Grant Funding*, 4; Shawn Reese, *Risk-Based Funding in Homeland Security Grant Legislation*, RL33050 (Washington, DC: Congressional Research Service, August 29, 2005), 2.

134. Department of Homeland Security, *Review of the Port Security Grant Program*, OIG-05-10 (Washington, DC: Office of Inspector General, January 2005), 4.

135. De Rugy, *What Does Homeland Security Spending Buy?* 26.

136. Department of Homeland Security, "News Release: DHS Introduces Risk-Based Formula for Urban Areas Security Initiative Grants" (Washington, DC: Department of Homeland Security, January 3, 2006).

137. Department of Homeland Security, *Homeland Security Grant Program:*

*Allocation Methodology* (Washington, DC: Department of Homeland Security, May 30, 2006).

138. Transcript, "Homeland Security Chief Says U.S. Prepared for 2006 Storm Season," *NewsHour with Jim Lehrer,* PBS, June 1, 2006.

139. Michael Saul, "Feds to City: Drop Dead," *Daily News,* May 31, 2006.

140. Herman B. Leonard and Arnold M. Howitt, "Katrina as Prelude: Preparing for and Responding to Katrina-Class Disturbances in the United States," *Journal of Homeland Security and Emergency Management* 3, no. 2 (2006): 2.

141. Executive Office of the President, *National Security Strategy of the United States* (Washington, DC: Executive Office of the President, September 17, 2002), 6. This was affirmed in a later study by the Government Accountability Office: Government Accountability Office, *DHS' Efforts to Enhance First Responders' All-Hazards Capabilities Continue to Evolve,* 5.

142. Mark Fischetti, "Drowning New Orleans," *Scientific American,* October 2001, 76.

143. For an outstanding description of the immediate aftermath, see Brinkley, *The Great Deluge.*

144. Ervin, *Open Target,* 182.

145. In a *Newsweek* poll conducted September 29–30, 2005, 57 percent of respondents said that the federal government's failures in responding to Katrina were the result of bad management or cronyism.

146. The firm, New Bridge Strategies, was created in 2003. The webpage that described its aims, http://www.newbridgestrategies.com/whoweare.asp, was removed in 2005.

147. Spencer Hsu, "Leaders Lacking Disaster Experience; 'Brain Drain' at Agency Cited," *Washington Post,* September 9, 2005, A1; Senate Homeland Security and Governmental Affairs Committee, *Hurricane Katrina: A Nation Still Unprepared* (Washington, DC: Senate Homeland Security and Governmental Affairs Committee, May 2006), 214–215.

148. David Cohen, "Amateur Government," *Journal of Public Administration Research and Theory* 8, no. 4 (1998): 450–497; James Pfiffner, "Political Appointees and Career Executives: The Democracy-Bureaucracy Nexus in the Third Century," *Public Administration Review* 47, no. 1 (1987): 57–65; Paul Charles Light, *Thickening Government: Federal Hierarchy and the Diffusion of Accountability* (Washington, DC: Brookings Institution Press, 1995). David Lewis finds that agencies led by political appointees get systematically lower grades for management performance than those led by career officials. David E. Lewis, *Political Appointments, Bureau Chiefs, and Federal Management Performance* (Princeton, NJ: Woodrow Wilson School of Public and International Affairs, 2005).

149. John Barry, "The Prologue, and Maybe the Coda," *New York Times,* September 4, 2005. For a more detailed description of the response to the 1927 flood, see Kevin Kosar, *Disaster Response and Appointment of a Recovery Czar: The Executive Branch's Response to the Flood of 1927,* RL33126 (Washington, DC: Congressional Research Service, October 25, 2005).

150. Richard Sylves and William Cumming, "FEMA's Path to Homeland Security: 1979–2003," *Journal of Homeland Security and Emergency Management* 1, no. 2 (2004): 1.

151. Leonard and Howitt, "Katrina as Prelude," 4.

152. General Accounting Office, *Disaster Assistance: Information on Federal Costs and Approaches for Reducing Them*, GAO/T-RCED-98-139 (Washington, DC: General Accounting Office, March 26, 1998).

153. Thomas Garrett and Russell Sobel, "The Political Economy of FEMA Disaster Payments," *Economic Inquiry* 41, no. 3 (2003): 496–509.

154. For example, see General Accounting Office, *Disaster Assistance: Improvements Needed in Determining Eligibility for Public Assistance*, GAO/T-RCED-96-166 (Washington, DC: General Accounting Office, April 30, 1996).

155. Joe M. Allbaugh, *Testimony before the Veterans Affairs, Housing and Urban Development and Independent Agencies Subcommittee of the Senate Appropriations Committee* (Washington, DC: Federal Emergency Management Agency, May 16, 2001), available online at http://www.fema.gov/library/jma051601.shtm (accessed March 20, 2006).

156. Anthony Crupi, "Cable News Nets, Weather Channel Earn Stunning Ratings for Katrina Coverage," *MediaWeek,* August 31, 2005. In the week following landfall, Fox News experienced a 65 percent increase in viewership; CNN, a 246 percent increase. Coverage in the print media also soared. For a discussion of post-Katrina newspaper coverage, and the negative perceptions of federal government that were often conveyed within this coverage, see Freedman Consulting, *Covering Katrina: Trends in Katrina Media Coverage* (Washington, DC: Partnership for Public Service, August 18, 2006).

157. Brinkley, *The Great Deluge,* 454.

158. Transcript, *Anderson Cooper 360 Degrees,* CNN, September 1, 2005, available online at http://transcripts.cnn.com/TRANSCRIPTS/0509/01/acd.01.html (accessed August 6, 2006).

159. A Pew Research Center poll conducted September 6–7, 2005, found that 67 percent of respondents believed that President Bush could have done more in relief efforts. The federal government's performance was rated more harshly than that of state and local governments. In an Associated Press/Ipsos poll conducted September 16–18, 2005, 70 percent of Americans said that the federal government should have been better prepared for Katrina. A Fox News/Opinion Dynamics poll conducted September 13–14, 2005, found that 48 percent of registered voters thought that the federal government had sole or shared responsibility for post-Katrina problems. A Gallup poll conducted September 5–6, 2005, found that 31 percent of respondents thought that President Bush and federal agencies were most responsible for post-Katrina problems; 25 percent held state and local officials most responsible.

160. Senate Homeland Security and Governmental Affairs Committee, *Hurricane Katrina,* 217.

161. Ibid., 216; Select Bipartisan Committee, *A Failure of Initiative* (Washing-

ton, DC: Select Bipartisan Committee to Investigate the Preparation for and Response to Hurricane Katrina, February 2006), 151–158; Robert Block, "U.S. Had Plan for Crisis Like Katrina," *Wall Street Journal*, September 19, 2005, A3.

162. Homeland Security Advisory Council, *Summary of Inaugural Meeting* (Washington, DC: Department of Homeland Security, June 30, 2003).

163. Justin Rood, "FEMA's Decline," *Government Executive*, September 28, 2005.

164. Hsu, "Leaders Lacking Disaster Experience."

165. R. G. Edmonson, "DHS Releases National Response Plan," *Journal of Commerce Online*, January 6, 2005.

166. Department of Homeland Security, *National Response Plan* (Washington, DC: Department of Homeland Security, December 2004), i.

167. Eric Lipton, Christopher Drew, Scott Shane, and David Rohde, "Breakdowns Marked Path from Hurricane to Anarchy," *New York Times*, September 11, 2005.

168. Government Accountability Office, *Hurricane Katrina: Preliminary Observations Regarding Preparedness, Response and Recovery*, GAO-06-442T (Washington, DC: Government Accountability Office, March 8, 2006), 9, 12; Senate Homeland Security and Governmental Affairs Committee, *Hurricane Katrina*, 554–558.

169. Federal Emergency Management Agency, *Hurricane Pam Exercise Concludes* (Washington, DC: FEMA, July 23, 2004).

170. Senate Homeland Security and Governmental Affairs Committee, *Hurricane Katrina*, chap. 8; Lipton et al., "Breakdowns Marked Path from Hurricane to Anarchy."

171. Senate Homeland Security and Governmental Affairs Committee, *Hurricane Katrina*, chap. 27; Leonard and Howitt, "Katrina as Prelude," 4.

172. These are described well by Brinkley, *The Great Deluge*.

173. Leonard and Howitt, "Katrina as Prelude," 12.

174. Tom Planchet, "Katrina Blog Part II," WWLTV–New Orleans, September 2, 2005, available online at http://www.wwltv.com/local/stories/WWLBLOGII .1626ad7d.html (accessed August 10, 2006).

175. Bill Adair, "Ten Years Ago, Her Angry Plea Got Hurricane Aid Moving," *St. Petersburg Times*, August 20, 2002.

176. "Put to Katrina's Test," *Los Angeles Times*, September 11, 2005. See also Susan Glasser and Michael Grunwald, "The Steady Buildup to a City's Chaos," *Washington Post*, September 11, 2005, A1.

177. Peter Gosselin and Janet Hook, "A Comeback for Big Government," *Los Angeles Times*, September 10, 2005.

178. "Frustration Boils; Mayor Nagin, Blanco Irate about Delays," *Baton Rouge Advocate*, September 2, 2005, 1-A.

179. Transcript, *CNN Live Saturday*, CNN, September 10, 2005, available online at http://transcripts.cnn.com/TRANSCRIPTS/0509/10/cst.11.html (accessed August 10, 2006).

180. "Lt. Gen. Honore a 'John Wayne Dude,'" *CNN.com*, September 3, 2005, http://www.cnn.com/2005/US/09/02/honore.profile/ (accessed August 10, 2006).

181. "Put to Katrina's Test," *Los Angeles Times,* September 11, 2005.

182. Eric Lipton, Eric Schmitt, and Thom Shanker, "Political Issues Snarled Plans for Troop Aid," *New York Times,* September 9, 2005.

183. Senate Homeland Security and Governmental Affairs Committee, *Hurricane Katrina,* chap. 26.

184. "Put to Katrina's Test."

185. Senate Homeland Security and Governmental Affairs Committee, *Hurricane Katrina,* 487.

186. Several polls taken immediately after Katrina showed that a large majority of Americans preferred to have relief efforts funded by borrowing or cuts to other programs, rather than by tax increases.

187. Executive Office of the President, "President Discusses Hurricane Relief in Address to the Nation" (Washington, DC: Executive Office of the President, September 15, 2005).

188. Executive Office of the President, "President's Remarks during Hurricane Briefing in Texas" (Washington, DC: Executive Office of the President, September 25, 2005); Ann Scott Tyson, "Pentagon Plans to Beef Up Domestic Rapid-Response Plans," *Washington Post,* October 13, 2005, A4. Bush also suggested that active-duty military forces might be used to enforce quarantine in case of a flu epidemic. Executive Office of the President, "President Holds Press Conference" (Washington, DC: Executive Office of the President, October 4, 2005).

189. Eric Schmitt and Thom Shanker, "Military May Propose an Active-Duty Force for Relief Efforts," *New York Times,* October 11, 2005.

190. In October 2006, Bush signed the National Defense Authorization Act of 2007, which broadened the Insurrection Act by giving the federal government the authority to use the armed forces to restore order after natural disasters, epidemics, public-health emergencies, terrorist attacks, or "other conditions." See section 1076 of the act.

**Notes to Chapter 4**

1. Office of the Press Secretary, "Press Briefing by Ari Fleischer" (Washington, DC: Executive Office of the President, March 18, 2003).

2. Anne Krueger, "Trading Phobias: Governments, NGOs and the Multilateral System" (St. Leonard's, Australia: Centre for Independent Studies, 2000), available online at http://www.cis.org.au/Events/JBL/JBL00.htm (accessed March 18, 2006). Krueger was First Deputy Managing Director of the International Monetary Fund from 2001 to 2006.

3. Barry C. Lynn, *End of the Line: The Rise and Coming Fall of the Global Corporation* (New York: Doubleday, 2005), 234. A similar argument is made more briefly by Stephen Flynn, *The Continued Vulnerability of the Global Maritime Transportation System* (Washington, DC: Council on Foreign Relations, March 9, 2006), available online at http://www.cfr.org/publication/10074/continued_vulnerability_of_the_global_maritime_transportation_system.html (accessed March 9, 2006). One meas-

ure of the openness of an economy is the value of total trade (that is, exports and imports) as a percentage of GDP. For the United States, this measure increased slightly, from 8 percent to 11 percent, between 1950 and 1970. It increased to 26 percent by 2000. See Penn World Tables, http://pwt.econ.upenn.edu.

4. Stanley L. Engerman and Robert E. Gallman, *The Cambridge Economic History of the United States,* 3 vols. (New York: Cambridge University Press, 1996).

5. Jack Feinstein, "Managing Reliability in Electric Power Companies," in *Seeds of Disaster, Roots of Response,* ed. Philip E. Auerswald, Lewis M. Branscomb, Todd M. La Porte, and Erwann O. Michel-Kerjan, 164–193 (New York: Cambridge University Press, 2006), 166; Eric Schlosser, *Fast Food Nation: The Dark Side of the All-American Meal* (New York: Perennial, 2002); George Ritzer, *The McDonaldization of Society* (Thousand Oaks, CA: Pine Forge, 2004).

6. This is the core of Lynn's argument in *End of the Line.* "The global economy," says Eric Beinhocker, "is orders of magnitude more complex than any other physical or social structure ever built by humankind." Eric D. Beinhocker, *The Origin of Wealth: Evolution, Complexity, and the Radical Remaking of Economics* (Boston: Harvard Business School Press, 2006), 6.

7. See, for example, Todd Purdum, "Go Ahead, Try to Stop K Street," *New York Times,* January 8, 2006, 1; Zachary Coile, "Lobbying Reform Easier Said than Done," *San Francisco Chronicle,* January 16, 2006, A1; George Will, "How to Evict the Rent-Seekers," *Chicago Sun-Times,* January 11, 2006, 39.

8. The average for 2001 to 2005 was 19.6 percent of GDP; for 1976 to 2000, 21.3 percent of GDP. Data from historical tables of the president's budget for fiscal year 2007.

9. Debra Mayberry, "Just How Many Lobbyists Are There in Washington, Anyway?" *Washington Post,* January 29, 2006, B3. A discussion of the lobbyist industry, and difficulties in gauging its size and rate of growth, is provided by Burdett A. Loomis and Michael Struemph, *Organized Interests, Lobbying, and the Industry of Politics: A First-Cut Overview* (Lawrence: University of Kansas, April 2003).

10. For a discussion of trends up to the early 1990s, see John P. Heinz, *The Hollow Core: Private Interests in National Policy Making* (Cambridge, MA: Harvard University Press, 1993), 10.

11. Norman Ornstein, "The House That Jack Built," *New York Times Book Review,* January 14, 2007, 25.

12. It is, as economists say, a "normal good"—the richer we are, the more we spend on it.

13. Data obtained from opensecrets.org.

14. *Buckley v. Valeo,* 424 U.S. 1 (1976).

15. The growing significance of broadcast advertising costs in campaign budgets up to the 1990s is described by Stephen Ansolabehere, Roy Behr, and Shanto Iyengar, *Mass Media and Elections: An Overview* (Los Angeles: Center for American Politics and Public Policy, 1990), 1; Joseph Cantor and Denis Rutkus, *Free and Reduced-Rate Television Time for Political Candidates* (Washington, DC: Congressional Research Service, July 1997). Ansolabehere and colleagues review argu-

ments about the role of advertising costs in inflating campaign budgets, although they are skeptical of these claims, in Stephen Ansolabehere, Alan Gerber, and James Snyder Jr., *Does TV Advertising Explain the Rise of Campaign Spending?* (Boston: MIT, October 2001). For an argument about the need for nuance in assessing the significance of advertising costs, see Dwight Morris, *Testimony on Campaign Finance Reform* (Washington, DC: House of Representatives Committee on Energy and Commerce, June 20, 2001), available online at http://energycommerce.house .gov/107/hearings/06202001Hearing290/Morris444.htm (accessed September 24, 2006).

16. The difficulties encountered in tracing the effect of lobbying and campaign contributions are described by David Lowery and Virginia Gray, "A Neopluralist Perspective on Research on Organized Interests," *Political Research Quarterly* 57, no. 1 (2004): 165–166.

17. Matthew Fellowes and Patrick Wolf, "Funding Mechanisms and Policy Instruments: How Business Campaign Contributions Influence Congressional Votes," *Political Research Quarterly* 57, no. 2 (2004): 315–324.

18. Jeffrey Berry, "Interest Groups and Gridlock," in *Interest Group Politics*, ed. Allan J. Cigler and Burdett A. Loomis, 333–353 (Washington, DC: CQ Press, 2002), 338; Lowery and Gray, "A Neopluralist Perspective," 167. For a comparable argument with regard to interest-group activity at the state level, see Virginia Gray and David Lowery, "Interest Representation and Democratic Gridlock," *Legislative Studies Quarterly* 20, no. 4 (1995): 531–552.

19. "It may seem a paradox," says one extensive study of private interest groups in Washington, "but the principal result of the vast amount of interest group activity may be stability in systems of policy formation." Heinz, *The Hollow Core*, 413.

20. Research on the connection between economic conditions and support for the president and members of Congress is voluminous. For early work finding that economic downturns have an important effect on popular support for incumbent presidents, see Howard Bloom and Douglas Price, "Voter Response to Short-Run Economic Conditions," *American Political Science Review* 69, no. 4 (1975): 1240–1254; Donald Kinder and D. Roderick Kiewiet, "Sociotropic Politics: The American Case," *British Journal of Political Science* 11, no. 2 (1981): 129–161. On the role of economic conditions in determining support for members of Congress, see Kevin Grier and Joseph McGarrity, "The Effect of Macroeconomic Fluctuations on the Electoral Fortunes of House Incumbents," *Journal of Law and Economics* 41, no. 1 (1998): 143–161. Two key issues in this literature are the extent to which support is driven by retrospective or prospective views of the economy and the extent to which such views may be influenced or tempered by other considerations, such as media coverage, party identification, or political campaigning. For an argument that voters appear to have a retrospective, and fairly short-term, perspective on the economy, see Helmut Norpoth, "Presidents and the Prospective Voter," *Journal of Politics* 58, no. 3 (1996): 776–792. For a contrary view, emphasizing the importance of prospective judgments, see Michael MacKuen, Robert Erikson, and James A.

Stimson, "Peasants or Bankers? The American Electorate and the U.S. Economy," *American Political Science Review* 86, no. 3 (1992): 597–611. For a critique of this analysis, see Harold Clarke and Marianne Stewart, "Prospections, Retrospections, and Rationality: The 'Bankers' Model of Presidential Approval Reconsidered," *American Journal of Political Science* 38, no. 4 (1994): 1104–1123.

21. G. Patrick Lynch, "Presidential Elections and the Economy 1872 to 1996," *Political Research Quarterly* 52, no. 4 (1999): 825–844.

22. In a December 1992 Gallup poll, only 17 percent of Americans said that George Bush's policies had helped the economy. In an earlier poll, most Clinton supporters said that they could not vote for Bush because of his handling of the economy.

23. Clinton won only 43 percent of the popular vote in 1992.

24. Elizabeth Drew, *On the Edge: The Clinton Presidency* (New York: Simon and Schuster, 1994), 57–75.

25. Brian Newman, "Bill Clinton's Approval Ratings," *Political Research Quarterly* 55, no. 4 (2002): 781–804.

26. The University of Michigan's Index of Consumer Sentiment dropped from 108 in November 2000 to 91 in August 2001. This was equal to the index's decline between January 1989 and August 1990.

27. Wayne Washington, "Bush Seeks Cover as Economy Falls," *Boston Globe,* September 10, 2001.

28. Richard Berke and David Sanger, "Bush's Aides Seek to Focus Efforts on the Economy," *New York Times,* September 9, 2001.

29. As measured by the University of Michigan's Index of Consumer Sentiment.

30. For an assessment of the impact of the 9/11 attacks on layoffs, see Linda Levine, *The Worker Adjustment and Retraining Notification Act* (Washington, DC: Congressional Research Service, February 20, 2004), appendix.

31. Harumi Ito and Darin Lee, *Assessing the Impact of the September 11 Terrorist Attacks on U.S. Airline Demand* (Providence, RI: Brown University, February 3, 2004).

32. U.S. Airways eventually declared bankruptcy in August 2002, and United Airlines followed in December 2002.

33. Public Law 107-38.

34. The Air Transportation Safety and System Stabilization Act (Public Law 107-42) was introduced in Congress on September 21, 2001, and signed into law by the president on September 22.

35. Executive Office of the President, "President's Radio Address" (Washington, DC: Office of the Press Secretary, September 22, 2001).

36. Executive Office of the President, "President Discusses Economic Recovery in New York City" (Washington, DC: Office of the Press Secretary, October 3, 2001).

37. Job Creation and Worker Assistance Act of 2002, Public Law 107-147.

38. Anne Kornblut, "Bush Announces New Air Security Plan, Urges Americans to Return to the Skies," *Boston Globe,* September 28, 2001.

39. Executive Office of the President, "At O'Hare, President Says 'Get on Board'" (Washington, DC: Office of the Press Secretary, September 27, 2001).

40. Kathleen Cassedy, "O'Rourke of TIA on Travel Industry Recovery," conference report (New York: Association of Travel Marketing Executives, 2002).

41. Travel Industry Association of America, "News Release: More than Two-Thirds of American Population Saw President Bush Travel Recovery Ad" (Washington, DC: Travel Industry Association of America, January 11, 2002).

42. Speech to the American Society of Newspaper Editors in 1925. "Coolidge Declares Press Must Foster America's Idealism," *New York Times*, January 18, 1925, 1.

43. Address to Congress, January 6, 1941.

44. Executive Office of the President, "President Addresses Military Families, Discusses War on Terror" (Washington, DC: Office of the Press Secretary, August 24, 2005).

45. Executive Office of the President, "President's Address to the Nation" (Washington, DC: Office of the Press Secretary, September 11, 2006).

46. Executive Office of the President, "President Discusses Economic Recovery in New York City."

47. Statement of Senator Mitch McConnell, *Congressional Record,* September 19, 2001, p. S9485.

48. Gail Makinen, *The Economic Effects of 9/11: A Retrospective Assessment* (Washington, DC: Congressional Research Service, September 2002), 6, 51–52. In 2003, savings bonds of all types accounted for about 3 percent of total government debt. There is an ongoing debate about the efficiency of this financing mechanism. General Accounting Office, *Savings Bonds: Actions Needed to Increase the Reliability of Cost-Effectiveness Measures* (Washington, DC: General Accounting Office, June 2003), 1.

49. Margaret Carlson, "Patriotic Splurging," *Time.com,* October 15, 2001.

50. Martin Feldstein, "The Return of Saving," *Foreign Affairs* 85, no. 3 (2006): 87–88.

51. International Monetary Fund, *IMF Concludes 2002 Article IV Consultation with the United States* (Washington, DC: International Monetary Fund, August 5, 2002).

52. Thomas Ilgen, "Better Living through Chemistry: The Chemical Industry in the World Economy," *International Organization* 37, no. 4 (1983): 651. On the role of the chemical industry, see Fred Aftalion, *A History of the International Chemical Industry,* 2nd ed. (Philadelphia: Chemical Heritage Press, 2001).

53. General Accounting Office, *Homeland Security: Voluntary Initiatives Are Under Way at Chemical Facilities, but the Extent of Security Preparedness Is Unknown,* GAO-03-439 (Washington, DC: General Accounting Office, March 2003), 30.

54. Agency for Toxic Substances and Disease Registry, *Industrial Chemicals and Terrorism: Human Health Threat Analysis, Mitigation and Prevention* (Washington, DC: Department of Health and Human Services, April 1999), 7.

55. Gilmore Commission, *First Annual Report of the Advisory Panel to Assess*

*Domestic Response Capabilities for Terrorism Involving Weapons of Mass Destruction* (Santa Monica, CA: Rand Corporation, December 1999).

56. Department of Justice, *Assessment of the Increased Risk of Terrorist or Other Criminal Activity Associated with Posting Off-Site Consequence Analysis Information on the Internet* (Washington, DC: Department of Justice, April 18, 2000), 2.

57. General Accounting Office, *Security of Chemical Facilities,* GAO-03-24R (Washington, DC: General Accounting Office, 2003).

58. Eric Pianin, "Study Assesses Risk of Attack on Chemical Plant," *Washington Post,* March 12, 2002.

59. George Tenet, *Testimony before the Senate Select Committee on Intelligence* (Washington, DC: Central Intelligence Agency, February 6, 2002).

60. Robert Stephan, *Statement before the Subcommittee on Economic Security, Infrastructure Protection, and Cyber Security* (Washington, DC: Department of Homeland Security, June 15, 2005), 2.

61. General Accounting Office, *Homeland Security,* 4.

62. In the words of Senator James Inhofe. Bob Dart, "Oklahoma Senator Stands Firm against Tougher Air Standards," *Atlanta Journal-Constitution,* July 25, 1997, 10A. Representative Tom DeLay, House majority leader, also called the EPA "the Gestapo of government." Janet Hook, "House Rejects Bid to Curtail EPA," *Chicago Sun-Times,* July 29, 1995.

63. Michael Weisskopf, "The Hill May Be a Health Hazard for Safety Agency," *Washington Post,* July 23, 1995, A1.

64. Rep. Billy Tauzin, "Letter to the Honorable Tom Ridge, Director of Homeland Security" (Washington, DC: House Committee on Energy and Commerce, June 19, 2002).

65. General Accounting Office, *Homeland Security,* 4; "EPA Drops Chemical Security Effort," *Washington Post,* October 3, 2002, A17.

66. Linda-Jo Schierow, *Chemical Facility Security* (Washington, DC: Congressional Research Service, March 24, 2006), 24–25.

67. DHS assumed these responsibilities under Homeland Security Presidential Directive 7, December 17, 2003. See also Dana Shea, *Legislative Approaches to Chemical Facility Security,* RL33043 (Washington, DC: Congressional Research Service, April 12, 2006), 6–7.

68. National Performance Review, *Reinvention's Next Steps: Governing in a Balanced Budget World; Speech by Vice President Al Gore and Supporting Background Papers* (Washington, DC: National Performance Review, March 4, 1996).

69. Carol Andress, *Testimony before the Senate Committee on Homeland Security and Government Affairs* (Washington, DC: Environmental Defense Fund, July 13, 2005), 7.

70. Schierow, *Chemical Facility Security,* 37.

71. General Accounting Office, *Homeland Security*; Government Accountability Office, *DHS Is Taking Steps to Enhance Security at Chemical Facilities, but Additional Authority Is Needed,* GAO-06-150 (Washington, DC: Government Accountability Office, January 2006); Government Accountability Office, *Homeland Security:*

*DHS Is Addressing Security at Chemical Facilities, but Additional Authority Is Needed,* GAO-06-899T (Washington, DC: Government Accountability Office, June 21, 2006).

72. Tom Ridge and Christie Whitman, "Letter to the Editor," *Washington Post,* October 6, 2006, B6.

73. Executive Office of the President, "President Urges Congress to Pass Iraq Resolution Promptly" (Washington, DC: Office of the Press Secretary, September 24, 2002).

74. Executive Office of the President, *The National Strategy for the Physical Protection of Critical Infrastructures and Key Assets* (Washington, DC: Executive Office of the President, February 2003), 66.

75. Jeff Stein, "Is Homeland Security Keeping America Safe?" *CQ Weekly,* June 14, 2003.

76. Michael Grass and Brody Mullins, "K Street Files," *Roll Call,* June 4, 2003.

77. Schierow, *Chemical Facility Security,* 38–39.

78. Martin Kady, "Cox Blames 'Political Season,' Recalcitrant House Members for Homeland Panel's Problems," *CQ Weekly,* July 24, 2004, 1806.

79. In July 2005, the Senate adopted a resolution that Congress should pass legislation to regulate chemical-plant security, and a few months later the House approved a similar statement. Schierow, *Chemical Facility Security,* 41–42.

80. Richard Falkenrath, *Statement before the Senate Committee on Homeland Security and Governmental Affairs* (Washington, DC: Brookings Institution, April 27, 2005). Falkenrath also observed that the Bush administration clearly had authority to regulate the transportation of dangerous chemicals but had failed to exercise that authority.

81. Schierow, *Chemical Facility Security,* 38.

82. Michael Chertoff, "Remarks at the National Chemical Security Forum" (Washington, DC: Department of Homeland Security, March 21, 2006).

83. Jon Corzine, "News Release: Corzine Applauds Adoption of Mandatory Chemical Plant Security Measures" (Washington, DC: Office of Senator Jon Corzine, November 29, 2005).

84. Department of Homeland Security Appropriations Act, 2007, Public Law 109-295, section 550.

85. Susan Collins and Peter King, "Letter to the Editor," *New York Times,* September 25, 2006, 22. The administration issued draft rules on chemical-plant safety in December 2006, which were widely criticized for giving too much leeway to the chemical industry. Robert Block, "U.S. Allows Chemical Plants Leeway in Terror Order, *Wall Street Journal,* December 22, 2006, A3.

86. Massoud Amin, "North America's Electricity Infrastructure: Are We Ready for More Perfect Storms?" *IEEE Security and Privacy* 1, no. 5 (2003): 19.

87. Institute for Security Technology Studies, *Cyber Security of the Electric Power Industry* (Hanover, NH: Dartmouth College, December 2002), 4; Feinstein, "Managing Reliability," 164.

88. T. J. Glauthier, *Testimony before the House Committee on Science* (Washington, DC: Electricity Innovation Institute, September 25, 2003).

89. Feinstein, "Managing Reliability," 165.

90. Office of Technology Assessment, *Physical Vulnerability of Electric System to Natural Disasters and Sabotage*, OTA-E-453 (Washington, DC: Office of Technology Assessment, June 1990).

91. Energy Information Administration, *Annual Energy Outlook 2006* (Washington, DC: Energy Information Administration, February 2006).

92. "Not Enough Juice," *Industry Standard*, July 31, 2000.

93. For a discussion of Enron's role in promoting liberalization in the electricity industry, see Bethany McLean and Peter Elkind, *The Smartest Guys in the Room: The Amazing Rise and Scandalous Fall of Enron* (New York: Portfolio, 2004).

94. Feinstein, "Managing Reliability," 188; Michael Kormos and Thomas Bowe, "Coordinated and Uncoordinated Crisis Responses by the Electric Industry," in *Seeds of Disaster, Roots of Response*, ed. Philip E. Auerswald, Lewis M. Branscomb, Todd M. La Porte, and Erwann O. Michel-Kerjan, 194–210 (New York: Cambridge University Press, 2006), 199.

95. See the 2006 decision of the U.S. Supreme Court in *New York, et al. v. Federal Energy Regulatory Commission, et al.* See also John German, "Market Restructuring and Increasing Complexity of the Power Grid Raise Concerns about Power Reliability," *Sandia Lab News*, February 11, 2000.

96. President's Commission on Critical Infrastructure Protection, *Critical Foundations: Protecting America's Infrastructures* (Washington, DC: President's Commission on Critical Infrastructure Protection, October 1997), 27. The task of assessing the system's vulnerabilities has given rise to sophisticated exercises in modeling. See, for example, Javier Salmeron, Kevin Wood, and Ross Baldick, "Analysis of Electric Grid Security under Terrorist Threat," *IEEE Transactions on Power Systems* 19, no. 2 (2004): 905–912.

97. Kormos and Bowe, "Coordinated and Uncoordinated Crisis Responses," 198.

98. Alexander Farrell, Lester Lave, and Granger Morgan, "Bolstering the Security of the Electric Power System," *Issues in Science and Technology* 18, no. 3 (2002): 49–56. Samuel Varnado, *Testimony before the House Committee on Energy and Commerce* (Albuquerque, NM: Sandia National Laboratories, July 9, 2002).

99. North American Electric Reliability Council, *SQL Slammer Worm: Lessons Learned for Consideration by the Electricity Sector* (Princeton, NJ: North American Electric Reliability Council, June 20, 2003).

100. In 2005, former White House adviser Richard Clarke warned that a cyber-attack could have consequences equal to the 1984 Bhopal disaster. Nathaniel Hoopes, "New Focus on Cyber-Terrorism," *Christian Science Monitor*, August 16, 2005. Al Qaeda is said to have given careful consideration to cyber-attacks. Dan Verton, *Black Ice: The Invisible Threat of Cyber-Terrorism* (New York: McGraw-Hill/Osborne, 2003), 84–85.

101. Massoud Amin, "Balancing Market Priorities with Security Issues," *IEEE Power and Energy Magazine*, July/August 2004, 30–38; Institute for Security Tech-

nology Studies, *Cyber Security of the Electric Power Industry*, 5; Farrell, Lave, and Morgan, "Bolstering the Security," 4; Task Force on Electric System Reliability, "Maintaining Reliability in a Competitive U.S. Electricity Industry" (Washington, DC: U.S. Department of Energy, 1998).

102. Amin, "Balancing Market Priorities," 33.

103. Feinstein, "Managing Reliability," 191.

104. Ibid., 172–175.

105. Task Force on Electric System Reliability, "Maintaining Reliability." See also Farrell, Lave, and Morgan, "Bolstering the Security," 4.

106. Federal Energy Regulatory Commission, *Policy Statement Regarding Regional Transmission Groups* (Washington, DC: Federal Energy Regulatory Commission, 1993).

107. *New York, et al. v. Federal Energy Regulatory Commission, et al.*, U.S. Supreme Court, judgment issued March 4, 2002.

108. A NERC spokesman said at the time that the new council "would do away with the need for any legislated controls." Gene Smith, "Electric Utilities Form Group," *New York Times,* June 12, 1968.

109. Task Force on Electric System Reliability, "Maintaining Reliability."

110. Paul Joskow, *U.S. Energy Policy during the 1990s* (Cambridge, MA: MIT Center for Energy and Environmental Policy Research, 2001), 3, 17, 41–42.

111. Department of Energy, *National Transmission Grid Study* (Washington, DC: Department of Energy, May 2002), 27.

112. Federal Energy Regulatory Commission, *Notice of Proposed Rulemaking, Docket Rm01-12-000* (Washington, DC: Federal Energy Regulatory Commission, July 31, 2002), 5, 304–306.

113. Federal Energy Regulatory Commission, *White Paper on Wholesale Power Market Platform* (Washington, DC: Federal Energy Regulatory Commission, April 28, 2003).

114. Elizabeth Anne Moler, *Unintended Consequences of Delaying FERC's Standard Market Design* (Cambridge, MA: Harvard Electricity Policy Group, September 2003), 1.

115. Richard Schwartz, "FERC Halts Effort to Set Electricity Standards," *Houston Chronicle,* July 20, 2005.

116. U.S.-Canada Power System Outage Task Force, *Final Report on the August 14, 2003 Blackout in the United States and Canada* (Washington, DC: U.S. Department of Energy, 2004), 6, 44, 147.

117. Executive Office of the President, "President Visits Detroit Edison Monroe Power Plant" (Washington, DC: Office of the Press Secretary, September 15, 2003). Vice President Cheney's Energy Policy Development Group had earlier endorsed the idea of mandatory standards. National Energy Policy Development Group, *Report* (Washington, DC: Executive Office of the President, May 2001), 7.6.

118. Energy Policy Act of 2005, Public Law 109-58, section 1211.

119. The Energy Policy Act said that standard-setting authority should be

given to an "Electric Reliability Organization" selected by FERC. NERC was selected as this organization in July 2006. FERC is required to defer to NERC's technical judgment except with regard to the effect of a standard on competition.

120. Joseph Kelliher, *Statement on Implementation of Reliability Provisions of Energy Policy Act of 2005* (Washington, DC: Federal Energy Regulatory Commission, November 1, 2005).

121. I simplify slightly: some U.S. grids are connected to Canadian and Mexican grids, creating a problem of international coordination, as the 2003 blackout showed.

122. There are two recent histories of the shipping container: Brian J. Cudahy, *Box Boats: How Container Ships Changed the World* (New York: Fordham University Press, 2006); Marc Levinson, *The Box: How the Shipping Container Made the World Smaller and the World Economy Bigger* (Princeton, NJ: Princeton University Press, 2006).

123. Data on the value of goods imported by the United States is provided by the Bureau of Economic Analysis of the Department of Commerce.

124. Levinson, *The Box,* 7.

125. U.S. officials continued to make this claim as late as 2005. Robert Bonner, *Remarks to the Council on Foreign Relations* (Washington, DC: U.S. Customs and Border Protection, January 11, 2005).

126. U.S. news reports neglected to mention that Rizk had packed all his household goods in the container, including a dishwasher, clothes, and family photos. " 'Container Boy' Freed from Jail, on Way Back to Canada," *Vancouver Province,* November 16, 2001.

127. Liat Collins and Arieh O'Sullivan, "Going for a Mega-Attack," *Jerusalem Post,* March 26, 2004, 3.

128. Stephen Flynn, "Beyond Border Control," *Foreign Affairs* 79, no. 6 (2000): 63.

129. Charles Meade and Roger Molander, *Considering the Effects of a Catastrophic Terrorist Attack* (Santa Monica, CA: Rand Corporation, 2006). Earlier studies of the impact of similar terrorist attacks were completed by the consulting firms Booz Allen Hamilton and Abt Associates, with similarly bleak findings. See Todd Konkel, "Container Security: Preventing a Nuclear Catastrophe," *Journal of International Policy Solutions* 3 (spring 2005): 4–5.

130. On staffing requirements and possible technical innovations in container design, see Flynn, "Beyond Border Control," 87, 93–96.

131. Office of Inspector General, *Audit of Targeting Oceangoing Cargo Containers,* OIG-05–26 (Washington, DC: Department of Homeland Security, July, 2005), 2.

132. Richard Stana, *Statement on the Status of Efforts to Improve the Automated Targeting System,* GAO-06-591T (Washington, DC: Government Accountability Office, March 30, 2006), 5.

133. Jon Haveman, Ethan Jennings, Howard Shatz, and Greg Wright, "The Container Security Initiative and Ocean Container Threats," *Journal of Homeland Security and Emergency Management* 4, no. 1 (2007): 1–19.

134. Richard Stana, *Statement: Key Cargo Security Programs Can Be Improved,* GAO-05-466T (Washington, DC: Government Accountability Office, May 26, 2005), 20; Ted Bridis, "Security Lapses Found at U.S. Ports," Associated Press, March 12, 2006.

135. Stephen Flynn, *The Ongoing Neglect of Maritime Transportation Security* (Washington, DC: Council on Foreign Relations, August 25, 2004).

136. Government Accountability Office, *Container Security: A Flexible Staffing Model and Minimum Equipment Models Would Improve Overseas Targeting and Inspection Efforts,* GAO-05-557 (Washington, DC: Government Accountability Office, April 2005), 20.

137. Ibid.; Stana, *Statement: Key Cargo Security Programs;* Jon Haveman, Howard Shatz, and Ernesto Vilchis, "U.S. Port Security Policy after 9/11: Overview and Evaluation," *Journal of Homeland Security and Emergency Management* 2, no. 4 (2005): 1–24.

138. In 2005, 5 percent of the 11.3 million containers arriving at U.S. ports were either physically inspected or screened by imaging machines. Pamela Prah, "Port Security," *CQ Researcher,* April 21, 2006.

139. Richard Stana, *Statement Regarding Challenges Faced in Targeting Oceangoing Cargo Containers for Inspection,* GAO-04-557T (Washington, DC: General Accounting Office, March 31, 2004); Stana, *Statement on the Status of Efforts;* Government Accountability Office, *Container Security,* 21.

140. Prah, "Port Security."

141. Stana, *Statement: Key Cargo Security Programs,* 16; Audrey Hudson, "U.S. Eyes Privatizing Cargo Security Work," *Washington Times,* March 21, 2006.

142. Government Accountability Office, *Partnership Program Grants Importers Reduced Scrutiny with Limited Assurance of Improved Security,* GAO-05-404 (Washington, DC: Government Accountability Office, March 2005), 4; Stana, *Statement: Key Cargo Security Programs,* 3; Leigh B. Boske, *Port and Supply-Chain Initiatives in the United States and Abroad* (Austin, TX: Lyndon B. Johnson School of Public Affairs, September 2006), 59.

143. National Performance Review, *The New OSHA* (Washington, DC: National Performance Review, February 21, 1995).

144. "The Safety Challenge," *Government Executive,* February 1, 1999, 77–80.

145. *Chamber of Commerce of the United States et al. v. U.S. Department of Labor et al.,* U.S. Court of Appeals (DC Circuit), Case 98-1036, judgment issued April 9, 1999.

146. Some people in the private sector already regarded C-TPAT as "an involuntary voluntary program." R. G. Edmonson, "Inside the Port Security Act," *Journal of Commerce,* September 18, 2006, 12.

147. Andrew Howell, *Statement on the Greenlane Maritime Cargo Security Act* (Washington, DC: U.S. Chamber of Commerce, April 5, 2006).

148. The Port Security Improvement Act of 2006.

149. Bridis, "Security Lapses Found at U.S. Ports."

150. Flynn, *The Continued Vulnerability.*

## Notes to Chapter 5

1. Bob Woodward, *Bush at War* (New York: Simon and Schuster, 2002), 73.

2. Karen DeYoung, "A Fight against Terrorism—and Disorganization," *Washington Post*, August 9, 2006, A1.

3. For a criticism of the reliance on the language of war in the U.S. case, and a discussion of the treatment of counterterrorism efforts by the British government, see Michael Howard, "What's in a Name? How to Fight Terrorism," *Foreign Affairs* 81, no. 1 (2002): 8.

4. Executive Office of the President, "Vice President's Remarks to the Traveling Press" (Washington, DC: Office of the Vice President, December 20, 2005).

5. Woodward, *Bush at War,* 15. See the ensuing discussion for repeated instances in which Bush characterizes the oncoming difficulties as a war.

6. Executive Office of the President, "Statement by the President in His Address to the Nation" (Washington, DC: Office of the Press Secretary, September 11, 2001).

7. Woodward, *Bush at War,* 63.

8. Michael R. Gordon and Bernard E. Trainor, *Cobra II: The Inside Story of the Invasion and Occupation of Iraq* (New York: Pantheon Books, 2006), 15–23. David Rothkopf observes that it "is beyond dispute [that] the president made the decision to seriously consider going after Iraq within days or weeks of the [9/11] attacks." David J. Rothkopf, *Running the World: The Inside Story of the National Security Council and the Architects of American Power* (New York: PublicAffairs, 2005), 433. Zbigniew Brzezinski observes that "a de facto consensus in favor of military action emerged by early 2002." Zbigniew Brzezinski, *Second Chance: Three Presidents and the Crisis of American Superpower* (New York: Basic Books, 2007), 143.

9. Executive Office of the President, *National Security Strategy of the United States* (Washington, DC: Executive Office of the President, September 17, 2002).

10. "Wherry Says Acheson Is 'Risk' and 'Must Go,'" *New York Times*, March 22, 1950.

11. Rothkopf, *Running the World,* 391.

12. National Commission on Terrorist Attacks upon the United States, *Final Report* (New York: Barnes and Noble Books, 2004), 95.

13. U.S. Commission on National Security/21st Century, *Road Map for National Security: Imperative for Change* (Washington, DC: U.S. Commission on National Security/21st Century, February 15, 2001), 47.

14. President's Commission on an All-Volunteer Armed Force, *The Report of the President's Commission on an All-Volunteer Armed Force* (Washington, DC: U.S. Government Printing Office, 1970), 17.

15. Caspar W. Weinberger, "Excerpts from Address of Weinberger," *New York Times,* November 29, 1984, A1.

16. Colin Powell, "U.S. Forces: Challenges Ahead," *Foreign Affairs* 71, no. 5 (1992): 32–46.

17. Dana Priest, *The Mission: Waging War and Keeping Peace with America's Military* (New York: Norton, 2003), 52.

18. A useful summary of these actions is provided by David Halberstam, *War in a Time of Peace: Bush, Clinton, and the Generals* (New York: Scribner, 2001), 457. The retreat from the Powell Doctrine during the Clinton administration is described in that book and in Priest, *The Mission.*

19. Josef Joffe, *Überpower: The Imperial Temptation of America* (New York: Norton, 2006), 30–36.

20. A 1980 Gallup poll found a brief resurgence in support for the draft. In the 1990s and 2000s, however, polls found that 80 to 90 percent of Americans opposed its reinstatement. Opposition softened during the two Iraq wars, but a majority still opposed the draft.

21. Milton Friedman, "The Case for Abolishing the Draft," *New York Times,* May 14, 1967, 3–9.

22. Walter Oi, "The Economic Cost of the Draft," *American Economic Review* 57, no. 2 (1967): 39–62.

23. President's Commission on an All-Volunteer Armed Force, *Report of the President's Commission,* 6, 23.

24. "The Army, after Iraq," *New York Times,* March 18, 2007, 11.

25. For a tabulation of protests, prosecutions and editorial coverage during the Vietnam era, see: John Hagan and Ilene Bernstein, "Conflict in Context: The Sanction of Draft Resisters, 1963–1976," *Social Problems* 27, no. 1 (1979): 109–122, 111.

26. For a rare case of conscientious objection by an officer during the Iraq war, see John Kifner and Timothy Egan, "Officer Faces Court-Martial for Refusing to Deploy to Iraq," *New York Times,* July 23, 2006.

27. Department of Defense, *Population Representation in the Military Services, Fiscal Year 1998* (Washington, DC: Office of the Assistant Secretary of Defense [Force Management Policy], November 1999), chap. 7. For a critical assessment of claims about biases in representation within the armed services, see Tim Kane, *Who Are the Recruits? The Demographic Characteristics of U.S. Military Enlistment, 2003–2005* (Washington, DC: Heritage Foundation, October 27, 2006).

28. Sidney Verba and Norman H. Nie, *Participation in America: Political Democracy and Social Equality* (Chicago: University of Chicago Press, 1987); Eliot Cohen, "Constraints on America's Conduct of Small Wars," *International Security* 9, no. 2 (1984): 157.

29. This phrase about the military's transition is borrowed from James Kitfield, *Prodigal Soldiers* (Washington, DC: Simon and Schuster, 1995), 303. For further discussion of this transformation, see Michael Adas, *Dominance by Design: Technological Imperatives and America's Civilizing Mission* (Cambridge, MA: Belknap, 2006), 339–382.

30. U.S. Air Force, *Reaching Globally, Reaching Powerfully: The United States Air Force in the Gulf War* (Washington, DC: Department of the Air Force, September 1999).

31. S. J. Deitchman, "Completing the Transformation of U.S. Military Forces," *Issues in Science and Technology* 20, no. 4 (2004): 62–68.

32. Erik Gartzke, "Democracy and the Preparation for War: Does Regime Type Affect States' Anticipation of Casualties?" *International Studies Quarterly* 45, no. 3 (2001): 468.

33. General William Westmoreland anticipated this shift in 1969: with technological innovation, the need for "large forces" would dissipate. Adas, *Dominance by Design,* 350.

34. Department of Defense, *Joint Vision 2010* (Washington, DC: Joint Chiefs of Staff, June 1996), 18.

35. Data from the U.S. Census Bureau's 2007 Statistical Abstract, "National Security and Veterans Affairs: Military Personnel and Expenditures," available online at http://www.census.gov/compendia/statab/national_security_veterans_affairs/military_personnel_and_expenditures/. The total number of military fatalities from all causes is not available for 2006, but it is likely that it remains comparable to figures for the latter years of the Cold War. The increase in fatalities from hostile acts is largely offset by a substantial decline in accidental and self-inflicted deaths. An important caveat is that these comparisons overlook the number of soldiers wounded in action in Iraq and Afghanistan: this number exceeded twenty-four thousand by 2007. Casualty data can also be found in the "Personnel and Procurement Reports and Data Files," Defense Manpower Data Center website, http://siadapp.dmdc.osd.mil.

36. Scott Gartner and Gary Segura, "War, Casualties and Public Opinion," *Journal of Conflict Resolution* 42, no. 3 (1998): 278–300; John Mueller, "The Iraq Syndrome," *Foreign Affairs* 84, no. 6 (2005): 44–54.

37. David Kennedy, "Prepared Remarks for 2005 Class Day Luncheon" (Stanford, CA: Stanford University, June 11, 2005).

38. Frederick Perry Powers, "The Reform of the Federal Service," *Political Science Quarterly* 3, no. 2 (1888): 249.

39. During the 9/11 crisis, this view was most forcefully articulated by Robert D. Kaplan, in *Imperial Grunts: The American Military on the Ground* (New York: Random House, 2005) and in "The Media and Medievalism," *Policy Review* 128 (2004): 47–57.

40. David Brooks, "Heroes Abroad, Unknown at Home," *New York Times,* November 27, 2005.

41. A history of Congress's statutory actions is provided in Government Accountability Office, *Medicare Prescription Drug, Improvement, and Modernization Act of 2003: Use of Appropriated Funds for Flyer and Print and Television Advertisements,* B-302504 (Washington, DC: Government Accountability Office, March 10, 2004).

42. Kitfield, *Prodigal Soldiers,* 209–214, 304; David C. King and Zachary Karabell, *The Generation of Trust: Public Confidence in the U.S. Military since Vietnam* (Washington, DC: AEI Press, 2003), chap. 6.

43. Janet Myers, "Y&R Uses Ayer's Theme as Army's New Agency," *Advertis-*

*ing Age*, February 2, 1987, 1–2; Thomas Mucha, "The Essentials of Remaking Your Brand," *Business 2.0*, April 2003, 43.

44. Bob Garfield, "The Top 100 Advertising Campaigns," *Advertising Age*, March 29, 1999, 18.

45. Paula Span, "The Marines Go Medieval," *Washington Post*, March 22, 1992, W25.

46. King and Karabell, *The Generation of Trust*, 81.

47. General Accounting Office, *Military Recruiting: DOD Needs to Establish Objectives and Measures to Better Evaluate Advertising's Effectiveness* (Washington, DC: General Accounting Office, September 2003), 4, 10.

48. Mark Ross, " 'America's Army': Be All That You Can Be, Short of Joining Up," *Atlanta Journal-Constitution*, September 3, 2005, FE1.

49. Patrick M. Regan, "War Toys, War Movies, and the Militarization of the United States, 1900–1985," *Journal of Peace Research* 31, no. 1 (1994): 53.

50. Lawrence H. Suid, *Guts and Glory: The Making of the American Military Image in Film*, rev. and exp. ed. (Lexington: University Press of Kentucky, 2002), chap. 25; King and Karabell, *The Generation of Trust*, chap. 5.

51. Data for 2005 obtained from the Entertainment Software Association, http://www.theesa.com/facts/index.php.

52. J. C. Herz and Michael Macedonia, "Computer Games and the Military: Two Views," *Defense Horizons*, April 2002, 1–8.

53. Matthew Baum, *Soft News Goes to War: Public Opinion and American Foreign Policy in the New Media Age* (Princeton, NJ: Princeton University Press, 2003), 194–195.

54. H. Bruce Franklin, "From Realism to Virtual Reality: Images of America's Wars," in *Seeing through the Media: The Persian Gulf War*, ed. Susan Jeffords and Lauren Rabinovitz, 25–44 (New Brunswick, NJ: Rutgers University Press, 1994), 42.

55. Adas, *Dominance by Design*, 363.

56. Paul Gronke and Peter Feaver, *Uncertain Confidence: Civilian and Military Attitudes about Civil-Military Relations* (Portland, OR: Reed College, 1999), 6.

57. Baum, *Soft News Goes to War*, 223.

58. Executive Office of the President, "President Bush Delivers Graduation Speech at West Point" (Washington, DC: Executive Office of the President, June 1, 2002). The National Security Strategy released by the White House in September 2002 also announced the Bush administration's determination to "exercise our right to self-defense by acting preemptively" against nations or groups that threatened national security. Executive Office of the President, *National Security Strategy of the United States*, 6.

59. Executive Office of the President, "Inaugural Address" (Washington, DC: Executive Office of the President, January 20, 2005).

60. Anne Applebaum, "The Sources of American Conduct," *American Interest* 1, no. 1 (2005): 14–16. A similar claim is made by Ivo H. Daalder and James M. Lindsay, *America Unbound: The Bush Revolution in Foreign Policy* (Hoboken, NJ: Wiley, 2005), 12.

61. James Mann, *Rise of the Vulcans* (New York: Viking, 2004), xii.

62. Philip Stephens, "The West Pays a Heavy Price for Foreign Policy Realism," *Financial Times,* October 14, 2005, 19.

63. Woodward, *Bush at War,* 77. For a discussion of the role of the United States in the extraordinary rendition of a Syrian-Canadian, see Arar Commission, *Report of the Events Relating to Maher Arar: Analysis and Recommendations* (Ottawa, Canada: Commission of Inquiry into the Actions of Canadian Officials in Relation to Maher Arar, September 18, 2006). For the condemnation of Syria as one of the lesser partners in the "Axis of Evil," see John Bolton, "Remarks to the Heritage Foundation: 'Beyond the Axis of Evil: Additional Threats from Weapons of Mass Destruction'" (Washington, DC: Office of the Undersecretary of State for Arms Control and International Security, May 6, 2002).

64. On U.S. support for Musharraf, see Woodward, *Bush at War,* 82–83, 115.

65. Peter Baker, "The Realities of Exporting Democracy," *Washington Post,* January 25, 2006, A1; Gordon and Trainor, *Cobra II,* 111. Gordon and Trainor also report that CENTCOM chief Tommy Franks, attempting to obtain support for the Iraq invasion, sought to "get [the King of Jordan] everything he needs to keep stability in Jordan." Ibid., 110.

66. Robert Jervis, "Why the Bush Doctrine Cannot Be Sustained," *Political Science Quarterly* 120, no. 3 (2005): 371; Dana Priest, "Foreign Network at Front of CIA's Terror Fight," *Washington Post,* November 18, 2005, A1; Josh White, "Rumsfeld Arrives in Kabul after Talks in Tajikistan," *Washington Post,* July 11, 2006, A14; Isabel Gorst, "Washington Seeks to Smooth Kyrgyz Relations as Central Asian States Flex Their Muscles," *Financial Times,* August 12, 2006, 6.

67. Thomas Ricks, *Fiasco: The American Military Adventure in Iraq* (New York: Penguin, 2006), 38.

68. Stephen Kinzer, *Overthrow: America's Century of Regime Change from Hawaii to Iraq* (New York: Times Books, 2006); John Prados, *JFK and the Diem Coup* (Washington, DC: National Security Archive, 2003). For a review of the U.S. attitude toward preemption and unilateralism in earlier years, see John Lewis Gaddis, *Surprise, Security, and the American Experience* (Cambridge, MA: Harvard University Press, 2004).

69. On the less well-known covert programs in Japan, see Karen Gatz, ed., *Foreign Relations of the United States, 1964–1968,* vol. 29, part 2 (Washington, DC: U.S. Government Printing Office, 2006), 1.

70. Michael Byers, *War Law: Understanding International Law and Armed Conflicts* (New York: Grove, 2006), 87–89.

71. Bernard Gwertzman, "Shultz Supports Armed Reprisals," *New York Times,* January 16, 1986, A1.

72. Executive Office of the President, "Remarks by the President on American Security in a Changing World" (Washington, DC: Office of the Press Secretary, August 5, 1996).

73. Tim Weiner, "Raids Are Seen as One Battle in a Long Fight," *New York Times,* August 23, 1998, 1.

74. Executive Office of the President, "State of the Union Address" (Washington, DC: Office of the Press Secretary, January 29, 2002).

75. Executive Office of the President, "Press Gaggle with Scott McClellan" (Washington, DC: Office of the Press Secretary, February 10, 2005). Gordon and Trainor observe that the Bush administration was downplaying the North Korean threat in October 2002 because it recognized that "there was no good military option." Gordon and Trainor, *Cobra II*, 130–131.

76. Sheryl Gay Stolberg, "For Bush, Many Questions on Iraq and North Korea," *New York Times*, October 10, 2006.

77. Glen Kessler, "Rice Key to Reversal on Iran," *Washington Post*, June 4, 2006, A17.

78. Executive Office of the President, "State of the Union Address" (Washington, DC: Office of the Press Secretary, January 31, 2006). Bush defended his policy in Iraq by inviting *New York Times* columnist David Brooks to "think about what the world could look like 50 years from now, with Islamic radicals either controlling the world's oil supply or not." David Brooks, "Ends without Means," *New York Times*, September 14, 2006, A27.

79. BP, *Statistical Review of World Energy 2006* (London: BP, 2006), available online at http://www.bp.com (accessed November 3, 2006).

80. A National Intelligence Assessment prepared at the request of the National Security Council and completed in December 2000 restated the intelligence community's determination that Iraq retained stockpiles of chemical weapons and the capacity to produce biological as well as chemical weapons. Senate Intelligence Committee, *Report on the U.S. Intelligence Community's Prewar Intelligence Assessments on Iraq*, S.Rep. 108-301 (Washington, DC: U.S. Senate Select Committee on Intelligence, July 9, 2004), 196–197; Gordon and Trainor, *Cobra II*, 125. Denis MacShane, a minister in Britain's Labour government responsible for European affairs, later wrote, "every European leader . . . said that Saddam and WMD were a major problem. Those who opposed intervention . . . did not deny the existence of WMD; they simply argued that a full-scale invasion would make matters worse." Denis MacShane, "How to Write about Iraq," *Prospect*, December 2006, available online at http://www.prospect-magazine.co.uk/printarticle.php?id=7981.

81. Ricks, *Fiasco*, 12.

82. Andrew Bacevich, *The New American Militarism* (New York: Oxford University Press, 2005), 193. Bob Woodward calls it an "undeclared war." Bob Woodward, *State of Denial* (New York: Simon and Schuster, 2006), 93.

83. Peter Malanczuk, "The Kurdish Crisis and Allied Intervention in the Aftermath of the Second Gulf War," *European Journal of International Law* 2, no. 2 (1991): 131; Byers, *War Law*, 98–99.

84. Eric Schmitt, "Raid on Iraq," *New York Times*, January 14, 1993, A8.

85. Michael Knights, "The Long View of No-Fly and No-Augmentation Zones," *PolicyWatch*, March 24, 2003.

86. Eric Schmitt, "U.S. Puts Limits on Its Military Buildup in Gulf," *New York Times*, October 20, 1994, A5.

87. See Military Personnel Historical Reports provided by the Department of Defense in the "Personnel and Procurement Reports and Data Files," Defense Manpower Data Center website, http://siadapp.dmdc.osd.mil.

88. Eric Schmitt, "The Day's Weapon of Choice, the Cruise Missile, Is Valued for Its Accuracy," *New York Times*, January 17, 1993, A8.

89. Gordon and Trainor, *Cobra II*, 13.

90. James Bennet, "Clinton Describes Goals for a Strike on Iraqi Arsenals," *New York Times*, February 18, 1998, A1.

91. Barbara Crossette, "Pressing for Iraqi's Overthrow, U.S. Appeals for Arab Support," *New York Times*, December 9, 1998, A8.

92. David Malone says that U.S. policy toward Iraq in the 1990s was characterized by a "creeping unilateralism [that] sheltered the seeds" of the 2003 conflict. David Malone, *The International Struggle over Iraq: Politics in the UN Security Council 1980–2005* (New York: Oxford University Press, 2006), 103.

93. A 1999 report for the UK House of Commons noted that the legal basis for no-fly zones was "ambiguous" and that authority for use of force was "subject to discussion." Tim Youngs and Mark Oakes, *Iraq: "Desert Fox" and Policy Developments* (London: House of Commons Library, February 10, 1999), 25, 36.

94. Transcript, *NewsHour with Jim Lehrer*, PBS, November 11, 2004.

95. Jon Alterman, *Thinking Out Loud: Policies toward Iraq* (Washington, DC: United States Institute of Peace, February 17, 1999).

96. Gordon and Trainor, *Cobra II*, 25–27, 78–79, 199. Ricks observes that many senior Army officers involved in the 2002 invasion planning "had worked at CENTCOM during the 1990s, and so were familiar with the series of war plans refined there during the decade." Ricks, *Fiasco*, 33.

97. Gordon and Trainor, *Cobra II*, 27.

98. Ibid., 105.

99. A Gallup poll found 70 percent in favor in June 1993; 72 percent in October 1994; 61 percent in February 1998, shortly after Iraq and the United Nations reached agreement on further weapons inspections; and 74 percent in 1999.

100. "Iraqis Fire Artillery," *New York Times*, December 27, 1998.

101. Elizabeth Becker, "U.S. Pilots over Iraq Given Wider Leeway to Fight Back," *New York Times*, January 27, 1999, A8.

102. Bacevich, *The New American Militarism*, 196.

103. Michael Gordon, "A Decade beyond the Gulf War," *New York Times*, February 18, 2001, 10.

104. James Dao, "Attack on Iraq," *New York Times*, February 17, 2001, A6.

105. Woodward, *State of Denial*, 22.

106. Gordon, "A Decade beyond the Gulf War."

107. National Commission on Terrorist Attacks, *Final Report*, 336.

108. Ken Adelman, "Cakewalk in Iraq," *Washington Post*, February 13, 2002, A27.

109. Frank Newport, *Only a Third Believe War against Terror Being Won* (Washington, DC: Gallup Poll, August 24, 2006); Suzanne Parker, "Toward an Under-

standing of 'Rally' Effects: Public Opinion in the Persian Gulf War," *Public Opinion Quarterly* 59, no. 4 (1995): 526–546. The Gallup Poll later observed that the public's "optimism about winning against terrorism is highly related to major military offensives. When the United States invaded Afghanistan in October 2001, and when the United States invaded Iraq in March 2003, the perception that the United States and its allies were winning the war against terrorism shot up well above the fifty percent mark." Newport, *Only a Third Believe War against Terror Being Won.*

110. Merrill McPeak, "Leave the Flying to Us," *Washington Post,* June 5, 2003.

111. Gordon and Trainor, *Cobra II,* 72.

112. Iraq Body Count, "Press Release: Iraq Death Toll in Third Year of Occupation Is Highest Yet" (London: Iraq Body Count, March 9, 2006).

113. Iraq Study Group, *The Way Forward: A New Approach* (Washington, DC: Vintage, 2006), 5.

114. In February 2007, the Internal Displacement Monitoring Centre estimated that about 860,000 Iraqis had been displaced because of conflict since 2003. Roughly one million more were already displaced before the 2003 invasion. http://www.internal-displacement.org/.

115. Director of National Intelligence, *Declassified Key Judgments of the National Intelligence Estimate "Trends in Global Terrorism: Implications for the United States" Dated April 2006* (Washington, DC: Office of the Director of National Intelligence, September 2006), 2.

116. International Monetary Fund, *Country Report: Iraq* (Washington, DC: International Monetary Fund, August 2006), 4.

117. In November 2006, Transparency International reported that Iraq ranked 160th out of the 163 countries included in its annual Corruption Perceptions Index. Its position on the index worsened every year after 2003.

118. On the eve of the 2006 midterm elections, most Americans believed that the situation in Iraq was out of control and that Bush lacked a clear plan for responding, according to a Gallup poll.

119. Commission on Post-Conflict Reconstruction, *Play to Win: Final Report of the Commission* (Washington, DC: Center for Strategic and International Studies and Association of the U.S. Army, January 2003), 11. This diagnosis was affirmed, four years later, by the Special Inspector General for Iraq Reconstruction, *Iraq Reconstruction: Lessons in Program and Project Management* (Washington, DC: Special Inspector General for Iraq Reconstruction, March 2007).

120. U.S. Central Command, *Desert Crossing Seminar: After Action Report* (MacDill AFB, FL: U.S. Central Command, 1999). The document was obtained by the National Security Archive in response to a Freedom of Information Act request and publicly released in November 2006.

121. Anthony Zinni later said that in 2002 "I called CENTCOM and said, You need to dust off Desert Crossing. They said, What's that? Never heard of it. So in a matter of just a few years ago it was gone. The corporate memory." Leslie Evans, "Straight Talk from General Anthony Zinni" (Los Angeles, CA: Burkle Center for

International Relations, May 14, 2004), available online at http://www.international
.ucla.edu/bcir/news/print.asp?parentid=11162 (accessed August 10, 2006). See
also Gordon and Trainor, *Cobra II*, 26–27, 139.

122. Gordon and Trainor, *Cobra II*, 66–67.

123. Ricks, *Fiasco*, 151, 242.

124. Gordon and Trainor, *Cobra II*, 25, 139.

125. Ibid., 68, 70, 74.

126. Special Inspector General for Iraq Reconstruction, *Iraq Reconstruction:
Lessons Learned in Human Capital Management* (Washington, DC: Special Inspector
General for Iraq Reconstruction, February 2006), 6.

127. Future of Iraq Project, *The Future of Iraq Project: Overview* (Washington,
DC: Department of State, May 12, 2003). This was one of several documents released by the State Department in August 2006 in response to a Freedom of Information Act request filed by the National Security Archive.

128. Ricks, *Fiasco*, 103.

129. Gordon and Trainor, *Cobra II*, 140–141. The Joint Chiefs of Staff, meanwhile, set up a special group, JTF-4, to make plans for the postwar military command. Difficulties would later arise because of the lack of coordination between
JTF-4's work and planning by Lieutenant General David McKiernan, commander
of land forces in Iraq. Ibid., 143–144. Ricks provides a different explanation of JTF-
4, describing it as a CENTCOM project. Ricks, *Fiasco*, 78. Woodward says that the
Office of Secretary of Defense asserted ownership of the issue in September 2002
and that CENTCOM leaders were happy to be relieved of the responsibility. Woodward, *State of Denial*, 90–92.

130. Ricks, *Fiasco*, 78; Gordon and Trainor, *Cobra II*, 142; Woodward, *State of
Denial*, 208. Franks called Feith "the dumbest fucking guy on the planet." Tommy
Franks, *American Soldier* (New York: Regan Books, 2004), 362.

131. Rand, *Iraq: Translating Lessons into Future DoD Policies* (Santa Monica, CA:
Rand, February 2005), 9.

132. National Security Presidential Directive 24, January 20, 2003. On the
adoption of this directive, see Woodward, *State of Denial*, 112–113. On Feith's su-
pervisory role, see L. Elaine Halchin, *The Coalition Provisional Authority (CPA): Origin, Characteristics, and Institutional Authorities* (Washington, DC: Congressional Research Service, June 6, 2005), 2. Jay Garner, however, said in March 2003 that once
his team entered Iraq, "General Franks will be my boss." Department of Defense,
*Backgrounder on Reconstruction and Humanitarian Assistance in Post-War* (Washington, DC: Department of Defense, March 11, 2003).

133. Woodward, *Bush at War*, 283.

134. Special Inspector General for Iraq Reconstruction, *Iraq Reconstruction:
Lessons Learned in Human Capital Management*, 7, 12–13. Garner's position was formally approved only two weeks before the invasion. Halchin, *The Coalition Provisional Authority*, 2.

135. Woodward, *State of Denial*, 126–129, 150–152, 157–158; Gordon and Trainor, *Cobra II*, 158–159.

136. Department of Defense, *Backgrounder on Reconstruction and Humanitarian Assistance in Post-War.*

137. Woodward, *State of Denial,* 166–174, 180–181, 193; Steven Weisman, "U.S. Set to Name Civilian to Oversee Iraq," *New York Times,* May 2, 2003, 18. The CPA was recognized in a CENTCOM order issued by General Franks on April 17. Special Inspector General for Iraq Reconstruction, *Iraq Reconstruction: Lessons in Contracting and Procurement* (Washington, DC: Special Inspector General for Iraq Reconstruction, July 2006), 23.

138. Special Inspector General for Iraq Reconstruction, *Iraq Reconstruction: Lessons Learned in Human Capital Management,* 11.

139. Halchin, *The Coalition Provisional Authority,* 1.

140. Ibid., 10, 12, 20.

141. Celeste Ward, *The Coalition Provisional Authority's Experience with Governance in Iraq* (Washington, DC: United States Institute of Peace, May 2005), 10.

142. CPA Inspector General, *Management of Personnel Assigned to the Coalition Provisional Authority in Baghdad, Iraq* (Arlington, VA: Office of the CPA Inspector General, June 25, 2004), i.

143. Special Inspector General for Iraq Reconstruction, *Iraq Reconstruction: Lessons Learned in Human Capital Management,* 16.

144. Ibid., 21; Special Inspector General for Iraq Reconstruction, *Seventh Quarterly Report* (Washington, DC: Office of the Special Inspector General for Iraq Reconstruction, 2005), 79.

145. Ariana Cha, "In Iraq, the Opportunity of a Lifetime," *Washington Post,* May 23, 2004, A1.

146. A. Juhasz, "Ambitions of Empire: The Bush Administration Economic Plan for Iraq," *Left Turn,* February/March 2004, 27–32.

147. Rajiv Chandrasekaran, "Best-Connected Were Sent to Rebuild Iraq," *Washington Post,* September 17, 2006, A1.

148. Anne Henderson, *The Coalition Provisional Authority's Experience with Economic Reconstruction in Iraq: Lessons Identified* (Washington, DC: United States Institute of Peace, April 2005), 11.

149. Stephen Glain, "Fast Track Plan to Sell State-Owned Firms in Iraq Is Put on Hold," *Boston Globe,* September 18, 2003, E1.

150. Special Inspector General for Iraq Reconstruction, *Iraq Reconstruction: Lessons Learned in Human Capital Management,* 37–39.

151. Ricks, *Fiasco,* 173, 209, 324; Woodward, *State of Denial,* 292–297, 308.

152. Ward, *The Coalition Provisional Authority's Experience with Governance in Iraq,* 6.

153. Ibid., 5; Larry Diamond, "What Went Wrong in Iraq," *Foreign Affairs* 83, no. 5 (2004).

154. CPA Private Security Company Working Group, *Minutes of Meeting* (Baghdad, Iraq: Coalition Provisional Authority, March 30, 2004).

155. Special Inspector General for Iraq Reconstruction, *Iraq Reconstruction: Lessons Learned in Human Capital Management,* 10.

156. Henderson, *The Coalition Provisional Authority's Experience with Economic Reconstruction in Iraq*, 13.

157. Halchin, *The Coalition Provisional Authority*, 3.

158. Woodward, *State of Denial*, 208–209, 212; Ricks, *Fiasco*, 179, 181.

159. Woodward, *State of Denial*, 274.

160. Peter Slevin and Mike Allen, "Rice to Lead Effort to Speed Iraqi Aid," *Washington Post*, October 7, 2003, A1; Woodward, *State of Denial*, 209.

161. Ricks, *Fiasco*, 255.

162. Coalition Provisional Authority Order Number 1, *De-Ba'athification of Iraqi Society*, May 16, 2003.

163. Coalition Provisional Authority Order Number 2, *Dissolution of Entities*, May 23, 2003.

164. Invasion plans had assumed that Iraqi army forces could be used to maintain order after the invasion. Gordon and Trainor, *Cobra II*, 68, 73, 105.

165. Henderson, *The Coalition Provisional Authority's Experience with Economic Reconstruction in Iraq*, 15; Robert Perito, *The Coalition Provisional Authority's Experience with Public Security in Iraq* (Washington, DC: United States Institute of Peace, April 2005), 6; Council on Foreign Relations, *Backgrounder: Debaathification* (New York: Council on Foreign Relations, April 7, 2005), available online at http://www.cfr.org/publication.html?id=7853 (accessed October 15, 2006).

166. Ricks, *Fiasco*, 158–165; Woodward, *State of Denial*, 132–140, 193–198; Gordon and Trainor, *Cobra II*, 160–162, 483.

167. "Bremer's Change in De-Baathification Policy Benefits Iraqi Teachers," *Deutsche Press-Agentur*, April 23, 2004.

168. Patrick Tyler, "Opposition Groups to Help Create Assembly in Iraq," *New York Times*, May 6, 2003, A1; Woodward, *State of Denial*, 74–75.

169. Woodward, *Bush at War*, 341–342, 360.

170. Patrick Tyler, "In Reversal, Plan for Iraq Self-Rule Has Been Put Off," *New York Times*, May 17, 2003, A1.

171. Ward, *The Coalition Provisional Authority's Experience with Governance in Iraq*, 5; Diamond, "What Went Wrong in Iraq"; Gordon and Trainor, *Cobra II*, 479, 491.

172. L. Paul Bremer, "Iraq's Path to Sovereignty," *Washington Post*, September 8, 2003, A21.

173. Richard Bernstein, "France and Germany Differ with U.S. on Plan for Iraq," *New York Times*, September 5, 2003, 9.

174. Woodward, *State of Denial*, 249; Ricks, *Fiasco*, 254–255.

175. David Brooks, "Bush's Winning Strategy," *New York Times*, July 3, 2004, 15.

176. Executive Office of the President, "President Addresses the Nation" (Washington, DC: Office of the Press Secretary, September 7, 2003); Elisabeth Bumiller, "Bush, at UN, Defends Policy over Iraq," *New York Times*, September 24, 2003, A1.

177. David Sanger, "White House to Overhaul Iraq and Afghan Missions," *New York Times*, October 5, 2003, A1; Woodward, *State of Denial*, 254–259.

178. David Sanger, "America's Gamble: Faster Power Shift in Iraq," *New York Times,* November 16, 2003, 17.

179. Susan Sachs, "U.S. Is to Return Power to Iraqis as Early as June," *New York Times,* November 15, 2003, 1.

180. Commission on Post-Conflict Reconstruction, *Play to Win,* 7.

181. On the collapse of security and its consequences, see Perito, *The Coalition Provisional Authority's Experience with Public Security in Iraq,* 4, 7; Henderson, *The Coalition Provisional Authority's Experience with Economic Reconstruction in Iraq,* 8.

182. Ward, *The Coalition Provisional Authority's Experience with Governance in Iraq,* 6; Henderson, *The Coalition Provisional Authority's Experience with Economic Reconstruction in Iraq,* 15.

183. Diamond, "What Went Wrong in Iraq."

184. Gordon and Trainor, *Cobra II,* 155–162.

185. Ibid., 28–29, 168; Ricks, *Fiasco,* 117–123.

186. Richard Haass, director of policy planning in the State Department, later observed that there was no conscious decision to go to war against Iraq. "It was an accretion, a tipping point. A decision was not made—a decision happened, and you can't say when or how." George Packer, *The Assassins' Gate: America in Iraq* (New York: Farrar, Straus and Giroux, 2005), 45.

187. Department of Defense, "Secretary Rumsfeld Interview with Sir David Frost, BBC News" (Washington, DC: Department of Defense, June 13, 2005).

188. Woodward, *State of Denial,* 408, 455. For a similar criticism of the breakdown of national-security planning and deliberative processes, see Brzezinski, *Second Chance,* 142, 195.

189. Rand, *Iraq: Translating Lessons,* 6, 10.

190. Woodward, *State of Denial,* 400.

191. For variations, see ibid., 109, 295, 321, 381, 436.

### Notes to Chapter 6

1. John Burke, "The Bush Transition in Historical Context," *PS: Political Science and Politics* 35, no. 1 (2002): 25.

2. Ken Auletta, "Fortress Bush," *New Yorker,* January 19, 2004.

3. Jeremy Mayer, "The Presidency and Image Management: Discipline in Pursuit of Illusion," *Presidential Studies Quarterly* 34, no. 3 (2004): 624.

4. Elizabeth Drew, "Power Grab," *New York Review of Books,* June 22, 2006, 10–15.

5. Arthur M. Schlesinger Jr., *War and the American Presidency* (New York: Norton, 2004), 61.

6. John W. Dean, *Worse than Watergate* (New York: Little, Brown, 2004), 1. Dean later criticized the Bush administration for its authoritarian tendencies. John W. Dean, *Conservatives without Conscience* (New York: Viking, 2006).

7. Alan Elsner, "Bush Expands Government Secrecy, Arouses Critics," Reuters, September 3, 2002. Veteran journalist Haynes Johnson goes further still: se-

crecy under Bush, Johnson said, was the worst since Hoover. Haynes Johnson, *The Age of Anxiety* (Orlando, FL: Harcourt Books, 2005), 490.

8. Timothy Noah, "The Rumsfeld Death Watch," *Slate*, August 7, 2001; Johanna McGeary, "Odd Man Out," *Time*, September 10, 2001, 24–33.

9. David Brooks, "Let's Have an Argument," *Weekly Standard*, August 13, 2001, 9.

10. Richard Berke and David Sanger, "Bush's Aides Seek to Focus Efforts on the Economy," *New York Times*, September 9, 2001.

11. Thomas K. Kean, Lee Hamilton, and Benjamin Rhodes, *Without Precedent: The Inside Story of the 9/11 Commission* (New York: Knopf, 2006), 97.

12. John D. Ashcroft, *Never Again: Securing America and Restoring Justice* (New York: Center Street, 2006), 235.

13. The history of the commission is described by Kean, Hamilton, and Rhodes, *Without Precedent*.

14. Ibid., 157.

15. Alessandra Stanley, "Laying Blame and Passing the Buck, Dramatized," *New York Times*, September 8, 2006.

16. National Commission on Terrorist Attacks upon the United States, *Final Report* (New York: Barnes and Noble Books, 2004), 265.

17. Joseph Wilson, "What I Didn't Find in Africa," *New York Times*, July 6, 2003.

18. Faye Bowers and Peter Grier, "After Rare Move to Declassify Documents, Intelligence Wars May Transform Spying," *Christian Science Monitor*, July 21, 2003, 2. For detailed discussion of the discrepancies, see Joseph Cirincione, Jessica Mathews, and George Perkovich, *WMD in Iraq: Evidence and Implications* (Washington, DC: Carnegie Endowment for International Peace, January 2004), 16–17; John Prados, *Hoodwinked* (New York: New Press, 2004), 45–46.

19. Robert Novak, "The Mission to Niger," *Chicago Sun-Times*, July 14, 2003, 31.

20. Murray Waas, "Bush Directed Cheney to Counter War Critic," *National Journal*, July 3, 2006.

21. "Cheney was lost without Libby, many of the vice president's associates felt." Bob Woodward, *State of Denial* (New York: Simon and Schuster, 2006), 456–457. See also David Sanger and Eric Schmitt, "Cheney's Power No Longer Goes Unquestioned," *New York Times*, September 10, 2006; David J. Rothkopf, *Running the World: The Inside Story of the National Security Council and the Architects of American Power* (New York: PublicAffairs, 2005), 438. Libby was convicted of perjury and other charges in March 2007.

22. Ron Suskind, "Why Are These Men Laughing?" *Esquire*, January 2003, 96.

23. For a brief summary of the tensions between President Clinton and the military leadership, see Dana Priest, *The Mission: Waging War and Keeping Peace with America's Military* (New York: Norton, 2003), 42–45.

24. Executive Office of the President, "Remarks by the President and Secretary of Defense Donald Rumsfeld at Swearing-in Ceremony" (Washington, DC: Office of the Press Secretary, January 26, 2001).

25. Thomas Ricks, *Fiasco: The American Military Adventure in Iraq* (New York: Penguin, 2006), 68–69.

26. Donald Rumsfeld, "Remarks at the DoD Acquisition and Logistics Excellence Week Kickoff" (Washington, DC: Office of the Assistant Secretary of Defense [Public Affairs], September 10, 2001).

27. A critical appraisal of Rumsfeld's approach to management of the Defense Department is provided in several books, including Bob Woodward, *Bush at War* (New York: Simon and Schuster, 2002); Ricks, *Fiasco*; Michael R. Gordon and Bernard E. Trainor, *Cobra II: The Inside Story of the Invasion and Occupation of Iraq* (New York: Pantheon Books, 2006).

28. James Mann, *Rise of the Vulcans* (New York: Viking, 2004), 290–291.

29. Woodward, *State of Denial*, 57.

30. Ibid., 22.

31. Bob Woodward, *Plan of Attack* (New York: Simon and Schuster, 2004), 6. In his autobiography, Franks says that he told Rumsfeld, "It appears you no longer have confidence in me." Tommy Franks, *American Soldier* (New York: Regan Books, 2004), 466.

32. Ricks, *Fiasco*, 42–43. Similarly, Woodward says that Rumsfeld "drove the train" on troop levels. Woodward, *State of Denial*, 257.

33. Eric Schmitt, "U.S. Plan for Iraq Is Said to Include Attack on 3 Sides," *New York Times*, July 5, 2002, 1.

34. Frederick Kroesen, "Commentary," *Army*, September 2002, 16.

35. Anthony C. Zinni, "Transcript of Speech to the Middle East Institute" (Washington, DC: Middle East Institute, October 31, 2002).

36. Thomas Ricks, " 'Stormin' Norman,' Gen. Schwarzkopf Is Skeptical about U.S. Action in Iraq," *Washington Post*, January 28, 2003, C1.

37. Seymour M. Hersh, "The Debate Within," *New Yorker*, March 11, 2002, 34.

38. Ricks, " 'Stormin' Norman,' "; Eric Shinseki, "Leadership and Command," *Army*, August 2003, 64.

39. The intelligence community comprises all federal agencies or offices engaged in the collection and analysis of intelligence, the most prominent of which is the Central Intelligence Agency. Until 2004, the head of the CIA, titled the Director of Central Intelligence, was nominally the overseer of the intelligence community as well.

40. Woodward, *Plan of Attack*, 179.

41. House Select Committee on Intelligence, *Report on the Intelligence Authorization Act for Fiscal Year 2005*, H.Rep. 108-558 (Washington, DC: House of Representatives, June 21, 2004), 24, 25.

42. Tom Hamburger and Peter Wallsten, "Cheney, CIA Long at Odds," *Los Angeles Times*, October 20, 2005.

43. Richard Cheney, "Remarks by the Vice President to the Veterans of Foreign Wars 103rd National Convention" (Washington, DC: Office of the Press Secretary, August 26, 2002).

44. James Risen, "How Pair's Finding on Terror Led to Clash on Shaping Intelligence," *New York Times,* April 28, 2004, 1.

45. Commission to Assess the Ballistic Missile Threat to the United States, *Report* (Washington, DC: Central Intelligence Agency, July 15, 1998). Paul Wolfowitz also participated in the inquiry.

46. Bradley Graham, "Iran, North Korea Missile Gains Spur Warning," *Washington Post,* July 16, 1998, A1.

47. James Risen, "India's A-Tests Prompt CIA to Review Its Warning Systems," *New York Times,* July 4, 1998, A3.

48. Paul Pillar, "Intelligence, Policy and the War in Iraq," *Foreign Affairs* 85, no. 2 (2006): 15.

49. In July 2002 Condoleezza Rice told Richard Haass, director of policy planning in the State Department, that "the decision's been made." John Burke, "Condoleezza Rice as NSC Advisor: A Case Study of the Honest Broker Role," *Presidential Studies Quarterly* 35, no. 3 (2005): 563. A leaked UK government memorandum (the "Downing Street Memorandum") also reported that in Washington, "military action was now seen as inevitable. . . . the intelligence and facts were being fixed around the policy."

50. Executive Office of the President, "The Vice President Appears on NBC's *Meet the Press*" (Washington, DC: Office of the Vice President, December 9, 2001).

51. Woodward, *Plan of Attack,* 247–250.

52. The CIA provided Congress with a classified National Intelligence Estimate (NIE) on Iraq on October 1, 2002. It became clear to some readers that the NIE contained some statements that weakened the administration's case for war. Dana Priest, "Analysts Discount Attack by Iraq," *Washington Post,* October 9, 2002, A1. On October 4, Tenet's office released an unclassified white paper that was later found to have omitted critical reservations contained in the NIE. On October 7, Tenet provided Senator Bob Graham with an unclassified letter on the Iraqi threat, and Iraqi connections to al Qaeda, that were also stated more strongly than in the NIE. See generally Prados, *Hoodwinked.* On October 8, Tenet gave an interview to the *New York Times* in which he emphasized that "there is no inconsistency" between the CIA's assessment and the president's views. Alison Mitchell, "CIA Sees Terror after Iraq Action," *New York Times,* October 9, 2002, A1.

53. Commission on Intelligence Capabilities of the United States Regarding Weapons of Mass Destruction, *Report to the President* (Washington, DC: Commission on Intelligence Capabilities, March 31, 2005), 188–192. The Senate Intelligence Committee observed that after September 11, the CIA was under "under tremendous pressure . . . to avoid missing a credible threat." Senate Intelligence Committee, *Report on the U.S. Intelligence Community's Prewar Intelligence Assessments on Iraq,* S.Rep. 108-301 (Washington, DC: U.S. Senate Select Committee on Intelligence, July 9, 2004), 363. Prados observes that Cheney's visits were "extremely unusual." Prados, *Hoodwinked,* 34.

54. For a description of the work done by Feith's unit, see Eric Schmitt and Thom Shanker, "A CIA Rival; Pentagon Sets Up Intelligence Unit," *New York Times*, October 24, 2002, 1; Department of Defense, "DoD Briefing on Policy and Intelligence Matters" (Washington, DC: U.S. Department of Defense, June 4, 2002); Seymour M. Hersh, "Selective Intelligence," *New Yorker*, May 12, 2003, 44; Prados, *Hoodwinked*, 288–308; Senator Carl Levin, *Report of an Inquiry into the Alternative Analysis of the Issue of an Iraq–Al Qaeda Relationship* (Washington, DC: Office of Senator Carl Levin, October 21, 2004). On CIA analysts' view of the Iraq–al Qaeda connection, see Senate Intelligence Committee, *Report on the U.S. Intelligence Community's Prewar Intelligence Assessments on Iraq*, 305–307. See also the excerpt of an interview with Paul Pillar in Gordon and Trainor, *Cobra II*, 127.

55. Senate Intelligence Committee, *Report on the U.S. Intelligence Community's Prewar Intelligence Assessments on Iraq*, 362.

56. Ibid., 308; Levin, *Report of an Inquiry into the Alternative Analysis*, 16–24.

57. Feith's PowerPoint slides were released following an inquiry by the Defense Department's inspector general in February 2007. Department of Defense, *Review of the Pre-Iraqi War Activities of the Office of the Under Secretary of Defense for Policy*, 07-INTEL-04 (Washington, DC: Office of the Inspector General, February 9, 2007), 9.

58. M. E. Sprengelmeyer, "Cheney under Attack," *Denver Post*, January 24, 2004, 27A. Cheney was referring to a summary provided by Feith's office to the Senate Intelligence Committee and later leaked to the magazine the *Weekly Standard*. The phrase "alternative intelligence assessments" was used by the Defense Department's inspector general to describe Feith's work. Department of Defense, *Review of the Pre-Iraqi War Activities*, 5.

59. Woodward, *Plan of Attack*, 288–290, 297–300, 309.

60. Ibid., 284.

61. Woodward, *Bush at War*, 61.

62. L. Paul Bremer and Malcolm McConnell, *My Year in Iraq: The Struggle to Build a Future of Hope* (New York: Simon and Schuster, 2006), 208.

63. Woodward, *Plan of Attack*, 284.

64. Mann, *Rise of the Vulcans*, 270.

65. Woodward, *Plan of Attack*, 164.

66. Woodward, *State of Denial*, 126.

67. Ricks, *Fiasco*, 105. When Rumsfeld contemplated replacing Jay Garner in March 2003, one candidate briefly considered was former secretary of state George Shultz; a knock against Shultz was the prospect that he might "be more tolerant of State's viewpoints." Woodward, *State of Denial*, 167.

68. Woodward, *State of Denial*, 162.

69. Newt Gingrich, *Transforming the State Department: The Next Challenge for the Bush Administration* (Washington, DC: American Enterprise Institute, April 22, 2003), available online at http://www.aei.org/publications/pubID.16992,filter.all/pub_detail.asp (accessed November 3, 2006).

70. John Maynard Keynes, *The General Theory of Employment, Interest and Money* (New York: Harcourt, Brace, 1936), chap. 24.

71. David K. Johnson, *The Lavender Scare* (Chicago: University of Chicago Press, 2004), 72.

72. Seymour Martin Lipset, "The Radical Right: A Problem for American Democracy," *British Journal of Sociology* 6, no. 2 (1955): 176–209; E. Digby Baltzell, *The Protestant Establishment: Aristocracy and Caste in America* (New York: Random House, 1964).

73. William Douglas, "UN Ambassador Nominee Faces Tough Hearing," *Seattle Times,* April 11, 2005, A5.

74. Woodward, *Bush at War,* 11.

75. The influential early works on this subject include Anthony Downs, *Inside Bureaucracy* (Santa Monica, CA: Rand Corporation, 1964); Gordon Tullock, *The Politics of Bureaucracy* (Washington, DC: Public Affairs Press, 1965); William Niskanen, "The Peculiar Economics of Bureaucracy," *American Economic Review* 58, no. 2 (1968): 293–305.

76. Donald Devine, "Burgeoning Bureaucracy," *Washington Times,* September 8, 1989, F1. See also Donald J. Devine, *Reagan's Terrible Swift Sword: Reforming and Controlling the Federal Bureaucracy* (Ottawa, IL: Jameson Books, 1991).

77. James Pfiffner, "Political Appointees and Career Executives: The Democracy-Bureaucracy Nexus in the Third Century," *Public Administration Review* 47, no. 1 (1987): 59.

78. George Nesterczuk, Donald Devine, and Robert Moffit, *Taking Charge of Federal Personnel* (Washington, DC: Heritage Foundation, January 10, 2001), available online at http://www.heritage.org/Research/GovernmentReform/BG1404.cfm (accessed September 23, 2006).

79. John O'Connor, "I'm the Guy They Call Deep Throat," *Vanity Fair,* July 2005, 86. Woodward quickly wrote a book about his relationship with Felt: Bob Woodward, *The Secret Man* (New York: Simon and Schuster, 2005).

80. Transcript, *This Week with George Stephanopoulos,* ABC News, June 26, 2005.

81. O'Connor, "I'm the Guy They Call Deep Throat."

82. Amanda Ripley and Maggie Sieger, "The Special Agent," *Time,* December 30, 2002, 34.

83. O'Connor, "I'm the Guy They Call Deep Throat."

84. Patricia Sullivan, "Watergate-Era FBI Chief L. Patrick Gray III Dies at 88," *Washington Post,* July 7, 2005, B6.

85. John Morriss, "New Nader Group Seeking Tipsters," *New York Times,* January 27, 1971, 32.

86. For a review of the early academic literature on whistleblowing by government employees, see James Bowman, "Whistle Blowing: Literature and Resource Materials," *Public Administration Review* 43, no. 3 (1983): 271–276. A more recent review of the Whistleblower Protection Act is provided by L. Paige Whitaker, *The Whistleblower Protection Act: An Overview* (Washington, DC: Congressional Research Service, March 12, 2007). There are important limitations to the protection

provided by law; most notably, employees working in the FBI or intelligence agencies are not able to rely on the law. In March 2007, Congress approved a bill (HR 985) that would extend whistleblower protections to these employees.

87. Rosemary O'Leary, *The Ethics of Dissent: Managing Guerrilla Government* (Washington, DC: CQ Press, 2006).

88. Chitra Ragavan, "The Case of a '20th Hijacker'?" *U.S. News and World Report,* December 24, 2001, 20. More details about the "Phoenix memorandum" were leaked to the Associated Press in April 2002.

89. Michael Weisskopf, "The Whistle-Blower," *Time,* June 3, 2003, 24.

90. Sen. Chuck Grassley, "Letter to the Hon. Patrick Leahy on Rowley Testimony" (Washington, DC: Office of Senator Chuck Grassley, May 31, 2002).

91. Lisa Myers, "9/11 Commission Interviews FBI Officials Who Contradict Ashcroft Testimony," *MSNBC Nightly News,* June 22, 2004, available online at http://www.msnbc.com/id/5271234/.

92. Eric Lichtblau, "Whistle-Blowing Said to Be Factor in FBI Firing," *New York Times,* July 29, 2004, 1.

93. David Rose, "Defectors Tricked Us with WMD Lies," *Observer* (London), May 30, 2004, 23.

94. See, for example, an article based on interviews with "more than a dozen current and former senior government officials": Jonathan Landay and Warren Strobel, "Officials Had No Plan B for Postwar Iraq," *Pittsburgh Post-Gazette,* July 13, 2003, A6.

95. Felicity Barringer, "U.S. Diplomat Resigns, Protesting 'Our Fervent Pursuit of War,'" *New York Times,* February 27, 2003, 13. Kiesling also wrote a book criticizing the administration's foreign policy: John Brady Kiesling, *Diplomacy Lessons: Realism for an Unloved Superpower* (Washington, DC: Potomac Books, 2006).

96. Neela Banerjee, "State Dept. Official Apologizes for Criticism of Iraq Policy," *New York Times,* October 23, 2006.

97. Warren Strobel, Jonathan Landay, and John Walcott, "Some in Government Doubt Iraq Evidence," *Pittsburgh Post-Gazette,* October 9, 2002, A10.

98. Judith Miller, "My Four Hours Testifying in the Federal Grand Jury Room," *New York Times,* October 16, 2005, 31.

99. Woodward, *State of Denial,* 233.

100. "Cheney Must Go," *Salon.com,* July 16, 2003, available online at http://dir.salon.com/story/news/feature/2003/07/16/vips/.

101. Senate Intelligence Committee, *Report on the U.S. Intelligence Community's Prewar Intelligence Assessments on Iraq.* The report was released in July, but the Intelligence Committee had prolonged discussions with the CIA about declassification of its contents in the preceding three months.

102. See, for example, President Bush's statements on January 27, 2004: Executive Office of the President, "President Bush Welcomes President Kwasniewski to White House" (Washington, DC: Office of the Press Secretary, January 27, 2004).

103. Michael Scheuer, *Imperial Hubris: Why the West Is Losing the War on Terror* (Washington, DC: Brassey's, 2004).

104. Ibid., ix, 213.

105. The book was on the *New York Times* nonfiction bestseller list from August 1 to September 19, 2004.

106. Dana Priest, "Bringing Change, Not by the Book," *Washington Post*, November 25, 2004, A4.

107. Dana Priest, "CIA Officer Criticizes Agency's Handling of Bin Laden," *Washington Post*, November 9, 2004, A28.

108. Douglas Jehl, "U.S. Intelligence Shows Pessimism on Iraq's Future," *New York Times*, September 16, 2004, 1.

109. Paul Pillar said later that the agency's prewar assessments

> foretold a long, difficult, and turbulent transition. It projected that a Marshall Plan–type effort would be required to restore the Iraqi economy, despite Iraq's abundant oil resources. It forecast that in a deeply divided Iraqi society, with Sunnis resentful over the loss of their dominant position and Shiites seeking power commensurate with their majority status, there was a significant chance that the groups would engage in violent conflict unless an occupying power prevented it. And it anticipated that a foreign occupying force would itself be the target of resentment and attacks—including by guerrilla warfare—unless it established security and put Iraq on the road to prosperity in the first few weeks or months after the fall of Saddam.

Pillar, "Intelligence, Policy and the War in Iraq."

110. Executive Office of the President, "President Bush Meets with Prime Minister Allawi in New York" (Washington, DC: Office of the Press Secretary, September 21, 2004).

111. Executive Office of the President, "President Bush and Prime Minister Allawi Press Conference" (Washington, DC: Office of the Press Secretary, September 23, 2004).

112. Robert Novak, "Is CIA at War with Bush?" *Chicago Sun-Times*, September 27, 2004, 49. Pillar said that he believed his speech was given on an off-the-record basis.

113. Douglas Jehl and David Sanger, "Prewar Assessment on Iraq Saw Chance of Strong Divisions," *New York Times*, September 28, 2004, 1.

114. Warren Strobel, "Fresh CIA Analysis: No Evidence Saddam Colluded with Al-Qaida," *Seattle Times*, October 4, 2004, A9.

115. Douglas Jehl, "CIA–White House Tensions Are Unusually Public," *New York Times*, October 2, 2004, 12.

116. David Brooks, "The CIA versus Bush," *New York Times*, November 13, 2004.

117. Douglas Jehl, "New CIA Chief Tells Workers to Back Administration Policies," *New York Times*, November 17, 2004, 1.

118. The most prominent resignations were those of Stephen Kappes and Michael Sulick, senior officials in the agency's clandestine-services directorate.

119. Commission on Intelligence Capabilities, *Report to the President.*

120. George Tenet, *Statement on Silberman-Robb Commission* (Washington, DC: Federation of American Scientists, April 1, 2004).

121. Bob Drogin and Greg Miller, " 'Curveball' Debacle Ignites CIA Feud," *Los Angeles Times,* April 2, 2005, 1.

122. Dana Priest, "CIA Holds Terror Suspects in Secret Prisons," *Washington Post,* November 2, 2005, A1.

123. Jeffrey R. Smith, "Fired Officer Believed CIA Lied to Congress," *Washington Post,* May 14, 2006, A1; Sarah Baxter and Michael Smith, "CIA Chief Sacked for Opposing Torture," *Sunday Times,* February 12, 2006.

124. David Sanger and William Broad, "How to Listen for the Sound of Plutonium," *New York Times,* January 31, 2006, F1.

125. Porter Goss, "Loose Lips Sink Spies," *New York Times,* February 10, 2006, 25.

126. Baxter and Smith, "CIA Chief Sacked for Opposing Torture."

127. Maj. Gen. Antonio Taguba, *Article 15-6 Investigation of the 800th Military Police Brigade* (Washington, DC: United States Central Command, March 9, 2004).

128. "Rumsfeld Testifies before House Armed Services Committee," *Washington Post,* May 7, 2004, Web edition.

129. Seymour Hersh, "Chain of Command," *New Yorker,* May 17, 2004, 38.

130. Transcript, *Good Morning America,* ABC News, May 3, 2004. Karpinski also appeared on *Nightline* and CNN's *American Morning.*

131. Janis Karpinski, *One Woman's Army: The Commanding General of Abu Ghraib Tells Her Story* (New York: Miramax Books, 2005).

132. New York City Bar Association, *Human Rights Standards Applicable to the United States' Interrogation of Detainees* (New York: Association of the Bar of the City of New York, April 30, 2004).

133. Ken Silverstein, "U.S. Military Lawyers Felt 'Shut Out' of Prison Policy," *Los Angeles Times,* May 14, 2004; Neil Lewis and Eric Schmitt, "Lawyers Decided Bans on Torture Didn't Bind Bush," *New York Times,* June 8, 2004, 1; Dana Priest and Dan Morgan, "Rumsfeld Defends Rules for Prison," *Washington Post,* May 13, 2004, A1.

134. *World News Tonight,* ABC News, May 15, 2004; *20/20,* ABC News, June 25, 2004.

135. Jess Bravin, "Pentagon Report Set Framework for Use of Torture," *Wall Street Journal,* June 7, 2004, A1.

136. Lewis and Schmitt, "Lawyers Decided Bans on Torture Didn't Bind Bush"; Dana Priest and R. Jeffrey Smith, "Memo Offered Justification for Use of Torture," *Washington Post,* June 8, 2004, A1.

137. Richard Serrano, "Prison Interrogator's Gloves Came Off before Abu Ghraib," *Los Angeles Times,* June 9, 2004.

138. Executive Office of the President, "Press Briefing by White House Counsel Judge Alberto Gonzales, DoD General Counsel William Haynes, DoD Deputy General Counsel Daniel Dell'orto and Army Deputy Chief of Staff for Intelligence

General Keith Alexander" (Washington, DC: Office of the Press Secretary, June 22, 2004).

139. The Schlesinger report was released in August 2004: Steven Strasser, *The Abu Ghraib Investigations: The Official Reports of the Independent Panel and Pentagon on the Shocking Prisoner Abuse in Iraq* (New York: PublicAffairs, 2004), 30, 32. The Church report was given to Congress in March 2005: Vice Admiral A. T. Church, *Review of Department of Defense Detention Operations and Detainee Interrogation Techniques* (Washington, DC: Department of Defense, March 7, 2005).

140. Neil A. Lewis, "Military's Opposition to Harsh Interrogation Is Outlined," *New York Times,* July 27, 2005, A21. An Armed Services subcommittee chaired by Senator Lindsey Graham also had hearings in which the services' lawyers expressed their reservations. Josh White, "Military Lawyers Fought Policy on Interrogations," *Washington Post,* July 15, 2005, A1.

141. Neil Lewis, "2 Prosecutors Faulted Trials for Detainees," *New York Times,* August 1, 2005, A1. In March 2007, Hicks pled guilty before a military commission at Guantánamo Bay to the charge of providing material support to a terrorist organization.

142. Jeffrey R. Smith, "Top Military Lawyers Oppose Plan for Special Courts," *Washington Post,* August 3, 2006, A11; Charles Babington and Jeffrey R. Smith, "Bush's Detainee Plan Is Criticized," *Washington Post,* September 8, 2006, A9.

143. Mark Mazzetti and Neil Lewis, "Military Lawyers Caught in the Middle on Tribunals," *New York Times,* September 19, 2006, A1.

144. Jane Mayer, "The Memo," *New Yorker,* February 27, 2006, 32–41.

145. Joseph Hoar, Robert G. Gard Jr., Lee F. Gunn, Claudia Kennedy, and Al Konetz, "Letter to the Hon. Arlen Specter Regarding Nomination of William J. Haynes II" (Washington, DC: July 7, 2006).

146. The Senate did not confirm the nomination before the 2006 elections, and the administration subsequently decided not to renominate Haynes.

147. Complaints surfaced even in the first days of invasion. Vernon Loeb and Thomas Ricks, "Questions Raised about Invasion Force," *Washington Post,* March 25, 2003, A17.

148. Thomas Ricks, "Ex-Envoy Criticizes Bush's Postwar Policy," *Washington Post,* September 5, 2003, A16.

149. Tom Clancy, Anthony C. Zinni, and Tony Koltz, *Battle Ready* (New York: Putnam's Sons, 2004), 426.

150. From June 13 to July 11, 2004.

151. Thom Shanker, "General Says Training of Iraqi Troops Suffered from Poor Planning and Staffing," *New York Times,* February 11, 2006, 6.

152. Paul Eaton, "A Top-Down Review for the Pentagon," *New York Times,* March 19, 2006, 12.

153. Greg Newbold, "Why Iraq Was a Mistake," *Time,* April 17, 2006, 42–44.

154. Transcript, *All Things Considered,* National Public Radio, April 13, 2006.

155. Transcript, *American Morning,* CNN, April 12, 2006, available online at

http://transcripts.cnn.com/TRANSCRIPTS/0604/12/ltm.02.html (accessed May 10, 2006); Thomas Ricks, "Rumsfeld Rebuked by Retired Generals," *Washington Post*, April 13, 2006, A1.

156. "Retired Maj. General: We Need a New Secretary of Defense," *CNN.com*, April 13, 2006, http://www.cnn.com/2006/POLITICS/04/13/swannack/ (accessed May 20, 2006).

157. James Risen's *State of War*, published in January 2006; Gordon and Trainor's *Cobra II*, in March; Ron Suskind's *The One-Percent Doctrine*, in June; Thomas Ricks's *Fiasco*, in July; George Packer's *The Assassin's Gate*, in September; and Bob Woodward's *State of Denial*, in September.

158. Zbigniew Brzezinski, *Second Chance: Three Presidents and the Crisis of American Superpower* (New York: Basic Books, 2007), 146.

159. Graydon Carter, "Editor's Letter," *Vanity Fair*, December 2006, 84–86. The two books were David Halberstam's *The Best and the Brightest* and Frances Fitzgerald's *Fire in the Lake*.

160. Woodward, *State of Denial*, 404. Jones subsequently confirmed the comment. Thomas Ricks, "U.S. European Commander Confirms Quotes in Book," *Washington Post*, October 5, 2006, A18.

161. Michael Gordon, "U.S. Central Command Charts Sharp Movement of the Civil Conflict in Iraq toward Chaos," *New York Times*, November 1, 2006, 12.

162. "Time for Rumsfeld to Go," *Army Times*, November 4, 2006.

163. Matthew Stannard, "Daniel Ellsberg Sees a New Trend: Telling All While the Issue Is Hot," *San Francisco Chronicle*, March 29, 2004, A1.

164. Ron Suskind, *The Price of Loyalty: George W. Bush, the White House, and the Education of Paul O'Neill* (New York: Simon and Schuster, 2004). The book topped the *New York Times* nonfiction bestseller list from February 1 to February 29, 2004.

165. From April 11 to May 2, 2004.

166. Rachel Donadio, "Richard Clarke's Unsecret Agent," *New York Observer*, April 5, 2004, 1.

167. Sharon Waxman, "Sony Pictures Buys Richard Clarke's Book for the Screen," *New York Times*, April 10, 2004, B7.

168. Alasdair Roberts, *Blacked Out: Government Secrecy in the Information Age* (New York: Cambridge University Press, 2006), 74.

169. Woodward, *Plan of Attack*. Woodward's book held the top spot from May 9 to May 23, 2004.

170. Steven Weisman, "Airing of Powell's Misgivings Tests Cabinet Ties," *New York Times*, April 19, 2004, 1.

171. Woodward, *Plan of Attack*, 292.

172. Brian Knowlton, "Former Powell Aide Says Bush Policy Is Run by 'Cabal,'" *New York Times*, October 21, 2005.

173. Plame and her publisher eventually agreed to abandon this agreement, and Plame negotiated a new agreement for a comparable amount with another publisher. Motoko Rich, "Ex-CIA Officer in New Book Talks," *New York Times*, June

1, 2006; Michael Powell, "Next for the CIA's Least Secret Officer: A Quieter Life," *New York Times*, March 8, 2007, A18.

174. Peter Edidin, "The CIA Leak, Onscreen," *New York Times*, March 3, 2007, B8.

175. Scott Shane, "With Only Reputations at Stake, Talk on CIA Report Turns on How Much to Publish," *New York Times*, August 26, 2005. Tenet did not accept this offer but later negotiated an agreement with another publisher.

176. Paul de la Garza, "Franks Lands a $5-Million Book Deal," *St. Petersburg Times*, October 9, 2003, 1A.

177. Gordon and Trainor, *Cobra II*, 486.

178. Woodward, *Bush at War*, 413.

179. It stayed at the top of the *New York Times* list for two weeks, August 22 and August 29, 2004.

180. Douglas Feith, *War and Decision* (New York: Regan Books/HarperCollins, 2008).

181. Franks, *American Soldier*, 427, 429, 585.

182. Larry Jay Diamond, *Squandered Victory: The American Occupation and the Bungled Effort to Bring Democracy to Iraq* (New York: Times Books, 2005); Bremer and McConnell, *My Year in Iraq*.

183. Karen DeYoung, *Soldier: The Life of Colin Powell* (New York: Knopf, 2006).

184. For a discussion of the extent to which Woodward's book evidenced the collapse of discipline within the Bush administration, see David Sanger, "White House Disputes Book's Account of Rifts on Iraq," *New York Times*, September 30, 2006.

185. J. David Kuo, "Deep Throat's Unmasking, and Ours," *Beliefnet.com*, 2005, http://www.beliefnet.com/story/167/story_16789_1.html (accessed November 15, 2006).

186. J. David Kuo, *Tempting Faith: An Inside Story of Political Seduction* (New York: Free Press, 2006).

187. Department of Defense, "Secretary Rumsfeld Press Conference in Phoenix, Arizona" (Washington, DC: Office of the Assistant Secretary of Defense [Public Affairs], August 26, 2004).

188. Gail Chaddock and David Cook, "9/11 Panel Sets Sights on Talking to Al Qaeda Members," *Christian Science Monitor*, May 12, 2004, 2.

189. This point was strongly reinforced by the trial of I. Lewis Libby, which illustrated how "our patriotic guardians of wartime secrets wantonly leak them to manipulate public opinion, protect their backsides or smear an adversary." Max Frankel, "The Washington Back Channel," *New York Times Magazine*, March 25, 2007, 10.

190. Trent Lott and Ron Wyden, "Hiding the Truth in a Cloud of Black Ink," *New York Times*, August 26, 2004, 27. The report was released in July 2004: Senate Intelligence Committee, *Report on the U.S. Intelligence Community's Prewar Intelligence Assessments on Iraq*.

## Notes to Chapter 7

1. John Yoo, "How the Presidency Regained Its Balance," *New York Times*, September 17, 2006.

2. Lydia Saad, "Bush No Longer Seen as Effective Manager," Gallup News Service, May 4, 2006.

3. John Yoo, *The Powers of War and Peace: The Constitution and Foreign Affairs after 9/11* (Chicago: University of Chicago Press, 2005).

4. Arthur M. Schlesinger Jr., *The Imperial Presidency* (Boston: Houghton Mifflin, 1973).

5. Arthur M. Schlesinger Jr., *War and the American Presidency* (New York: Norton, 2004), xiv, 45.

6. Peter H. Irons, *War Powers: How the Imperial Presidency Hijacked the Constitution* (New York: Metropolitan Books, 2005), 5.

7. Andrew Rudalevige, "Charting a New Imperial Presidency," *Presidential Studies Quarterly* 36, no. 3 (2006): 506–524.

8. John W. Dean, *Worse than Watergate* (New York: Little, Brown, 2004); John W. Dean, *Conservatives without Conscience* (New York: Viking, 2006).

9. Strictly speaking, Johnson dealt with the Freedom of Information Act for a little over a year. (It went into force in July 1967.) However, this was a weaker form of the law. It was strengthened considerably after Nixon's resignation in 1974.

10. As noted earlier, there have been similar shifts in public opinion in other developed countries.

11. For a brief discussion of the importance of informal trust, see Richard Sennett, *The Culture of the New Capitalism* (New Haven, CT: Yale University Press, 2006), 66–67. For an extended discussion of the role of trust, see Francis Fukuyama, *Trust: The Social Virtues and the Creation of Prosperity* (New York: Free Press, 1995).

12. Executive Office of the President, "Press Conference by the President" (Washington, DC: Office of the Press Secretary, November 8, 2006).

13. This argument is also made by Kenneth Anderson, "Law and Terror," *Policy Review* 139 (2006): 3–24. See also Benjamin Wittes, *José Padilla: Would-Be Terrorist or White House Victim?*(Washington, DC: Brookings Institution, March 6, 2007). In November 2006, Richard Posner observed that "the structure of U.S. counterterrorism is in disarray" even five years after the attacks. Richard A. Posner, "The Constitution vs. Counterterrorism," *National Security Law Report* 28, no. 4 (2006): 1–2.

14. Saad, "Bush No Longer Seen as Effective Manager."

15. Senate Committee on Homeland Security and Governmental Affairs, "Press Release: DHS Inspector General Releases Report Recommending Merger of Border Protection and Immigration and Customs Enforcement Agencies" (Washington, DC: Senate Committee on Homeland Security and Governmental Affairs, November 10, 2005).

16. Michael Brown, *Deposition for the House Select Committee to Investigate the Preparation for and Response to Hurricane Katrina* (Washington, DC: House Select

Committee to Investigate the Preparation for and Response to Hurricane Katrina, February 11, 2006).

17. David Rose, "Neo Culpa," *Vanity Fair*, January 2007.

18. Bob Woodward, *Plan of Attack* (New York: Simon and Schuster, 2004), 414.

19. David Ignatius, "A Foreign Policy out of Focus," *Washington Post*, September 2, 2003, A21.

20. Robert Novak, "That Cleansing Process Has Been Inhibited by the CIA's Fear Factor as an Extraordinary Leak Machine," *Chicago Sun-Times*, November 18, 2004, 49.

21. National Commission on Terrorist Attacks upon the United States, *Final Report* (New York: Barnes and Noble Books, 2004), 421.

22. Bob Woodward, *State of Denial* (New York: Simon and Schuster, 2006), 241.

23. James R. Beniger, *The Control Revolution* (Cambridge, MA: Harvard University Press, 1986), 7.

24. Thomas Ricks, *Fiasco: The American Military Adventure in Iraq* (New York: Penguin, 2006), 115–116.

25. Iraq Study Group, *The Way Forward: A New Approach* (Washington, DC: Vintage, 2006), xiv.

26. State of the Union Address, January 23, 1996.

27. Senate Select Committee on Intelligence, *Report 110-75* (Washington, DC: Senate Select Committee on Intelligence, 100th Cong., 1st sess., May 31, 2007).

28. "The Democrats' Pledge," *New York Times*, May 9, 2008, 24; see also "Chance for Reform," *Washington Post*, May 9, 2007, A16.

29. Josh White and Shailagh Murray, "Guantanamo Ruling Renews the Debate over Detainees," *Washington Post*, June 6, 2007, A3.

30. "The Terrorism Index," *Foreign Policy* 155 (2006): 49–55.

31. Joseph Carroll, "Big Government Greater Threat than Big Labor, Big Business," Gallup News Service, January 5, 2007.

# Index

9/11 attacks: ACLU membership increase following, 33–34; airline industry following, 89; Armitage on, 17; censorship following, 185n31; Cheney on, 17; consumer confidence following, 89; control over narrative about, 136–138; as a crisis of authority, 2–3, 21–22, 57; foreign response, 2, 49; governance following, 84; Pearl Harbor compared to, 15–16; as a security crisis, 1–2; simultaneity of news and events, 16; on Sydney, Australia (hypothetical), 106; unemployment following, 89; warnings of, 137, 149

9/11 attacks, U.S. government response to: 9/11 Commission, 136–137; airline baggage/passenger screening systems, 44–45, 57; avoidance of imposing costs on politically important constituencies, 171; bureaucratic coordination problems, 19; bureaucratic inertia, 171; call for sacrifices, xi, 91; Cheney on, 106; civil liberties intrusions, 18–19, 25–26; context of, x–xi; continuities and discontinuities in, x; conventional view of, ix–xi, 17–18, 117–118; data-mining programs, 25; diffusion of information about, 16; displacement of harms onto foreigners, 18–19, 26, 49; dysfunctionality in, 170–171; emergency appropriations, 89; failure to establish rules for waging counterterrorism, 169; foreign policy responses, 20–21, 117–118, 131–132; governmental surveillance, 25; historical parallels, 24–27, 47–48; homeland security, 19, 23; impatience in, 106, 133–134; importance of, ix; impracticability of bold domestic action, 23; invasion of Iraq, 107–108; long-term inter-

ests of the U.S. undermined, 23; market economy's effect on, 19–20; neoliberalism adhered to, 171; opportunism, 131–132; Patriot Act, 36; preventive detention of citizens, 33, 57; privacy rights infringements, 18; pro-consumption publicity blitz, 90–91; profiling, 25; Terrorist Surveillance Program, 49; War on Terrorism, 21, 107, 132

9/11 Commission, 136–137
*60 Minutes* (television show), 157, 159, 161

Abd al-Hadi al-Iraqi, 200n212
Abramoff, Jack, 86
Abrams, Floyd, 27
Abu Ghraib prison, 53, 154–155
Abu Nidal group, 119
Acheson, Dean, 146
ACLU. *See* American Civil Liberties Union
Adelman, Kenneth, 123, 170
*Advertising Age* (trade journal), 115
ADVISE program, 43
Afghanistan, 20, 52–53
*Against All Enemies* (Clarke), 159
airline baggage/passenger screening systems, 43–45, 57, 63–65
airline industry, 89–90
al-Haramain Islamic Foundation, 194n146
Al Jazeera, 151
al-Masri, Khaled, 199n206
al Qaeda: in Afghanistan, 20; American spokesman for, 184n28; among Guantánamo Bay detainees/prisoners, 52; Bush administration's dismissal of, 137; Gadahn and, 184n28; Geneva Conventions, 196n164; Iraqi connections, 143–144, 152, 153, 240n52; propaganda victory, 172; Rizk and, 102; targeting of

251

Hurricane Katrina, 77–83; Bush and,
George W., 213n159; disaster management, 77–83; energy shock following,
85; federal government's failures,
212n145, 213n159; homeland security,
19; inability of federal agencies to collaborate, 4–5; law-enforcement powers,
82; media coverage, 16, 79; militarization of policy problems, 59, 81–83
Hurricane Pam simulation, 77, 80
Hussein, Saddam: American public support for removal, 122; to European
leaders, 231n80; fall/toppling of, 20,
125, 244n109; persecution of Kurds, 120

illegal immigration, 108
*Imperial Hubris* (anonymous), 152
imperial presidency, 164–165, 174
Inspector General Act (1978), 10t
institutional complexity, 165
Insurrection Act, 82, 215n190
Integrated Deepwater System, 65–66
intelligence community: Bush administra-
tion's distrust of, 139, 142–144, 151–
154; CIA (*see* Central Intelligence
Agency); definition, 239n39; fragmentation of, 71–72; head of, 239n39; national
intelligence director, post of, 71–72
Intelligence Identities Protection Act, 138
Intelligence Reform and Terrorism
Prevention Act (2004), 71–72
intergovernment collaboration, 74–77
International Arabian Horse Association,
78
International Monetary Fund, 92, 124
intragovernment collaboration, 67–73
Iran: Axis of Evil, 20; ballistic-missile
threats from, 142; nuclear proliferation,
5, 21, 120
Iraq, 117–134; Abu Ghraib prison, 53,
154–155; al Qaeda connections, 143–
144, 152, 153, 240n52; American casualties, 228n35; American public support
for aggression, 122; Axis of Evil, 20; ballistic-missile threats from, 142; CIA's
prewar assessment, 244n109; Clinton
administration, 121; Coalition Provisional Authority (CPA) in, 127–130;
conflict with prior to invasion, 108,
120–123; containment of, 120; cruise-

missile attacks against, 122–123; Curveball intelligence, 153–154; debaathification of, 129; decision to go to war,
237n186; Desert Crossing war game,
125; detainees in, 53; displaced persons,
124; elections in, 129–130; Future of
Iraq Project, 125–126; Gingrich on, 145;
Governing Council, 129–130; insurgency in, 124–125, 130; invasion of,
107–108, 120, 122–124, 141–142, 152,
157, 231n80; looting, 130; no-fly zones,
120, 122; nuclear weapons capabilities,
142; opportunism in foreign policy,
117–123, 171; planning for, 124–127,
130–133, 141–142, 145, 151, 171; preemptive intervention doctrine, 134;
regime change, 121, 122, 133; sectarian
violence, 124; "slam dunk case" promised, 143; transfer of sovereignty to a
new government, 129–130; troop
requirements for, 131, 141–142, 160;
UN initiatives, 145; unit of command,
132–133; uranium ore from Niger,
137, 151–152, 160; victory in, 145;
weapons of mass destruction, 143,
152, 231n80
Iraq Study Group, 171–172
Irons, Peter, 164
*It Can Happen Here* (Conason), 1

Japanese Americans, internment of,
31–32
*John Doe v. Ashcroft*, 190n92
*John Doe v. Gonzales*, 190n92
Johnson, Haynes, 24–25
Johnson, Lyndon, 165
Johnson administration, Lyndon Baines,
36
Jones, Jim, 158
Judicial Watch, 136
Justice Department: al Qaeda training
manual, 48; chemical plants, vulnerability to attacks, 93; FBI translation unit,
misconduct in, 150–151; Geneva Conventions, interpretation of, 53; Guantánamo Bay detainees/prisoners, 50; National Security Letters, 190n91; Operation TIPS, 43; Patriot Act, 36, 40; Red
Scare (1919-1921), 29; Terrorist Surveillance Program (TSP), 47

# About the Author

ALASDAIR ROBERTS is Professor of Public Administration in the Maxwell School of Citizenship and Public Affairs at Syracuse University. He is also a fellow of the National Academy of Public Administration and an Honorary Senior Research Fellow at the School of Public Policy, University College, London. He received his Ph.D. in public policy from Harvard University and a law degree from the University of Toronto. He is the author of *Blacked Out: Government Secrecy in the Information Age,* winner of the 2007 Book Award from the American Society for Public Administration's Section on Public Administration Research, the 2007 Best Book Award of the Academy of Management's Public and Non-Profit Division, the International Political Science Association's 2007 Levine Book Prize, and the 2006 Louis Brownlow Book Award from the National Academy of Public Administration.